Two Scoops of Django

Best Practices For Django 1.8

Daniel Roy Greenfeld
Audrey Roy Greenfeld

Two Scoops of Django: Best Practices for Django 1.8
Third Edition, 2015-09-02

by Daniel Roy Greenfeld and Audrey Roy Greenfeld

First Printing, April 2015

For more information, visit `https://twoscoopspress.com`.

Printed at Repro India Ltd,
Mumbai

Dedication

For Malcolm Tredinnick
1971-2013
We miss you.

http://2scoops.co/malcolm-tredinnick-memorial

About the Dedication

Malcolm Tredinnick wasn't just a Django core developer and reviewer of "Two Scoops of Django: Best Practices for Django 1.5." To us, he was much, much more.

Daniel had worked with Malcolm Tredinnick in the summer of 2010, but we first met him in person at DjangoCon 2010. He was funny and charming, sharply opinionated but always a gentleman; we instantly became close friends.

In 2012, when we co-organized the first PyCon Philippines, as soon as we told him about it, Malcolm instantly declared he was coming. He gave two memorable talks and ran an impromptu all-day Django tutorial. He also pushed and encouraged the local community to work on Filipino language translations for Django, including Tagalog, Tausug, Cebuano, and more.

After the conference, we started working on a book about Django best practices. We gathered friends and colleagues to help us as technical reviewers. Malcolm Tredinnick became the most active of them. He was our mentor and forced us to dig deeper and work harder. He did this while working a day job as the leader of a combined Rails and Haskell team; Malcolm was a true programming language polyglot.

For our book, he provided so much assistance and guidance we tried to figure out a way to include him in the author credits. When we told him about our dilemma, he laughed it off saying, "For a book called 'Two Scoops', you can't have three authors." We suggested he share credit with us on a second book, and he refused, saying he preferred to just comment on our work. He said that he wanted people to have proper references, and for him, simply reviewing our work was contributing to the greater good. Eventually the two of us quietly planned to somehow coerce him into being a co-author on a future work.

After months of effort, we released the first iteration on January 17th, 2013. Malcolm stepped back from Two Scoops of Django, but we stayed in touch. Since Malcolm was unable to attend PyCon US 2013 we weren't sure when we would meet him again.

Two months later, on March 17th, 2013, Malcolm passed away.

We knew Malcolm for less than three years and yet he made an incredible difference in our lives. We've heard many similar stories in the community about Malcolm; He was a friend and mentor to countless others around the world. His last lesson to us went beyond code or writing, he taught us to never take for granted friends, family, mentors, and teachers.

Contents

Authors' Notes

A Few Words From Daniel Roy Greenfeld

In the spring of 2006, I was working for NASA on a project that implemented a Java-based RESTful web service that was taking weeks to deliver. One evening, when management had left for the day, I reimplemented the service in Python in 90 minutes.

I knew then that I wanted to work with Python.

I wanted to use Django for the web front-end of the web service, but management insisted on using a closed-source stack because "Django is only at version 0.9x, hence not ready for real projects." I disagreed, but stayed happy with the realization that at least the core architecture was in Python. Django used to be edgy during those heady days, and it scared people the same way that Node.js scares people today.

Nearly nine years later, Django is considered a mature, powerful, secure, stable framework used by incredibly successful corporations (Instagram, Pinterest, Mozilla, etc.) and government agencies (NASA, et al) all over the world. Convincing management to use Django isn't hard anymore, and if it is hard to convince them, finding jobs which let you use Django has become much easier. In my 8+ years of building Django projects, I've learned how to launch new web applications with incredible speed while keeping technical debt to an absolute minimum.

My goal in this book is to share with you what I've learned. My knowledge and experience have been gathered from advice given by core developers, mistakes I've made, successes shared with others, and an enormous amount of note taking. I'm going to admit that the book is opinionated, but many of the leaders in the Django community use the same or similar techniques.

This book is for you, the developers. I hope you enjoy it!

A Few Words From Audrey Roy Greenfeld

I first discovered Python in a graduate class at MIT in 2005. In less than 4 weeks of homework assignments, each student built a voice-controlled system for navigating between rooms in MIT's Stata Center, running on our HP iPaqs running Debian. I was in awe of Python and wondered why it wasn't used for everything. I tried building a web application with Zope but struggled with it.

A couple of years passed, and I got drawn into the Silicon Valley tech startup scene. I wrote graphics libraries in C and desktop applications in C++ for a startup. At some point, I left that job and picked up painting and sculpture. Soon I was drawing and painting frantically for art shows, co-directing a 140-person art show, and managing a series of real estate renovations. I realized that I was doing a lot at once and had to optimize. Naturally, I turned to Python and began writing scripts to generate some of my artwork. That was when I rediscovered the joy of working with Python.

Many friends from the Google App Engine, SuperHappyDevHouse, and hackathon scenes in Silicon Valley inspired me to get into Django. Through them and through various freelance projects and partnerships I discovered how powerful Django was.

Before I knew it, I was attending PyCon 2010, where I met my husband Daniel Roy Greenfeld. We met at the end of James Bennett's "Django In Depth" tutorial, and now this chapter in our lives has come full circle with the publication of this book.

Django has brought more joy to my life than I thought was possible with a web framework. My goal with this book is to give you the thoughtful guidance on common Django development practices that are normally left unwritten (or implied), so that you can get past common hurdles and experience the joy of using the Django web framework for your projects.

Introduction

Our aim in writing this book is to write down all of the unwritten tips, tricks, and common practices that we've learned over the years while working with Django.

While writing, we've thought of ourselves as scribes, taking the various things that people assume are common knowledge and recording them with simple examples.

A Word About Our Recommendations

Like the official Django documentation, this book covers how to do things in Django, illustrating various scenarios with code examples.

Unlike the Django documentation, this book recommends particular coding styles, patterns, and library choices. While core Django developers may agree with some or many of these choices, keep in mind that many of our recommendations are just that: personal recommendations formed after years of working with Django.

Throughout this book, we advocate certain practices and techniques that we consider to be the best approaches. We also express our own personal preferences for particular tools and libraries.

Sometimes we reject common practices that we consider to be anti-patterns. For most things we reject, we try to be polite and respectful of the hard work of the authors. There are the rare, few things that we may not be so polite about. This is in the interest of helping you avoid dangerous pitfalls.

We have made every effort to give thoughtful recommendations and to make sure that our practices are sound. We've subjected ourselves to harsh, nerve-wracking critiques from Django and Python core developers whom we greatly respect. We've had this book reviewed by more technical reviewers than the average technical book, and we've poured countless hours into revisions. That being said, there is always the possibility of errors or omissions. There is also the possibility that better practices may emerge than those described here.

We are fully committed to iterating on and improving this book, and we mean it. If you see any practices that you disagree with or anything that can be done better, we humbly ask that you send us your suggestions for improvements. The best way to send us feedback is to file an issue at `https://github.com/twoscoops/two-scoops-of-django-1.8/issues`.

Please don't hesitate to tell us what can be improved. We will take your feedback constructively. Errata will be published at `http://www.2scoops.co/1.8-errata/`.

Why Two Scoops of Django?

Like most people, we, the authors of this book, love ice cream. Every Saturday night we throw caution to the wind and indulge in ice cream. Don't tell anyone, but sometimes we even have some when it's not Saturday night!

Figure 1: Throwing caution to the wind.

We like to try new flavors and discuss their merits against our old favorites. Tracking our progress through all these flavors, and possibly building a club around it, makes for a great sample Django project.

When we do find a flavor we really like, the new flavor brings a smile to our face, just like when we find great tidbits of code or advice in a technical book. One of our goals for this book is to write the kind of technical book that brings the ice cream smile to readers.

Best of all, using ice cream analogies has allowed us to come up with more vivid code examples. We've had a lot of fun writing this book. You may see us go overboard with ice cream silliness here and there; please forgive us.

Before You Begin

If you are new to Django, this book will be helpful but large parts will be challenging for you. This book is not a tutorial. To use this book to its fullest extent, you should have an understanding of the Python programming language and have at least gone through the 6 page Django tutorial: `https://docs.djangoproject.com/en/1.8/intro/tutorial01/`. Experience with object-oriented programming is also very useful.

This Book Is Intended for Django 1.8 and Python 2.7.x/3.3.x

This book should work well with the Django 1.8 series, less so with Django 1.7, and so on. Even though we make no promises about functional compatibility, at least the general approaches from most of this book stand up over every post-1.0 version of Django.

As for the Python version, this book is tested on Python 2.7.x and Python 3.3.3+.

None of the content in this book, including our practices, the code examples, and the libraries referenced applies to Google App Engine (GAE). If you try to use this book as a reference for GAE development, you may run into problems.

Each Chapter Stands on Its Own

Unlike tutorial and walkthrough books where each chapter builds upon the previous chapter's project, we've written this book in a way that each chapter intentionally stands by itself.

We've done this in order to make it easy for you to reference chapters about specific topics when needed while you're working on a project.

The examples in each chapter are completely independent. They aren't intended to be combined into one project and are not a tutorial. Consider them useful, isolated snippets that illustrate and help with various coding scenarios.

Conventions Used in This Book

Code blocks like the following are used throughout the book:

Example 0.1

```
class Scoop(object):
    def __init__(self):
        self._is_yummy = True
```

To keep these snippets compact, we sometimes violate the PEP 8 conventions on comments and line spacing. Code samples are available online at `http://www.2scoops.co/1.8-code-examples/`.

Special "Don't Do This!" code blocks like the following indicate examples of bad code that you should avoid:

Bad Example 0.1

```
# DON'T DO THIS!
from rotten_ice_cream import something_bad
```

We use the following typographical conventions throughout the book:

- `Constant width` for code fragments or commands.
- *Italic* for filenames.
- **Bold** when introducing a new term or important word.

Boxes containing notes, warnings, tips, and little anecdotes are also used in this book:

TIP: Something You Should Know

Tip boxes give handy advice.

WARNING: Some Dangerous Pitfall

Warning boxes help you avoid common mistakes and pitfalls.

PACKAGE TIP: Some Useful Package Recommendation

Indicates notes about useful third-party packages related to the current chapter, and general notes about using various Python, Django, and front-end packages.
We also provide a complete list of packages recommended throughout the book in Appendix A: *Packages Mentioned In This Book.*

We also use tables to summarize information in a handy, concise way:

	Daniel Roy Greenfeld	Audrey Roy Greenfeld
Can be fed coconut ice cream	No	Yes
Favorite ice cream flavors of the moment	Ube	Cookies and Cream

Authors' Ice Cream Preferences

Core Concepts

When we build Django projects, we keep the following concepts in mind.

Keep It Simple, Stupid

Kelly Johnson, one of the most renowned and prolific aircraft design engineers in the history of aviation, said it this way about 50 years ago. Centuries earlier, Leonardo da Vinci meant the same thing when he said, "Simplicity is the ultimate sophistication."

When building software projects, each piece of unnecessary complexity makes it harder to add new features and maintain old ones. Attempt the simplest solution, but take care not to implement overly simplistic solutions that make bad assumptions. This concept is sometimes abbreviated as "KISS."

Fat Models, Utility Modules, Thin Views, Stupid Templates

When deciding where to put a piece of code, we like to follow the "Fat Models, Utility Modules, Thin Views, Stupid Templates" approach.

We recommend that you err on the side of putting more logic into anything but views and templates. The results are pleasing. The code becomes clearer, more self-documenting, less duplicated, and a lot more reusable. As for template tags and filters, they should contain the least amount of logic possible to function.

We cover this further in:

Fat Models section 6.5, *Understanding Fat Models*
Utility Modules section 29.2 *Optimize Apps with Utility Modules*
Thin Views subsection 16.3.3 *Try to Keep Business Logic Out of Views*
Stupid Templates I section 13.9, *Follow a Minimalist Approach*
Stupid Templates II chapter 14, *Template Tags and Filters*

Start With Django by Default

Before we consider switching out core Django components for things like alternative template engines, different ORMs, or non-relational databases, we first try an implementation using standard Django components. If we run into obstacles, we explore all possibilities before replacing core Django components.

See chapter 18, *Tradeoffs of Replacing Core Components* for more details.

Be Familiar with Django's Design Philosophies

It is good to periodically read the documentation on Django's design philosophy because it helps us understand why Django provides certain constraints and tools. Like any framework, Django is more than just a tool for providing views, it's a way of doing things designed to help us put together maintainable projects in a reasonable amount of time.

https://docs.djangoproject.com/en/1.8/misc/design-philosophies/

The Twelve-Factor App

A comprehensive approach to web-based application design, the *Twelve-Factor App* approach is growing in popularity amongst many senior and core Django developers. It is a methodology for building deployable, scalable applications worth reading and understanding. Parts of it closely match the practices espoused in Two Scoops of Django, and we like to think of it as suggested reading for any web-based application developer.

See `http://12factor.net`

Our Writing Concepts

When we wrote this book, we wanted to provide to the reader and ourselves the absolute best material possible. To do that, we adopted the following principles:

Provide the Best Material

We've done our absolute best to provide the best material possible, going to the known resources on every topic covered to vet our material. We weren't afraid to ask questions! Then we distilled the articles, responses and advice of experts into the content that exists in the book today. When that didn't suffice, we came up with our own solutions and vetted them with various subject matter experts. It has been a lot of work, and we hope you are pleased with the results.

If you are curious about the differences between this edition (Django 1.8) and the previous edition (Django 1.6) of the book, you can find the shortlist of changes at:

- `http://www.2scoops.co/1.8-change-list/`

Stand on the Shoulders of Giants

While we take credit and responsibility for our work, we certainly did not come up with all the practices described in this book on our own.

Without all of the talented, creative, and generous developers who make up the Django, Python, and general open source software communities, this book would not exist. We strongly believe in recognizing the people who have served as our teachers and mentors as well as our sources for information, and we've tried our best to give credit whenever credit is due.

Listen to Our Readers and Reviewers

In the previous editions of this book, we received a huge amount of feedback from a veritable legion of readers and reviewers. This allowed us to greatly improve the quality of the book. It is now at a level that we hoped for but never expected to achieve.

In return, we've shared credit at the back of the book and are continually working on ways to pay it forward by improving the lives of developers around the world.

If you have any questions, comments, or other feedback about this edition, please share your input by submitting issues in our issue tracker, at:

- `https://github.com/twoscoops/two-scoops-of-django-1.8/issues`

Also, at the end of the book is a link to leave a review for Two Scoops of Django on Amazon. Doing this will help others make an informed decision about whether this book is right for them.

Publish Issues and Errata

Nothing is perfect, even after extensive review cycles. We will be publishing issues and errata at the Two Scoops of Django 1.8 GitHub repo:

- `https://github.com/twoscoops/two-scoops-of-django-1.8`

1 Coding Style

A little attention to following standard coding style guidelines will go a long way. We highly recommend that you read this chapter, even though you may be tempted to skip it.

1.1 The Importance of Making Your Code Readable

Code is read more than it is written. An individual block of code takes moments to write, minutes or hours to debug, and can last forever without being touched again. It's when you or someone else visits code written yesterday or ten years ago that having code written in a clear, consistent style becomes extremely useful. Understandable code frees mental bandwidth from having to puzzle out inconsistencies, making it easier to maintain and enhance projects of all sizes.

What this means is that you should go the extra mile to make your code as readable as possible:

- Avoid abbreviating variable names.
- Write out your function argument names.
- Document your classes and methods.
- Comment your code.
- Refactor repeated lines of code into reusable functions or methods.
- Keep functions and methods short. A good rule of thumb is that scrolling should not be necessary to read an entire function or method.

When you come back to your code after time away from it, you'll have an easier time picking up where you left off.

Take those pesky abbreviated variable names, for example. When you see a variable called `balance_sheet_decrease`, it's much easier to interpret in your mind than an abbreviated variable like `bsd` or `bal_s_d`. These types of shortcuts may save a few seconds of typing, but that savings comes at the expense of hours or days of technical debt. It's not worth it.

1.2 PEP 8

PEP 8 is the official style guide for Python. We advise reading it in detail and learn to follow the PEP 8 coding conventions: http://www.python.org/dev/peps/pep-0008/

PEP 8 describes coding conventions such as:

- "Use 4 spaces per indentation level."
- "Separate top-level function and class definitions with two blank lines."
- "Method definitions inside a class are separated by a single blank line."

All the Python files in your Django projects should follow PEP 8. If you have trouble remembering the PEP 8 guidelines, find a plugin for your code editor that checks your code as you type.

When an experienced Python programmer sees gross violations of PEP 8 in a Django project, even if they don't say something mean, they are probably thinking bad things. Trust us on this one.

WARNING: Don't Change an Existing Project's Conventions

The style of PEP 8 applies to new Django projects only. If you are brought into an existing Django project that follows a different convention than PEP 8, then follow the existing conventions.

Please read the "A Foolish Consistency is the Hobgoblin of Little Minds" section of PEP 8 for details about this and other reasons to break the rules:

- http://2scoops.co/hobgoblin-of-little-minds

PACKAGE TIP: Use flake8 For Checking Code Quality

Created by Tarek Ziadé and now maintained by the PyCQA group, this is a very useful command-line tool for checking coding style, quality, and logic errors in projects. Use while developing locally and as a component of Continuous Integration.

1.2.1 The 79-Character Limit

"No joke, I still deal with consoles that are restricted to 80 characters."

– Barry Morrison, Systems Engineer and reviewer of every edition of this book.

According to PEP 8, the limit of text per line is 79 characters. This exists because it's a safe value that most text-wrapping editors and developer teams can accommodate without hurting the understandability of code.

However, PEP 8 also has a provision for relaxing this limit to 99 characters for exclusive team projects. We interpret this to mean projects that are not open source.

Our preference is as follows:

- On open source projects, there should be a hard 79-character limit. Our experience has shown that contributors or visitors to these projects will grumble about line length issues.
- On private projects, we relax the limit to 99 characters, taking full advantage of modern monitors.

Please read `http://www.python.org/dev/peps/pep-0008/#maximum-line-length`.

> **TIP: Aymeric Augustin on Line Length Issues**
>
> Django core developer Aymeric Augustin says, "Fitting the code in 79 columns is never a good reason to pick worse names for variables, functions, and classes. It's much more important to have readable variable names than to fit in an arbitrary limit of hardware from three decades ago."

1.3 The Word on Imports

PEP 8 suggests that imports should be grouped in the following order:

1. Standard library imports
2. Related third-party imports

3. Local application or library specific imports

When we're working on a Django project, our imports look something like the following:

Example 1.1

```
# Stdlib imports
from __future__ import absolute_import
from math import sqrt
from os.path import abspath

# Core Django imports
from django.db import models
from django.utils.translation import ugettext_lazy as _

# Third-party app imports
from django_extensions.db.models import TimeStampedModel

# Imports from your apps
from splits.models import BananaSplit
```

(Note: you don't actually need to comment your imports like this. The comments are just here to explain the example.)

The import order in a Django project is:

1. Standard library imports.
2. Imports from core Django.
3. Imports from third-party apps including those unrelated to Django.
4. Imports from the apps that you created as part of your Django project. (You'll read more about apps in chapter 4, *Fundamentals of App Design*.)

1.4 Use Explicit Relative Imports

When writing code, it's important to do so in such a way that it's easier to move, rename, and version your work. In Python, explicit relative imports remove the need for hardcoding a module's package, separating individual modules from being tightly coupled to the architecture around them. Since Django apps are simply Python packages, the same rules apply.

To illustrate the benefits of explicit relative imports, let's explore an example.

Imagine that the following snippet is from a Django project that you created to track your ice cream consumption, including all of the waffle/sugar/cake cones that you have ever eaten.

Oh no, your cones app contains hardcoded imports, which are bad!

Bad Example 1.1

```python
# cones/views.py
from django.views.generic import CreateView

# DON'T DO THIS!
# Hardcoding of the 'cones' package
# with implicit relative imports
from cones.models import WaffleCone
from cones.forms import WaffleConeForm
from core.views import FoodMixin

class WaffleConeCreateView(FoodMixin, CreateView):
    model = WaffleCone
    form_class = WaffleConeForm
```

Sure, your cones app works fine within your ice cream tracker project, but it has those nasty hardcoded imports that make it less portable and reusable:

- What if you wanted to reuse your cones app in another project that tracks your general dessert consumption, but you had to change the name due to a naming conflict (e.g. a conflict with a Django app for snow cones)?
- What if you simply wanted to change the name of the app at some point?

With hardcoded imports, you can't just change the name of the app; you have to dig through all of the imports and change them as well. It's not hard to change them manually, but before you dismiss the need for explicit relative imports, keep in mind that the above example is extremely simple compared to a real app with various additional utility modules.

Let's now convert the bad code snippet containing hardcoded imports into a good one containing explicit relative imports. Here's the corrected example:

Example 1.2

```
# cones/views.py
from __future__ import absolute_import
from django.views.generic import CreateView

# Relative imports of the 'cones' package
from .models import WaffleCone
from .forms import WaffleConeForm
from core.views import FoodMixin

class WaffleConeCreateView(FoodMixin, CreateView):
    model = WaffleCone
    form_class = WaffleConeForm
```

Another concrete advantage is that we can immediately tell our local/internal imports from global/external imports, highlighting the Python package as a unit of code.

TIP: Use "from __future__ import absolute_import"

Python 3 updates and improves how imports work, and it does this in a good way. Fortunately, it's been back-ported to Python 2.7 via the use of the `from __future__ import absolute_import` statement. Even if you don't plan to use Python 3, this is a great feature and allows for the *explicit relative* imports demonstrated in the table below.

To summarize, here's a table of the different Python import types and when to use them in Django projects:

Code	Import Type	Usage
`from core.views import FoodMixin`	absolute import	Use when importing from outside the current app
`from .models import WaffleCone`	explicit relative	Use when importing from another module in the current app

`from models import WaffleCone`	implicit relative	Often used when importing from another module in the current app, but not a good idea

Table 1.1: Imports: Absolute vs. Explicit Relative vs. Implicit Relative

Get into the habit of using explicit relative imports. It's very easy to do, and using explicit relative imports is a good habit for any Python programmer to develop.

> **TIP: Doesn't PEP 328 Clash With PEP 8?**
>
> See what Guido Van Rossum, BDFL of Python says about it:
>
> ➤ http://2scoops.co/guido-on-pep-8-vs-pep-328

Additional reading: http://www.python.org/dev/peps/pep-0328/

1.5 Avoid Using Import *

In 99% of all our work, we explicitly import each module:

Example 1.3

```
from django import forms
from django.db import models
```

Never do the following:

Bad Example 1.2

```
# ANTI-PATTERN: Don't do this!
from django.forms import *
from django.db.models import *
```

The reason for this is to avoid implicitly loading all of another Python module's locals into and over our current module's namespace, this can produce unpredictable and sometimes catastrophic results.

We do cover a specific exception to this rule in chapter 5, *Settings and Requirements Files.*

Let's look at the bad code example above. Both the Django forms and Django models libraries have a class called `CharField`. By implicitly loading both libraries, the models library overwrote the forms version of the class. This can also happen with Python built-in libraries and other third-party libraries overwriting critical functionality.

WARNING: Python Naming Collisions

You'll run into similar problems if you try to import two things with the same name, such as:

Bad Example 1.3

```
# ANTI-PATTERN: Don't do this!
from django.forms import CharField
from django.db.models import CharField
```

Using `import *` is like being that greedy customer at an ice cream shop who asks for a free taster spoon of all thirty-one flavors, but who only purchases one or two scoops. Don't import everything if you're only going to use one or two things.

If the customer then walked out with a giant ice cream bowl containing a scoop of every or almost every flavor, though, it would be a different matter.

Figure 1.1: Using `import *` in an ice cream shop.

1.6 Django Coding Style

This section covers both the official guidelines as well as unofficial but commonly-accepted Django conventions.

1.6.1 Consider the Django Coding Style Guidelines

It goes without saying that it's a good idea to be aware of common Django style conventions. In fact, internally Django has its own set of style guidelines that extend PEP 8:

➤ http://2scoops.co/1.8-coding-style

Additionally, while the following are not specified in the official standards, they are common enough in the Django community that you will probably want to follow them in your projects.

1.6.2 Use Underscores in URL Pattern Names Rather Than Dashes

We always try to use underscores (the "_" character) over dashes. This isn't just more Pythonic, it's friendlier to more IDEs and text editors. Note that we are referring to the name argument of `url()` here, not the actual URL typed into the browser.

The wrong way, with dashes in url names:

Bad Example 1.4

```
patterns = [
    url(regex='^add/$',
        view=views.add_topping,
        name='add-topping'),
    ]
```

The right way, with underscores in url names:

Example 1.4

```
patterns = [
    url(regex='^add/$',
        view=views.add_topping,
        name='add_topping'),
    ]
```

Note that we are referring to the name argument of `url()` here, not the actual URL typed into the browser. Dashes in actual URLs are fine (e.g. `regex='âdd-topping/$'`).

1.6.3 Use Underscores in Template Block Names Rather Than Dashes

For the same reasons as using underscores in URL pattern names, we recommend using underscores when defining names of template blocks: in this case they're more Pythonic and more editor-friendly.

1.7 Choose JS, HTML, and CSS Style Guides

1.7.1 JavaScript Style Guides

Unlike Python which has one official style guide, there is no official JavaScript style guide. Instead, a number of unofficial JS style guides have been created by various individuals and/or companies:

- idiomatic.js: Principles of Writing Consistent, Idiomatic JavaScript `https://github.com/rwaldron/idiomatic.js/`
- Pragmatic.js code style guidelines `https://github.com/madrobby/pragmatic.js`
- Airbnb JavaScript Style Guide `https://github.com/airbnb/javascript`
- Node.js Style Guide `https://github.com/felixge/node-style-guide`
- Code Conventions for the JavaScript Programming Language `http://javascript.crockford.com/code.html`

There is no consensus in the Django or JavaScript communities on any one of these, so just pick your favorite and stick with it.

However, if you are using a JavaScript framework with a style guide of its own, you should use that guide. For example, ember.js has its own style guide.

> **PACKAGE TIP: The JSCS Code Style Linter**
>
> JSCS (`http://jscs.info/`) is a tool for checking JavaScript code style. It has presets for the JS style rules of several style guides, including a few of those listed above. There are also JSCS plugins for various text editors and JSCS tasks for the Gulp and Grunt task runners.

1.7.2 HTML and CSS Style Guides

- Code Guide by @mdo for HTML and CSS: `http://codeguide.co`
- idomatic-css: Principles of Writing Consistent, Idiomatic CSS: `https://github.com/necolas/idiomatic-css`

> **PACKAGE TIP: CSScomb**
>
> CSScomb (`http://csscomb.com/`) is a coding style formatter for CSS. It checks for consistency against the rules for which you configure it for, and it checks the sort order of your CSS properties. Just as for JSCS, there are CSScomb text editor and task/build tool plugins, including for Brunch.

1.8 Never Code to the IDE (Or Text Editor)

There are developers who make decisions about the layout and implementation of their project based on the features of IDEs (Integrated Development Environment). This can make discovery of project code extremely difficult for anyone whose choice of development tool doesn't match the original author.

Always assume that the developers around you like to use their own tools and that your code and project layout should be transparent enough that someone stuck using Notepad or Nano will be able to navigate your work.

For example, introspecting **template tags** or discovering their source can be difficult and time consuming for developers not using a very, very limited pool of IDEs. Therefore, we follow the commonly-used naming pattern of `<app_name>_tags.py`.

1.9 Summary

This chapter covered our preferred coding style and explained why we prefer each technique.

Even if you don't follow the coding style that we use, please follow a consistent coding style. Projects with varying styles are much harder to maintain, slowing development and increasing the chances of developer mistakes.

2 The Optimal Django Environment Setup

This chapter describes what we consider the best local environment setup for intermediate and advanced developers working with Django.

2.1 Use the Same Database Engine Everywhere

A common developer pitfall is using **SQLite3** for local development and **PostgreSQL** (or **MySQL**) in production. This section applies not only to the SQLite3/PostgreSQL scenario, but to any scenario where you're using two different databases and expecting them to behave identically.

Here are some of the issues we've encountered with using different database engines for development and production:

2.1.1 You Can't Examine an Exact Copy of Production Data Locally

When your production database is different from your local development database, you can't grab an exact copy of your production database to examine data locally.

Sure, you can generate a SQL dump from production and import it into your local database, but that doesn't mean that you have an exact copy after the export and import.

2.1.2 Different Databases Have Different Field Types/Constraints

Keep in mind that different databases handle typing of field data differently. Django's ORM attempts to accommodate those differences, but there's only so much that it can do.

For example, some people use SQLite3 for local development and PostgreSQL in production, thinking that the Django ORM gives them the excuse not to think about the differences. Eventually they run into problems, since SQLite3 has dynamic, weak typing instead of strong typing.

Yes, the Django ORM has features that allow your code to interact with SQLite3 in a more strongly typed manner, but form and model validation mistakes in development will go uncaught (even in tests) until the code goes to a production server. You may be saving long strings locally without a hitch, for example, since SQLite3 won't care. But then in production, your PostgreSQL or MySQL database will throw constraint errors that you've never seen locally, and you'll have a hard time replicating the issues until you set up an identical database locally.

Most problems usually can't be discovered until the project is run on a strongly typed database (e.g. PostgreSQL or MySQL). When these types of bugs hit, you end up kicking yourself and scrambling to set up your local development machine with the right database.

TIP: Django+PostgreSQL Rocks

Most Django developers that we know prefer to use PostgreSQL for all environments: development, staging, QA, and production systems.

Depending on your operating system, use these instructions:

- Mac: Download the one-click Mac installer at `http://postgresapp.com`
- Windows: Download the one-click Windows installer at `http://postgresql.org/download/windows/`
- Linux: Install via your package manager, or follow the instructions at `http://postgresql.org/download/linux/`

PostgreSQL may take some work to get running locally on some operating systems, but we find that it's well worth the effort.

2.1.3 Fixtures Are Not a Magic Solution

You may be wondering why you can't simply use **fixtures** to abstract away the differences between your local and production databases.

Well, fixtures are great for creating simple hardcoded test data sets. Sometimes you need to pre-populate your databases with fake test data during development, particularly during the early stages of a project.

Fixtures are not a reliable tool for migrating large data sets from one database to another in a database-agnostic way. They are simply not meant to be used that way. Don't mistake the ability of fixtures to create basic data (`dumpdata/loaddata`) with the capability to migrate production data between database tools.

2.2 Use Pip and Virtualenv

If you are not doing so already, we strongly urge you to familiarize yourself with both pip and virtualenv. They are the de facto standard for Django projects, and most companies that use Django rely on these tools.

Pip is a tool that fetches Python packages from the **Python Package Index** and its mirrors. It is used to manage and install Python packages. It's like easy_install but has more features, the key feature being support for virtualenv.

Virtualenv is a tool for creating isolated Python environments for maintaining package dependencies. It's great for situations where you're working on more than one project at a time, and where there are clashes between the version numbers of different libraries that your projects use.

For example, imagine that you're working on one project that requires Django 1.7 and another that requires Django 1.8.

- Without virtualenv (or an alternative tool to manage dependencies), you have to reinstall Django every time you switch projects.
- If that sounds tedious, keep in mind that most real Django projects have at least a dozen dependencies to maintain.

Pip is already included in Python 3.4 and higher. Further reading and installation instructions can be found at:

- pip: `http://pip-installer.org`
- virtualenv: `http://virtualenv.org`

TIP: virtualenvwrapper

We also highly recommend `virtualenvwrapper` for Mac OS X and Linux or `virtualenvwrapper-win` for Windows. The project was started by Doug Hellman.

Personally, we think virtualenv without virtualenvwrapper can be a pain to use, because every time you want to activate a virtual environment, you have to type something long like:

Example 2.1

```
$ source ~/.virtualenvs/twoscoops/bin/activate
```

With virtualenvwrapper, you'd only have to type:

Example 2.2

```
$ workon twoscoops
```

Virtualenvwrapper is a popular companion tool to pip and virtualenv and makes our lives easier, but it's not an absolute necessity.

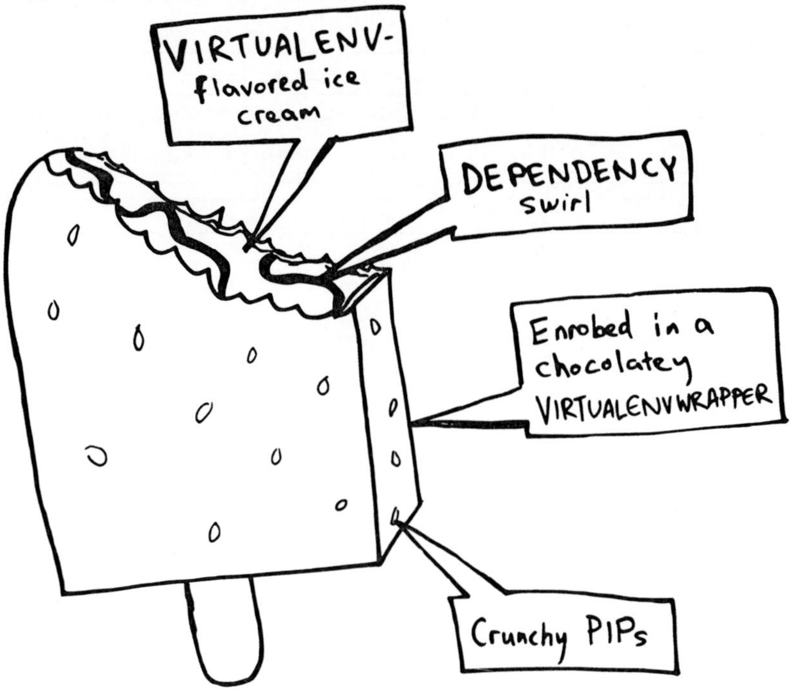

Figure 2.1: Pip, virtualenv, and virtualenvwrapper in ice cream bar form.

2.3 Install Django and Other Dependencies via Pip

The official Django documentation describes several ways of installing Django. Our recommended installation method is with pip and requirements files.

To summarize how this works: a requirements file is like a grocery list of Python packages that you want to install. It contains the name and desired version of each package. You use pip to install packages from this list into your virtual environment.

We cover the setup of and installation from requirements files in chapter 5, *Settings and Requirements Files.*

> **TIP: Setting PYTHONPATH**
>
> If you have a firm grasp of the command line and environment variables, you can set your virtualenv `PYTHONPATH` so that the ***django-admin.py*** command can be used to serve your site and perform other tasks.
>
> You can also set your virtualenv's `PYTHONPATH` to include the current directory with the latest version of pip. Running "`pip install -e .`" from your project's root directory will do the trick, installing the current directory as as package that can be edited in place.
>
> If you don't know how to set this or it seems complicated, don't worry about it and stick with ***manage.py***.
>
> Additional reading:
>
> - http://cs.simons-rock.edu/python/pythonpath.html
> - https://docs.djangoproject.com/en/1.8/ref/django-admin/

2.4 Use a Version Control System

Version control systems are also known as revision control or source control. Whenever you work on any Django project, you should use a version control system to keep track of your code changes.

Wikipedia has a detailed comparison of different version control systems:

- http://en.wikipedia.org/wiki/Comparison_of_revision_control_software

Of all the options, **Git** and **Mercurial** seem to be the most popular among Django developers. Both Git and Mercurial make it easy to create branches and merge changes.

When using a version control system, it's important to not only have a local copy of your code repository, but also to use a code hosting service for backups. For this, we recommend that you use GitHub (https://github.com/) or Bitbucket (https://bitbucket.org/).

2.5 Optional: Identical Environments

What works on a programmer's laptop might not work in production. But what if your local development environment was identical to your project's staging, test, and production environments?

Of course, if the production infrastructure consists of 10,000 servers, it's completely unrealistic to have another 10,000 local servers for development purposes. So when we say identical, we mean "as identical as realistically possible."

There are the environment differences that you can eliminate:

Operating system differences. If we're developing on a Mac or on Windows, and if our site is deployed on Ubuntu Linux, then there are huge differences between how our Django project works locally and how it works in production.

Python setup differences. Let's face it, many developers and sysadmins don't even know which version of Python they have running locally, although no one will admit it. Why? Because setting up Python properly and understanding your setup completely is hard.

Developer-to-developer differences. On large development teams, a lot of time can be wasted trying to debug differences between one developer's setup and another's.

The most common way to set up identical development environments is with Vagrant and VirtualBox.

2.5.1 Vagrant and VirtualBox

Vagrant is a popular tool for creating, configuring, and managing reproducible development environments. Vagrant's main benefit is that it makes working with **VirtualBox** (and other VM tools) much easier.

For example, if our development laptops run OS X but a project's configuration is Ubuntu-specific, we can use Vagrant and the project's Vagrantfile to quickly get a virtual Ubuntu development environment set up locally, complete with all the packages and setup configurations needed for the project.

- Set up identical local development environments for everyone on our project's dev team.

- Configure these local development environments in a way similar to our staging, test, and production servers.

The potential downsides are:

- Extra complexity that is not needed in many situations. For simpler projects where we're not too worried about OS-level differences, it's easier to skip this.
- On older development machines, running virtual instances can slow performance to a crawl. Even on newer machines, small but noticeable overhead is added.

TIP: Experimental: Using Isolated Docker Containers

Working with Docker is sort of like developing inside of a VM, except more lightweight. Docker containers share the host OS but have their own isolated process and memory space. Furthermore, since Docker uses AUFS, containers can be built quickly off of a snapshot plus deltas rather than building from scratch.

At Eventbrite, the architecture team uses Docker in conjunction with Vagrant to speed up development VM provisioning. However, Docker is still evolving rapidly and considered experimental.

2.6 Summary

This chapter covered using the same database in development as in production, pip, virtualenv, and version control systems. These are good to have in your tool chest, since they are commonly used not just in Django, but in the majority of Python software development.

3 How to Lay Out Django Projects

Project layout is one of those areas where core Django developers have differing opinions about what they consider best practice. In this chapter, we present our approach, which is one of the most commonly-used ones.

> **PACKAGE TIP: Django Project Templates**
>
> There are a number of project templates that really kickstart a Django project and follow the patterns described in this chapter. Here are two links that may be of use when we bootstrap a project:
>
> - `https://github.com/pydanny/cookiecutter-django`
>   Featured in this chapter.
> - `https://www.djangopackages.com/grids/g/cookiecutters/`
>   A list of alternate cookiecutter templates.

3.1 Django 1.8's Default Project Layout

Let's examine the default project layout that gets created when you run startproject and startapp:

Example 3.1

```
$ django-admin.py startproject mysite
$ cd mysite
$ django-admin.py startapp my_app
```

Here's the resulting project layout:

Example 3.2

```
mysite/
    manage.py
    my_app/
        __init__.py
        admin.py
        models.py
        tests.py
        views.py
    mysite/
        __init__.py
        settings.py
        urls.py
        wsgi.py
```

There are a number of problems with Django's default project layout. While useful for the tutorial, it's not quite as useful once you are trying to put together a real project. The rest of this chapter will explain why.

3.2 Our Preferred Project Layout

We rely on a three-tiered approach that builds on what is generated by the `django-admin.py startproject` management command. We place that inside another directory which serves as the git repository root. Our layouts at the highest level are:

Example 3.3

```
<repository_root>/
    <django_project_root>/
        <configuration_root>/
```

Let's go over each level in detail:

3.2.1 Top Level: Repository Root

The top-level *<repository_root>/* directory is the absolute root directory of the project. In addition to the *<django_project_root>* we also place other critical components like the *README.rst*, *docs/* directory, *.gitignore*, *requirements.txt* files, and other high-level files that are required for deployment.

Figure 3.1: Yet another reason why repositories are important.

> **TIP: Common Practice Varies Here**
>
> Some developers like to make the *<django_project_root>* the *<repository_root>* of the project.

3.2.2 Second Level: Project Root

This second level is the root of the actual Django project. All Python code files are inside this `<django_project_root>/` directory, its subdirectories, or below.

If using `django-admin.py startproject`, you would run the command from within the repository root. The Django project that it generates would then be the project root.

3.2.3 Third Level: Configuration Root

The *<configuration_root>* directory is where the settings module and base URLConf (*urls.py*) are placed. This must be a valid Python package (containing an *__init__.py* module).

The files in the configuration root are part of what is generated by the `django-admin.py startproject` command.

Figure 3.2: Three-tiered scoop layout.

3.3 Sample Project Layout

Let's take a common example: a simple rating site. Imagine that we are creating Ice Cream Ratings, a web application for rating different brands and flavors of ice cream.

This is how we would lay out such a project:

Example 3.4

```
icecreamratings_project/
    .gitignore
    Makefile
    docs/
    README.rst
    requirements.txt
    icecreamratings/
        manage.py
        media/  # Development ONLY!
        products/
```

```
    profiles/
    ratings/
    static/
    templates/
    config/
        __init__.py
        settings/
        urls.py
        wsgi.py
```

Let's do an in-depth review of this layout. As you can see, in the ***icecreamratings_project/*** directory, which is the ***<repository_root>*** , we have the following files and directories. We describe them in the table below:

File or Directory	Purpose
.gitignore	Lists the files and directories that Git should ignore. (This file is different for other version control systems. For example, if you are using Mercurial instead, you'd have an *.hgignore* file.)
README.rst and docs/	Developer-facing project documentation. You'll read more about this in chapter 23, ***Documentation***.
Makefile	Contains simple deployment tasks and macros. For more complex deployments you may want to rely on tools like `Invoke`, `Paver`, or `Fabric`.
requirements.txt	A list of Python packages required by your project, including the Django 1.8 package. You'll read more about this in chapter 21, ***Django's Secret Sauce: Third-Party Packages***.
icecreamratings/	The <django_project_root> of the project.

Table 3.1: Repository Root Files and Directories

When anyone visits this project, they are provided with a high-level view of the project. We've found that this allows us to work easily with other developers and even non-developers. For example, it's not uncommon for designer-focused directories to be created in the root directory.

Many developers like to make this at the same level as our ***<repository_root>***, and that's perfectly alright with us. We just like to see our projects a little more separated.

Inside the ***icecreamratings_project/icecreamratings*** directory, at the ***<django_project_root>***, we place the following files/directories:

File or Directory	Purpose
config/	The *<configuration_root>* of the project, where project-wide *settings*, *urls.py*, and *wsgi.py* modules are placed (We'll cover settings layout later in chapter 5, *Settings and Requirements Files*).
manage.py	If you leave this in, don't modify its contents. Refer to chapter 5, *Settings and Requirements Files* for more details.
media/	For use in development only: user-generated static media assets such as photos uploaded by users. For larger projects, this will be hosted on separate static media server(s).
products/	App for managing and displaying ice cream brands.
profiles/	App for managing and displaying user profiles.
ratings/	App for managing user ratings.
static/	Non-user-generated static media assets including CSS, JavaScript, and images. For larger projects, this will be hosted on separate static media server(s).
templates/	Where you put your site-wide Django templates.

Table 3.2: Django Project Files and Directories

TIP: Conventions for Static Media Directory Names

In the example above, we follow the official Django documentation's convention of using ***static/*** for the (non-user-generated) static media directory.

If you find this confusing, there's no harm in calling it ***assets/*** or ***site_assets/*** instead. Just remember to update your `STATICFILES_DIRS` setting appropriately.

3.4 What About the Virtualenv?

Notice how there is no virtualenv directory anywhere in the project directory or its subdirectories? That is completely intentional.

A good place to create the virtualenv for this project would be a separate directory where you keep all of your virtualenvs for all of your Python projects. We like to put all our environments in one directory and all our projects in another.

Figure 3.3: An isolated environment, allowing your ice cream to swim freely.

For example, on Mac OS X or Linux:

Example 3.5

```
~/projects/icecreamratings_project/
~/.envs/icecreamratings/
```

On Windows:

Example 3.6

```
c:\projects\icecreamratings_project\
c:\envs\icecreamratings\
```

If you're using virtualenvwrapper (Mac OS X or Linux) or virtualenvwrapper-win (Windows), that directory defaults to *~/.virtualenvs/* and the virtualenv would be located at:

Example 3.7

```
~/.virtualenvs/icecreamratings/
```

TIP: Listing Current Dependencies

If you have trouble determining which versions of dependencies you are using in your virtualenv, at the command line you can list your dependencies by typing:

Example 3.8

```
$ pip freeze --local
```

Also, remember, there's no need to keep the contents of your virtualenv in version control since it already has all the dependencies captured in ***requirements.txt***, and since you won't be editing any of the source code files in your virtualenv directly. Just remember that ***requirements.txt*** does need to remain in version control!

3.5 Going Beyond `startproject`

Django's `startproject` command allows you to create and use simple Django project templates. In Two Scoops of Django 1.6, we used this and tried to stay as vanilla as possible, providing a Django project template called `django-twoscoops-project` which worked with `startproject`.

Our previous project template was meant to generate all the boilerplate files referenced in the earlier parts of this chapter. However, as it grew more and more complex with contributions from readers, we hit its limitations and needed a more powerful project templating tool in order to create our ideal Django 1.8 starting project template.

In this section, we present our version of the ultimate Django project template, which is now a Cookiecutter template. We also present a popular alternative `startproject` template.

WARNING: What Will Happen to `django-twoscoops-project`?

Rather than updating `django-twoscoops-project` for Django 1.8, we've decided to focus on building and enhancing `cookiecutter-django`. `django-twoscoops-project` will no longer be updated, remaining on Django 1.6.

Here's why we think doing this is in your best interest:

- `django-twoscoops-project` ended up being too vanilla for us to use in our real-world projects. We stopped using it ourselves. Yet we had to keep `django-twoscoops-project` around as a vanilla template for Two Scoops 1.6 readers.
- Daniel ended up creating `cookiecutter-django` to address our need for an less plain, more customized, real-world Django project template.

3.5.1 Generating Project Boilerplate With Cookiecutter

In order to use our Django project template, you'll need a lightweight command-line tool called Cookiecutter. Cookiecutter is an advanced project templating tool that can be used for generating Django project boilerplate.

Here's how Cookiecutter works:

1. First, it asks you to enter a series of values, e.g the value for `project_name`.
2. Then it generates all your boilerplate project files based on the values you entered.

On Python 2.7+ or 3.3+, you'll first need to install Cookiecutter as per the instructions in the official Cookiecutter documentation.

TIP: Audrey on Cookiecutter

I originally created Cookiecutter in 2013 to meet my own Python package boilerplate creation needs. It was the first project to template file paths and file contents identically, an idea I thought was silly but decided to implement anyway.

There are now Cookiecutter templates for Python, C, C++, Common Lisp, JS, LaTeX/XeTeX, Berkshelf-Vagrant, HTML, Scala, 6502 Assembly, and more.

3.5.2 Our Favorite Project Template

The project template that we use for all our new Django 1.8 projects is `cookiecutter-django`.

Here's how you would use Cookiecutter to generate your boilerplate from `cookiecutter-django`:

Example 3.9

```
$ cookiecutter https://github.com/pydanny/cookiecutter-django

Cloning into 'cookiecutter-django'...
remote: Counting objects: 2358, done.
remote: Compressing objects: 100% (12/12), done.
remote: Total 2358 (delta 4), reused 0 (delta 0), pack-reused 2346
Receiving objects: 100% (2358/2358), 461.95 KiB, done.
Resolving deltas: 100% (1346/1346), done.

project_name (default is "project_name")? icecreamratings
repo_name (default is "icecreamratings")? icecreamratings_project
author_name (default is "Your Name")? Daniel and Audrey Roy Greenfeld
email (default is "audreyr@gmail.com")? hello@twoscoopspress.org
description (default is "A short description of the project.")? A website
 for rating ice cream flavors and brands.
domain_name (default is "example.com")? icecreamratings.audreyr.com
version (default is "0.1.0")? 0.1.0
timezone (default is "UTC")? America/Los_Angeles
now (default is "2015/01/13")? 2015/05/18
year (default is "2015")?
use_whitenoise (default is "y")?
github_username (default is "audreyr")? twoscoops
full_name (default is "Audrey Roy")? Daniel and Audrey Roy Greenfeld
```

After filling out all the values, in the directory where you ran Cookiecutter, it will create a directory for your project. In this case with the values entered above, the name of this directory will be *icecreamratings_project*.

The resulting project files will be roughly similar to the layout example we provided. The project will include settings, requirements, starter documentation, a starter test suite, and more.

TIP: What are all the other files?

Keep in mind that cookiecutter-django goes much further than the basic project layout components that we outlined earlier in this chapter. It's our ultimate Django project template that we use for our projects, so it has a lot of other bells and whistles.

It's a lot fancier than the `django-twoscoops-project` template that we created for Two Scoops of Django 1.6. We'd rather have you see our actual, real-life template that we use for our projects than a stripped-down, beginner-oriented template that we don't use.

You are welcome to fork `cookiecutter-django` and customize it to fit your own Django project needs.

3.5.3 An Alternative Template: `django-kevin`

Kevin Xu has maintained and enhanced his fork of the original "Two Scoops Project" layout, updating it for Django 1.8.

His alternative template is located at https://github.com/imkevinxu/django-kevin.

3.5.4 Other Alternatives

People can get very opinionated about their project layout being the "right" way, but as we mentioned, there's no one right way.

It's okay if a project differs from our layout, just so long as things are either done in a hierarchical fashion or the locations of elements of the project (docs, templates, apps, settings, etc) are documented in the root *README.rst*.

We encourage you to explore the forks of cookiecutter-django, django-kevin, and django-twoscoops-project, and to search for other Django project templates online. You'll learn all kinds of interesting tricks by studying other people's project templates.

Figure 3.4: Project layout differences of opinion can cause ice cream fights.

3.6 Summary

In this chapter, we covered our approach to basic Django project layout. We provided a detailed example to give you as much insight as possible into our practices.

Project layout is one of those areas of Django where practices differ widely from developer to developer and group to group. What works for a small team may not work for a large team with distributed resources. Whatever layout is chosen should be documented clearly.

4 | Fundamentals of Django App Design

It's not uncommon for new Django developers to become understandably confused by Django's usage of the word "app." So before we get into Django app design, it's very important that we go over some definitions.

A Django project is a web application powered by the Django web framework.

Django apps are small libraries designed to represent a single aspect of a project. A Django project is made up of many Django apps. Some of those apps are internal to the project and will never be reused; others are third-party Django packages.

INSTALLED_APPS is the list of Django apps used by a given project available in its INSTALLED_APPS setting.

Third-party Django packages are simply pluggable, reusable Django apps that have been packaged with the Python packaging tools. We'll begin coverage of them in chapter 21, *Django's Secret Sauce: Third-Party Packages.*

Figure 4.1: It'll make more sense when you turn the page.

Figure 4.2: Did that make sense? If not, read it again.

4.1 The Golden Rule of Django App Design

James Bennett volunteers as both a Django core developer and as its release manager. He taught us everything that we know about good Django app design. We quote him:

> "The art of creating and maintaining a good Django app is that it should follow the truncated Unix philosophy according to Douglas McIlroy: 'Write programs that do one thing and do it well.'"

In essence, **each app should be tightly focused on its task**. If an app can't be explained in a single sentence of moderate length, or you need to say 'and' more than once, it probably means the app is too big and should be broken up.

4.1.1 A Practical Example of Apps in a Project

Imagine that we're creating a web application for our fictional ice cream shop called "Two Scoops." Picture us getting ready to open the shop: polishing the countertops, making the first batches of ice cream, and building the website for our shop.

We'd call the Django project for our shop's website *twoscoops_project*. The apps within our Django project might be something like:

- A ***flavors*** app to track all of our ice cream flavors and list them on our website.
- A ***blog*** app for the official Two Scoops blog.
- An ***events*** app to display listings of our shop's events on our website: events such as Strawberry Sundae Sundays and Fudgy First Fridays.

Each one of these apps does one particular thing. Yes, the apps relate to each other, and you could imagine ***events*** or ***blog*** posts that are centered around certain ice cream flavors, but it's much better to have three specialized apps than one app that does everything.

In the future, we might extend the site with apps like:

- A ***shop*** app to allow us to sell pints by mail order.
- A ***tickets*** app, which would handle ticket sales for premium all-you-can-eat ice cream fests.

Notice how events are kept separate from ticket sales. Rather than expanding the ***events*** app to sell tickets, we create a separate ***tickets*** app because most events don't require tickets, and because event calendars and ticket sales have the potential to contain complex logic as the site grows.

Eventually, we hope to use the ***tickets*** app to sell tickets to Icecreamlandia, the ice cream theme park filled with thrill rides that we've always wanted to open.

Did we say that this was a fictional example? Ahem...well, here's an early concept map of what we envision for Icecreamlandia:

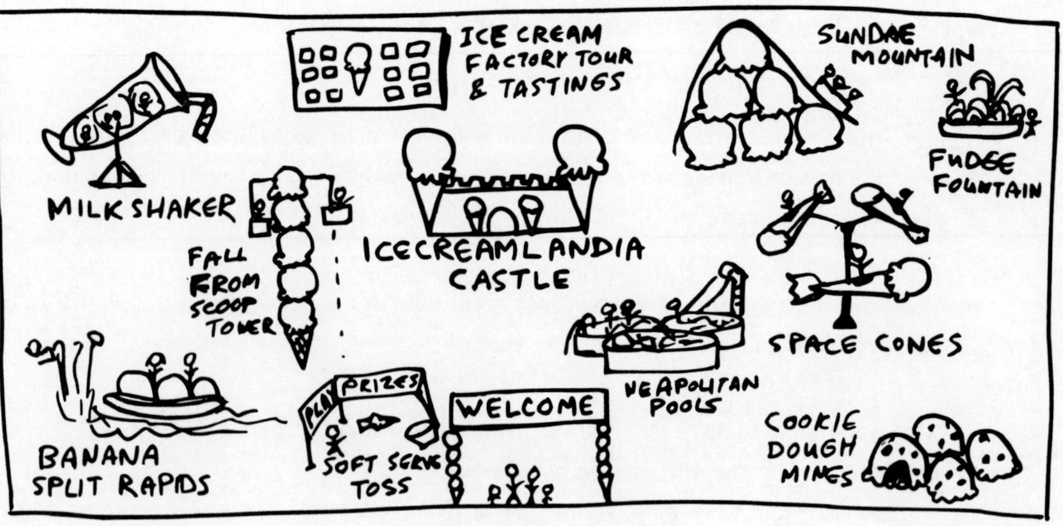

Figure 4.3: Our vision for Icecreamlandia.

4.2 What to Name Your Django Apps

Everyone has their own conventions, and some people like to use really colorful names. We like to use naming systems that are dull, boring, and obvious. In fact, we advocate doing the following:

When possible keep to single word names like ***flavors***, ***animals***, ***blog***, ***polls***, ***dreams***, ***estimates***, and ***finances***. A good, obvious app name makes the project easier to maintain.

As a general rule, the app's name should be a plural version of the app's main model, but there are many good exceptions to this rule, blog being one of the most common ones.

Don't just consider the app's main model, though. You should also consider how you want your URLs to appear when choosing a name. If you want your site's blog to appear at **http://www.example.com/weblog/**, then consider naming your app weblog rather than ***blog***, ***posts***, or ***blogposts***, even if the main model is `Post`, to make it easier for you to see which app corresponds with which part of the site.

Use valid, PEP 8-compliant, importable Python package names: short, all-lowercase names without numbers, dashes, periods, spaces, or special characters. If needed for readability, you can use underscores to separate words, although the use of underscores is discouraged.

4.3 When in Doubt, Keep Apps Small

Don't worry too hard about getting app design perfect. It's an art, not a science. Sometimes you have to rewrite them or break them up. That's okay.

Try and keep your apps small. Remember, it's better to have many small apps than to have a few giant apps.

Figure 4.4: Two small, single-flavor pints are better than a giant, 100-flavor container.

4.4 What Modules Belong in an App?

In this section we cover both the common and uncommon Python modules that belong in an app. For those with even a modicum of experience with Django, skipping to subsection 4.4.2 may be in order.

4.4.1 Common App Modules

Here are common modules seen in 99% of Django apps. These will prove very familiar to most readers, but we're placing this here for those just coming into the world of Django. For reference, any module ending with a slash ('/') represents a Python package, which can contain one or more modules.

Example 4.1

```
# Common modules
scoops/
    __init__.py
    admin.py
    forms.py
    management/
    migrations/
    models.py
    templatetags/
    tests/
    urls.py
    views.py
```

Over time a convention of module names has emerged for building Django apps. By following this convention across building of apps we set behaviors for ourselves and others, making examining each others code easier. While Python and Django are flexible enough that most of these don't need to be named according to this convention, doing so will cause problems. Probably not from an immediate technical perspective, but when you or others look at non-standard module names later, it will prove to be a frustrating experience.

4.4.2 Uncommon App Modules

Here are less common modules, which may or may not be familiar to many readers:

Example 4.2

```
# uncommon modules
scoops/
    behaviors.py
    constants.py
    context_processors.py
    decorators.py
    db/
```

```
exceptions
fields.py
factories.py
helpers.py
managers.py
middleware.py
signals.py
utils.py
viewmixins.py
```

What is the purpose of each module? Most of these should be obviously named, but we'll go over a few that might not be so clear.

behaviors.py : An option for locating model mixins per subsection 6.5.1.

constants.py : A good name for placement of app-level settings. If there are enough of them involved in an app, breaking them out into their own module can add clarity to a project.

decorators.py Where we like to locate our decorators. For more information on decorators, see section 9.3.

db/ Used in many projects for any custom model fields or components.

fields.py is commonly used for form fields, but is sometimes used for model fields when there isn't enough field code to justify creating a ***db/*** package.

factories.py Where we like to place our test data factories. Described in brief in subsection 22.3.5

helpers.py What we call helper functions. These are where we put code extracted from views (subsection 16.3.3) and models (section 6.5) to make them lighter. Synonymous with *utils.py*

managers.py When ***models.py*** grows too large, a common remedy is to move any custom model managers to this module.

signals.py While we argue against providing custom signals (see chapter 28), this can be a useful place to put them.

utils.py Synonymous with ***helpers.py***

viewmixins.py View modules and packages can be thinned by moving any view mixins to this module. See section 10.2.

For all of the modules listed in this section, their focus should be at the 'app-level', not global tools. Global-level modules are described in section 29.1, 'Create a Core App for Your Utilities'.

4.5 Summary

This chapter covered the art of Django app design. Specifically, each Django app should be tightly-focused on its own task, possess a simple, easy-to-remember name. If an app seems too complex, it should be broken up into smaller apps. Getting app design right takes practice and effort, but it's well worth the effort.

5 | Settings and Requirements Files

Django 1.8 has over 140 settings that can be controlled in the settings module, most of which come with default values. Settings are loaded when your server starts up, and experienced Django developers stay away from trying to change settings in production since they require a server restart.

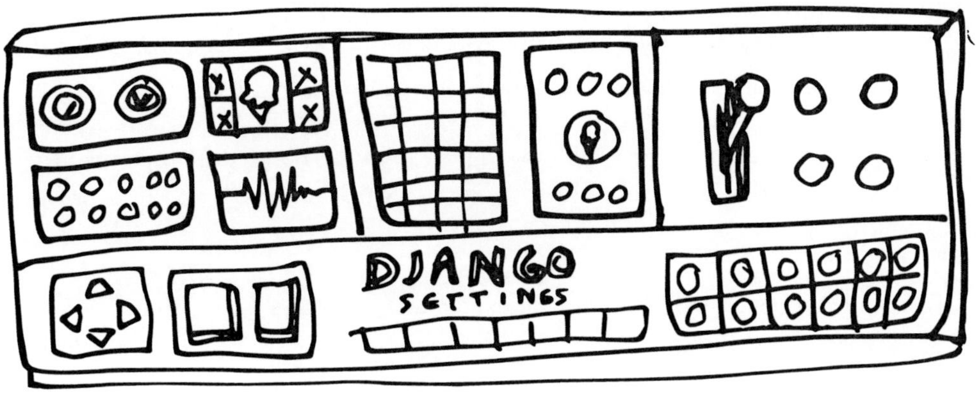

Figure 5.1: As your project grows, your Django settings can get pretty complex.

Some best practices we like to follow:

- **All settings files need to be version-controlled**. This is especially true in production environments, where dates, times, and explanations for settings changes absolutely must be tracked.
- **Don't Repeat Yourself**. You should inherit from a base settings file rather than cutting-and-pasting from one file to another.
- **Keep secret keys safe**. They should be kept out of version control.

5.1 Avoid Non-Versioned Local Settings

We used to advocate the non-versioned **local_settings anti-pattern**. Now we know better.

As developers, we have our own necessary settings for development, such as settings for debug tools which should be disabled (and often not installed to) staging or production servers.

Furthermore, there are often good reasons to keep specific settings out of public or private code repositories. The `SECRET_KEY` setting is the first thing that comes to mind, but API key settings to services like Amazon, Stripe, and other password-type variables need to be protected.

> **WARNING: Protect Your Secrets!**
>
> The `SECRET_KEY` setting is used in Django's cryptographic signing functionality, and needs to be set to a unique, unpredictable setting best kept out of version control. Running Django with a known `SECRET_KEY` defeats many of Django's security protections, which can lead to serious security vulnerabilities. For more details, read `https://docs.djangoproject.com/en/1.8/topics/signing/`.
>
> The same warning for `SECRET_KEY` also applies to production database passwords, AWS keys, OAuth tokens, or any other sensitive data that your project needs in order to operate.
>
> Later in this chapter we'll show how to handle the `SECRET_KEY` issue in the "Keep Secret Keys Out With Environment Settings" section.

A common solution is to create *local_settings.py* modules that are created locally per server or development machine, and are purposefully kept out of version control. Developers now make development-specific settings changes, including the incorporation of business logic without the code being tracked in version control. Staging and deployment servers can have location specific settings and logic without them being tracked in version control.

What could possibly go wrong?!?

Ahem...

- Every machine has untracked code.

- How much hair will you pull out, when after hours of failing to duplicate a production bug locally, you discover that the problem was custom logic in a production-only setting?
- How fast will you run from everyone when the 'bug' you discovered locally, fixed and pushed to production was actually caused by customizations you made in your own ***local_settings.py*** module and is now crashing the site?
- Everyone copy/pastes the same ***local_settings.py*** module everywhere. Isn't this a violation of Don't Repeat Yourself but on a larger scale?

Let's take a different approach. Let's break up development, staging, test, and production settings into separate components that inherit from a common base object in a settings file tracked by version control. Plus, we'll make sure we do it in such a way that server secrets will remain secret.

Read on and see how it's done!

5.2 Using Multiple Settings Files

> **TIP: History of This Setup Pattern**
>
> The setup described here is based on the so-called "The One True Way", from Jacob Kaplan-Moss' The Best (and Worst) of Django talk at OSCON 2011. See http://2scoops.co/the-best-and-worst-of-django.

Instead of having one ***settings.py*** file, with this setup you have a ***settings/*** directory containing your settings files. This directory will typically contain something like the following:

Example 5.1

```
settings/
    __init__.py
    base.py
    local.py
    staging.py
    test.py
    production.py
```

WARNING: Requirements + Settings

Each settings module should have its own corresponding requirements file. We'll cover this at the end of this chapter in section 5.5, 'Using Multiple Requirements Files.'

Settings file	Purpose
base.py	Settings common to all instances of the project.
local.py	This is the settings file that you use when you're working on the project locally. Local development-specific settings include `DEBUG` mode, log level, and activation of developer tools like django-debug-toolbar. Developers sometimes name this file *dev.py*.
staging.py	Staging version for running a semi-private version of the site on a production server. This is where managers and clients should be looking before your work is moved to production.
test.py	Settings for running tests including test runners, in-memory database definitions, and log settings.
production.py	This is the settings file used by your live production server(s). That is, the server(s) that host the real live website. This file contains production-level settings only. It is sometimes called *prod.py*.

Table 5.1: Settings files and their purpose

TIP: Multiple Files With Continuous Integration Servers

You'll also want to have a *ci.py* module containing that server's settings. Similarly, if it's a large project and you have other special-purpose servers, you might have custom settings files for each of them.

Let's take a look at how to use the shell and runserver management commands with this setup. You'll have to use the `--settings` command line option, so you'll be entering the following at the command-line.

To start the Python interactive interpreter with Django, using your *settings/local.py* settings file:

Example 5.2

```
python manage.py shell --settings=twoscoops.settings.local
```

To run the local development server with your ***settings/local.py*** settings file:

Example 5.3

```
python manage.py runserver --settings=twoscoops.settings.local
```

TIP: DJANGO_SETTINGS_MODULE and PYTHONPATH

A great alternative to using the `--settings` command line option everywhere is to set the `DJANGO_SETTINGS_MODULE` and `PYTHONPATH` environment variable to your desired settings module path. You'd have to set `DJANGO_SETTINGS_MODULE` to the corresponding settings module for each environment, of course.

For those with a more comprehensive understanding of virtualenv, another alternative is to set `DJANGO_SETTINGS_MODULE` and `PYTHONPATH` in the postactivate script. Then, once the virtualenv is activated, you can just type `python` from anywhere and import those values into your project. This also means that typing `django-admin.py` at the command-line works without the `--settings` option.

For the settings setup that we just described, here are the values to use with the `--settings` command line option or the `DJANGO_SETTINGS_MODULE` environment variable:

Environment	Option To Use With `--settings` (or `DJANGO_SETTINGS_MODULE` value)
Your local development server	`twoscoops.settings.local`
Your staging server	`twoscoops.settings.staging`
Your test server	`twoscoops.settings.test`
Your production server	`twoscoops.settings.production`

Table 5.2: Setting DJANGO_SETTINGS_MODULE per location

5.2.1 A Development Settings Example

As mentioned earlier, we need settings configured for development, such as selecting the console email backend, setting the project to run in DEBUG mode, and setting other configuration options that are used solely for development purposes. We place development settings like the following into ***settings/local.py***:

Example 5.4

```
# settings/local.py
from .base import *

DEBUG = True

EMAIL_BACKEND = 'django.core.mail.backends.console.EmailBackend'

DATABASES = {
    "default": {
        "ENGINE": "django.db.backends.postgresql_psycopg2",
        "NAME": "twoscoops",
        "USER": "",
        "PASSWORD": "",
        "HOST": "localhost",
        "PORT": "",
    }
}

INSTALLED_APPS += ("debug_toolbar", )
```

Now try it out at the command line with:

Example 5.5

```
python manage.py runserver --settings=twoscoops.settings.local
```

Open http://127.0.0.1:8000 and enjoy your development settings, ready to go into version control! You and other developers will be sharing the same development settings files, which for shared projects, is awesome.

Yet there's another advantage: No more '`if DEBUG`' or '`if not DEBUG`' logic to copy/paste around between projects. Settings just got a whole lot simpler!

At this point we want to take a moment to note that Django settings files are the single, solitary place we advocate using `import *`. The reason is that *for the singular case of Django setting modules we want to override all the namespace.*

5.2.2 Multiple Development Settings

Sometimes we're working on a large project where different developers need different settings, and sharing the same ***dev.py*** settings module with teammates won't do.

Well, it's still better tracking these settings in version control than relying on everyone customizing the same ***dev.py*** or ***local_settings.py*** module to their own tastes. A nice way to do this is with multiple dev settings files, e.g. ***dev_audrey.py*** and ***dev_pydanny.py***:

EXAMPLE 5.6

```
# settings/dev_pydanny.py
from .local import *

# Set short cache timeout
CACHE_TIMEOUT = 30
```

Why? It's not only good to keep all your own settings files in version control, but it's also good to be able to see your teammates' dev settings files. That way, you can tell if someone's missing a vital or helpful setting in their local development setup, and you can make sure that everyone's local settings files are synchronized. Here is what our projects frequently use for settings layout:

EXAMPLE 5.7

```
settings/
    __init__.py
    base.py
    dev_audreyr.py
    dev_pydanny.py
    local.py
```

```
staging.py
test.py
production.py
```

5.3 Separate Configuration From Code

One of the causes of the local_settings anti-pattern is that putting SECRET_KEY, AWS keys, API keys, or server-specific values into settings files has problems:

- Config varies substantially across deploys, code does not.
- Secret keys are configuration values, not code.
- Secrets often should be just that: secret! Keeping them in version control means that everyone with repository access has access to them.
- Platforms-as-a-service usually don't give you the ability to edit code on individual servers. Even if they allow it, it's a terribly dangerous practice.

To resolve this, our answer is to use **environment variables** in a pattern we like to call, well, **The Environment Variables Pattern**.

Every operating system supported by Django (and Python) provides the easy capability to create environment variables.

Here are the benefits of using environment variables for secret keys:

- Keeping secrets out of settings allows you to store every settings file in version control without hesitation. All of your Python code really should be stored in version control, including your settings.
- Instead of each developer maintaining an easily-outdated, copy-and-pasted version of the ***local_settings.py.example*** file for their own development purposes, everyone shares the same version-controlled ***settings/local.py*** .
- System administrators can rapidly deploy the project without having to modify files containing Python code.
- Most platforms-as-a-service recommend the use of environment variables for configuration and have built-in features for setting and managing them.

> **TIP: 12 Factor App: Store Config in the Environment**
>
> If you've read the 12 Factor App's article on configuration you'll recognize this pattern. For reference, see `http://12factor.net/config`. Some developers even advocate combining the use of environment variables with a single settings modules. We cover this practice in Appendix E under 12 Factor-Style Settings.

5.3.1 A Caution Before Using Environment Variables for Secrets

Before you begin setting environment variables, you should have the following:

- A way to manage the secret information you are going to store.
- A good understanding of how bash works with environment variables on servers, or a willingness to have your project hosted by a platform-as-a-service.

For more information, see `http://2scoops.co/wikipedia-env-variable`.

> **WARNING: Environment Variables Do Not Work With Apache**
>
> If your target production environment uses Apache, then you will discover that setting operating system environment variables as described below doesn't work. Confusing the issue is that Apache has its own environment variable system, which is almost but not quite what you'll need.
>
> If you are using Apache and want to avoid the local_settings anti-pattern, we recommend reading section 5.4, 'When You Can't Use Environment Variables,' later in this chapter.

5.3.2 How to Set Environment Variables Locally

On Mac and many Linux distributions that use **bash** for the shell, one can add lines like the following to the end of a *.bashrc*, *.bash_profile*, or *.profile*. When dealing with multiple projects using the same API but with different keys, you can also place these at the end of your virtualenv's *bin/activate* script:

EXAMPLE 5.8

```
$ export SOME_SECRET_KEY=1c3-cr3am-15-yummy
$ export AUDREY_FREEZER_KEY=y34h-r1ght-d0nt-t0uch-my-1c3-cr34m
```

On Windows systems, it's a bit trickier. You can set them one-by-one at the command line (**cmd.exe**) in a persistent way with the `setx` command, but you'll have to close and reopen your command prompt for them to go into effect. A better way is to place these commands at the end of the virtualenv's ***bin/activate.bat*** script so they are available upon activation:

EXAMPLE 5.9

```
> set SOME_SECRET_KEY 1c3-cr3am-15-yummy
```

PowerShell is much more powerful than the default Windows shell and comes with Windows Vista and above. Setting environment variables while using PowerShell:

For the current Windows user only:

EXAMPLE 5.10

```
[Environment]::SetEnvironmentVariable("SOME_SECRET_KEY",
                                "1c3-cr3am-15-yummy", "User")
[Environment]::SetEnvironmentVariable("AUDREY_FREEZER_KEY",
                    "y34h-r1ght-d0nt-t0uch-my-1c3-cr34m", "User")
```

Machine-wide:

EXAMPLE 5.11

```
[Environment]::SetEnvironmentVariable("SOME_SECRET_KEY",
                                "1c3-cr3am-15-yummy", "Machine")
[Environment]::SetEnvironmentVariable("AUDREY_FREEZER_KEY",
                    "y34h-r1ght-d0nt-t0uch-my-1c3-cr34m", "Machine")
```

For more information on Powershell, see http://2scoops.co/powershell

> **TIP: virtualenvwrapper Makes This Easier**
>
> Mentioned earlier in this book, **virtualenvwrapper**, simplifies per-virtualenv environment variables. It's a great tool. Of course, setting it up requires a more-than-basic understanding of the shell and Mac OS X, Linux, or Windows.

5.3.3 How to Set Environment Variables in Production

If you're using your own servers, your exact practices will differ depending on the tools you're using and the complexity of your setup. For the simplest 1-server setup for test projects, you can set the environment variables manually. But if you're using scripts or tools for automated server provisioning and deployment, your approach may be more complex. Check the documentation for your deployment tools for more information.

If your Django project is deployed via a platform-as-a-service, check the documentation for specific instructions. We've included Heroku instructions here so that you can see that it's similar for platform-as-a-service options.

On Heroku, you set environment variables with the following command, executed from your development machine:

Example 5.12

```
$ heroku config:set SOME_SECRET_KEY=1c3-cr3am-15-yummy
```

To see how you access environment variables from the Python side, open up a new Python prompt and type:

Example 5.13

```
>>> import os
>>> os.environ["SOME_SECRET_KEY"]
"1c3-cr3am-15-yummy"
```

To access environment variables from one of your settings files, you can do something like this:

Example 5.14

```
# Top of settings/production.py
import os
SOME_SECRET_KEY = os.environ["SOME_SECRET_KEY"]
```

This snippet simply gets the value of the SOME_SECRET_KEY environment variable from the operating system and saves it to a Python variable called SOME_SECRET_KEY.

Following this pattern means all code can remain in version control, and all secrets remain safe.

5.3.4 Handling Missing Secret Key Exceptions

In the above implementation, if the SECRET_KEY isn't available, it will throw a KeyError, making it impossible to start the project. That's great, but a KeyError doesn't tell you that much about what's actually wrong. Without a more helpful error message, this can be hard to debug, especially under the pressure of deploying to servers while users are waiting and your ice cream is melting.

Here's a useful code snippet that makes it easier to troubleshoot those missing environment variables. If you're using our recommended environment variable secrets approach, you'll want to add this to your *settings/base.py* file:

Example 5.15

```
# settings/base.py
import os

# Normally you should not import ANYTHING from Django directly
# into your settings, but ImproperlyConfigured is an exception.
from django.core.exceptions import ImproperlyConfigured

def get_env_variable(var_name):
    """Get the environment variable or return exception."""
    try:
        return os.environ[var_name]
```

```
    except KeyError:
        error_msg = "Set the {} environment variable".format(var_name)
        raise ImproperlyConfigured(error_msg)
```

Then, in any of your settings files, you can load secret keys from environment variables as follows:

Example 5.16

```
SOME_SECRET_KEY = get_env_variable("SOME_SECRET_KEY")
```

Now, if you don't have SOME_SECRET_KEY set as an environment variable, you get a traceback that ends with a useful error message like this:

Example 5.17

```
django.core.exceptions.ImproperlyConfigured: Set the SOME_SECRET_KEY
environment variable.
```

WARNING: Don't Import Django Components Into Settings Modules

This can have many unpredictable side effects, so avoid any sort of import of Django components into your settings. ImproperlyConfigured is the exception because it's the official Django exception for...well...improperly configured projects. And just to be helpful we add the name of the problem setting to the error message.

TIP: Using django-admin.py Instead of manage.py

The official Django documentation says that you should use *django-admin.py* rather than *manage.py* when working with multiple settings files: https://docs.djangoproject.com/en/1.8/ref/django-admin/

That being said, if you're struggling with *django-admin.py*, it's perfectly okay to develop and launch your site running it with *manage.py*.

5.4 When You Can't Use Environment Variables

The problem with using environment variables to store secrets is that it doesn't always work. The most common scenario for this is when using Apache for serving HTTP, but this also happens even in Nginx-based environments where operations wants to do things in a particular way. When this occurs, rather than going back to the **local_settings anti-pattern**, we advocate using non-executable files kept out of version control in a method we like to call the **secrets file pattern**.

To implement the **secrets file pattern**, follow these three steps:

1. Create a secrets file using the configuration format of choice, be it JSON, Config, YAML, or even XML.
2. Add a secrets loader (JSON-powered example below) to manage the secrets in a cohesive, explicit manner.
3. Add the secrets file name to the *.gitignore* or *.hgignore*.

5.4.1 Using JSON Files

Our preference is to use shallow JSON files. The JSON format has the advantage of being the format of choice for various Python and non-Python tools. To use the JSON format, first create a *secrets.json* file:

Example 5.18

```
{
    "FILENAME": "secrets.json",
    "SECRET_KEY": "I've got a secret!",
    "DATABASES_HOST": "127.0.0.1",
    "PORT": "5432"
}
```

To use the *secrets.json* file, add the following code to your base settings module.

Example 5.19

```
# settings/base.py
```

```python
import json

# Normally you should not import ANYTHING from Django directly
# into your settings, but ImproperlyConfigured is an exception.
from django.core.exceptions import ImproperlyConfigured

# JSON-based secrets module
with open("secrets.json") as f:
    secrets = json.loads(f.read())

def get_secret(setting, secrets=secrets):
    """Get the secret variable or return explicit exception."""
    try:
        return secrets[setting]
    except KeyError:
        error_msg = "Set the {0} environment variable".format(setting)
        raise ImproperlyConfigured(error_msg)

SECRET_KEY = get_secret("SECRET_KEY")
```

Now we are loading secrets from non-executable JSON files instead of from unversioned executable code. Hooray!

5.4.2 Using Config, YAML, and XML File Formats

While we prefer the forced simplicity of shallow JSON, others might prefer other file formats. We'll leave it up to the reader to create additional `get_secret()` alternatives that work with these formats. Just remember to be familiar with things like `yaml.safe_load()` and XML bombs. See section 26.9, 'Defend Against Python Code Injection Attacks.'

5.5 Using Multiple Requirements Files

Finally, there's one more thing you need to know about multiple settings files setup. It's good practice for each settings file to have its own corresponding requirements file. This means we're only installing what is required on each server.

To follow this pattern, recommended to us by Jeff Triplett, first create a ***requirements/*** directory in the **<repository_root>**. Then create '***.txt***' files that match the contents of your settings directory. The results should look something like:

Example 5.20

```
requirements/
    base.txt
    local.txt
    staging.txt
    production.txt
```

In the ***base.txt*** file, place the dependencies used in all environments. For example, you might have something like the following in there:

Example 5.21

```
Django==1.8.0
psycopg2==2.6
djangorestframework==3.1.1
```

Your ***local.txt*** file should have dependencies used for local development, such as:

Example 5.22

```
-r base.txt # includes the base.txt requirements file

coverage==3.7.1
django-debug-toolbar==1.3.0
```

The needs of a continuous integration server might prompt the following for a ***ci.txt*** file:

Example 5.23

```
-r base.txt # includes the base.txt requirements file

coverage==3.7.1
django-jenkins==0.16.4
```

Production installations should be close to what is used in other locations, so ***production.txt*** commonly just calls ***base.txt***:

Example 5.24

```
-r base.txt # includes the base.txt requirements file
```

5.5.1 Installing From Multiple Requirements Files

For local development:

Example 5.25

```
$ pip install -r requirements/local.txt
```

For production:

Example 5.26

```
$ pip install -r requirements/production.txt
```

5.5.2 Using Multiple Requirements Files With Platforms as a Service (PaaS)

See chapter 30, *Deployment:Platforms as a Service.*

> **TIP: Pin Requirements Exactly**
>
> All the pip requirements.txt examples in this chapter are explicitly set to a package version. This ensures a more stable project. We cover this at length in subsection 21.7.2, 'Add Package and Version Number to Your Requirements.'

5.6 Handling File Paths in Settings

If you switch to the multiple settings setup and get new file path errors to things like templates and media, don't be alarmed. This section will help you resolve these errors.

We humbly beseech the reader to never hardcode file paths in Django settings files. This is *really* bad:

Bad Example 5.1

```
# settings/base.py

# Configuring MEDIA_ROOT
# 'DONT DO THIS! Hardcoded to just one user's preferences
MEDIA_ROOT = "/Users/pydanny/twoscoops_project/media"

# Configuring STATIC_ROOT
# 'DONT DO THIS! Hardcoded to just one user's preferences
STATIC_ROOT = "/Users/pydanny/twoscoops_project/collected_static"

# Configuring TEMPLATES
# 'DONT DO THIS! Hardcoded to just one user's preferences
TEMPLATES = [
    {
        'BACKEND': 'django.template.backends.django.DjangoTemplates',
        DIRS = ("/Users/pydanny/twoscoops_project/templates",)
    },
]
```

The above code represents a common pitfall called **hardcoding**. The above code, called a **fixed path**, is bad because as far as you know, **pydanny** (Daniel Roy Greenfeld) is the only person who has set up their computer to match this path structure. Anyone else trying to use this example will see their project break, forcing them to either change their directory structure (unlikely) or change the settings module to match their preference (causing problems for everyone else including pydanny).

Don't hardcode your paths!

To fix the path issue, we dynamically set a project root variable intuitively named `BASE_DIR` at the top of the base settings module. Since BASE_DIR is determined in relation to the location of base.py, your project can be run from any location on any development computer or server.

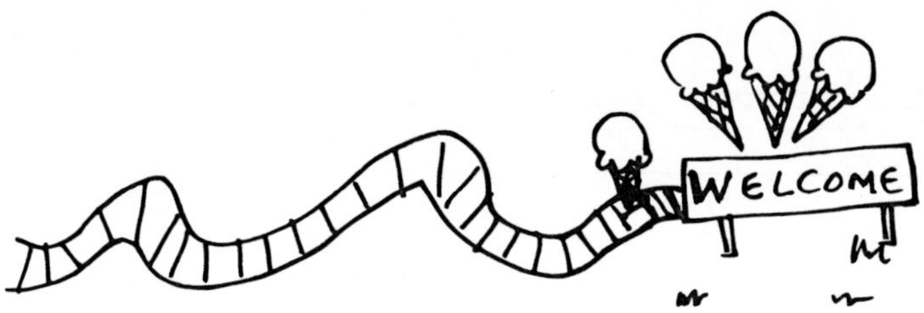

Figure 5.2: While we're at it, let's go down this path.

We find the cleanest way to set a BASE_DIR-like setting is with **Unipath** (http://pypi.python.org/pypi/Unipath/), a Python package that does elegant, clean path calculations:

EXAMPLE 5.27

```
# At the top of settings/base.py
from unipath import Path

BASE_DIR = Path(__file__).ancestor(3)
MEDIA_ROOT = BASE_DIR.child("media")
STATIC_ROOT = BASE_DIR.child("static")
STATICFILES_DIRS = (
    BASE_DIR.child("assets"),
)
TEMPLATES = [
    {
        'BACKEND': 'django.template.backends.django.DjangoTemplates',
        DIRS = (BASE_DIR.child("templates"),)
    },
]
```

If you really want to set your BASE_DIR with the Python standard library's os.path library, though, this is one way to do it in a way that will account for paths:

Example 5.28

```
# At the top of settings/base.py
from os.path import join, abspath, dirname

here = lambda *dirs: join(abspath(dirname(__file__)), *dirs)
BASE_DIR = here("..", "..")
root = lambda *dirs: join(abspath(BASE_DIR), *dirs)

# Configuring MEDIA_ROOT
MEDIA_ROOT = root("media")

# Configuring STATIC_ROOT
STATIC_ROOT = root("collected_static")

# Additional locations of static files
STATICFILES_DIRS = (
    root("assets"),
)

# Configuring TEMPLATE_DIRS
TEMPLATES = [
    {
        'BACKEND': 'django.template.backends.django.DjangoTemplates',
        DIRS = (root("templates"),)
    },
]
```

With your various path settings dependent on `BASE_DIR`, your file path settings should work, which means your templates and media should be loading without error.

TIP: How Different Are Your Settings From the Django Defaults?

If you want to know how things in your project differ from Django's defaults, use the `diffsettings` management command.

5.7 Summary

Remember, everything except for critical security related values ought to be tracked in version control.

Any project that's destined for a real live production server is bound to need multiple settings and requirements files. Even beginners to Django need this kind of settings/requirements file setup once their projects are ready to leave the original development machine. We provide our solution, as well as an Apache-friendly solution since it works well for both beginning and advanced developers.

Also, if you prefer a different shell than the ones provided, environment variables still work. You'll just need to know the syntax for defining them.

The same thing applies to requirements files. Working with untracked dependency differences increases risk as much as untracked settings.

6 Model Best Practices

Models are the foundation of most Django projects. Racing to write Django models without thinking things through can lead to problems down the road.

All too frequently we developers rush into adding or modifying models without considering the ramifications of what we are doing. The quick fix or sloppy "temporary" design decision that we toss into our code base now can hurt us in the months or years to come, forcing crazy workarounds or corrupting existing data.

So keep this in mind when adding new models in Django or modifying existing ones. Take your time to think things through, and design your foundation to be as strong and sound as possible.

PACKAGE TIP: Our Picks for Working With Models

Here's a quick list of the model-related Django packages that we use in practically every project.

- **django-model-utils** to handle common patterns like **TimeStampedModel**.
- **django-extensions** has a powerful management command called `shell_plus` which autoloads the model classes for all installed apps. The downside of this library is that it includes a lot of other functionality which breaks from our preference for small, focused apps.

6.1 Basics

6.1.1 Break Up Apps With Too Many Models

If there are 20+ models in a single app, think about ways to break it down into smaller apps, as it probably means your app is doing too much. In practice, we like to lower this number to no more than five models per app.

6.1.2 Be Careful With Model Inheritance

Model inheritance in Django is a tricky subject. Django provides three ways to do model inheritance: **abstract base classes, multi-table inheritance**, and **proxy models.**

WARNING: Django Abstract Base Classes <> Python Abstract Base Classes

Don't confuse Django abstract base classes with the abstract base classes in the Python standard library's abc module, as they have very different purposes and behaviors.

Here are the pros and cons of the three model inheritance styles. To give a complete comparison, we also include the option of using no model inheritance to begin with:

Model Inheritance Style	Pros	Cons
No model inheritance: if models have a common field, give both models that field.	Makes it easiest to understand at a glance how Django models map to database tables.	If there are a lot of fields duplicated across models, this can be hard to maintain.
Abstract base classes: tables are only created for derived models.	Having the common fields in an abstract parent class saves us from typing them more than once. We don't get the overhead of extra tables and joins that are incurred from multi-table inheritance.	We cannot use the parent class in isolation.

Multi-table inheritance: tables are created for both parent and child. An implied `OneToOneField` links parent and child.	Gives each model its own table, so that we can query either parent or child model. Also gives us the ability to get to a child object from a parent object: `parent.child`	Adds substantial overhead since each query on a child table requires joins with all parent tables. We strongly recommend against using multi-table inheritance. See the warning below.
Proxy models: a table is only created for the original model.	Allows us to have an alias of a model with different Python behavior.	We cannot change the model's fields.

Table 6.1: Pros and Cons of the Model Inheritance Styles

WARNING: Avoid Multi-Table Inheritance

Multi-table inheritance, sometimes called "concrete inheritance," is considered by the authors and many other developers to be a bad thing. We strongly recommend against using it. We'll go into more detail about this shortly.

Here are some simple rules of thumb for knowing which type of inheritance to use and when:

- If the overlap between models is minimal (e.g. you only have a couple of models that share one or two obvious fields), there might not be a need for model inheritance. Just add the fields to both models.
- If there is enough overlap between models that maintenance of models' repeated fields causes confusion and inadvertent mistakes, then in most cases the code should be refactored so that the common fields are in an abstract base model.
- Proxy models are an occasionally-useful convenience feature, but they're very different from the other two model inheritance styles.
- At all costs, everyone should avoid multi-table inheritance (see warning above) since it adds both confusion and substantial overhead. Instead of multi-table inheritance, use explicit `OneToOneFields` and `ForeignKeys` between models so you can control when joins are traversed.

6.1.3 Model Inheritance in Practice: The TimeStampedModel

It's very common in Django projects to include a `created` and `modified` timestamp field on all your models. We could manually add those fields to each and every model, but that's a lot of work and adds the risk of human error. A better solution is to write a `TimeStampedModel` to do the work for us:

Example 6.1

```
# core/models.py
from django.db import models

class TimeStampedModel(models.Model):
    """
    An abstract base class model that provides self-
    updating ``created`` and ``modified`` fields.
    """
    created = models.DateTimeField(auto_now_add=True)
    modified = models.DateTimeField(auto_now=True)

    class Meta:
        abstract = True
```

Take careful note of the very last two lines in the example, which turn our example into an abstract base class:

Example 6.2

```
class Meta:
    abstract = True
```

By defining `TimeStampedModel` as an abstract base class when we define a new class that inherits from it, Django doesn't create a `core_timestampedmodel` table when `migrate` is run.

Let's put it to the test:

Example 6.3

```python
# flavors/models.py
from django.db import models

from core.models import TimeStampedModel

class Flavor(TimeStampedModel):
    title = models.CharField(max_length=200)
```

This only creates one table: the `flavors_flavor` database table. That's exactly the behavior we wanted.

On the other hand, if `TimeStampedModel` was not an abstract base class (i.e. a concrete base class via multi-table inheritance), it would also create a `core_timestampedmodel` table. Not only that, but all of its subclasses including `Flavor` would lack the fields and have implicit foreign keys back to `TimeStampedModel` just to handle `created/modified` timestamps. Any reference to `Flavor` that reads or writes to the `TimeStampedModel` would impact two tables. (Thank goodness it's abstract!)

Remember, concrete inheritance has the potential to become a nasty performance bottleneck. This is even more true when you subclass a concrete model class multiple times.

Further reading:

- http://2scoops.co/1.8-model-inheritance

6.1.4 Database Migrations

Django comes with a powerful database change propagation library aptly called "**migrations**", or as we prefer to refer in the book, `django.db.migrations`. As of Django 1.7 `django.db.migrations` replaced the use of the third-party South library, but as both libraries share the same author (Andrew Godwin), usage and practices are quite similar.

Tips for creating migrations:

- As soon as a new app or model is created, take that extra minute to create the initial `django.db.migrations` for that new model. All we do is type `python manage.py makemigrations`.
- Examine the generated migration code before you run it, especially when complex changes are involved. Also review the SQL that will be used with the `sqlmigrate` command.
- Use the `MIGRATION_MODULES` setting to manage writing migrations for third-party apps that don't have their own `django.db.migrations`-style migrations.
- Don't worry about how many migrations are created. If the number of migrations becomes unwieldy, use `squashmigrations` to bring them to heel.

Deployment and management of migrations:

- Before deployment, check that you can rollback migrations! We can't always have perfect round-trips, but not being able to roll back to an earlier state really hurts bug tracking and sometimes deployment in larger projects.
- If a project has tables with millions of rows in them, do extensive tests against data of that size on staging servers before running a migration on a production server. Migrations on real data can take much, much, much more time than anticipated.
- If you are using MySQL:
  - You must back up the database before any schema change. MySQL lacks transaction support around schema changes, hence rollbacks are impossible.
  - If you can, put the project in read-only mode before executing the change.
  - If not careful, schema changes on heavily populated tables can take a long time. Not seconds or minutes, but hours.

Figure 6.1: Cones migrating south for the winter. Django's built-in migration system started out as an external project called South.

6.2 Django Model Design

One of the most difficult topics that receives the least amount of attention is how to design good Django models.

How do you design for performance without optimizing prematurely? Let's explore some strategies here.

6.2.1 Start Normalized

We suggest that readers of this book need to be familiar with **database normalization**. If you are unfamiliar with database normalization, make it your responsibility to gain an understanding, as working with models in Django effectively requires a working knowledge of this. Since a detailed explanation of the subject is outside the scope of this book, we recommend the following resources:

- `http://en.wikipedia.org/wiki/Database_normalization`
- `http://en.wikibooks.org/wiki/Relational_Database_Design/Normalization`

When you're designing your Django models, always start off normalized. Take the time to make sure that no model should contain data already stored in another model.

At this stage, use relationship fields liberally. Don't denormalize prematurely. You want to have a good sense of the shape of your data.

6.2.2 Cache Before Denormalizing

Often, setting up caching in the right places can save you the trouble of denormalizing your models. We'll cover caching in much more detail in chapter 24, *Finding and Reducing Bottlenecks*, so don't worry too much about this right now.

6.2.3 Denormalize Only if Absolutely Needed

It can be tempting, especially for those new to the concepts of data normalization, to denormalize prematurely. Don't do it! Denormalization may seem like a panacea for what causes problems in a project. However it's a tricky process that risks adding complexity to your project and dramatically raises the risk of losing data.

Please, please, please explore caching before denormalization.

When a project has reached the limits of what the techniques described in chapter 24, *Finding and Reducing Bottlenecks* can address, that's when research into the concepts and patterns of database denormalization should begin.

6.2.4 When to Use Null and Blank

When defining a model field, you have the ability to set the `null=True` and the `blank=True` options. By default, they are False.

Knowing when to use these options is a common source of confusion for developers.

We've put this guide together to serve as a guide for standard usage of these model field arguments.

Field Type	Setting null=True	Setting blank=True
`CharField`, `TextField`, `SlugField`, `EmailField`, `CommaSeparatedIntegerField`, `UUIDField`	*Don't do this.* Django's convention is to store empty values as the empty string, and to always retrieve NULL or empty values as the empty string for consistency.	*Okay.* Do this if you want the corresponding form widget to accept empty values. If you set this, empty values get stored as empty strings in the database.
`FileField`, `ImageField`	*Don't do this.* Django stores the path from `MEDIA_ROOT` to the file or to the image in a CharField, so the same pattern applies to FileFields.	*Okay.* The same pattern for CharField applies here.
`BooleanField`	*Don't do this.* Use `NullBooleanField` instead.	*Don't do this.*

Field Type	Setting null=True	Setting blank=True
`IntegerField`, `FloatField`, `DecimalField`, `DurationField`, etc	*Okay* if you want to be able to set the value to `NULL` in the database.	*Okay* if you want the corresponding form widget to accept empty values. If so, you will also want to set `null=True`.
`DateTimeField`, `DateField`, `TimeField`, etc.	*Okay* if you want to be able to set the value to `NULL` in the database.	*Okay* if you want the corresponding form widget to accept empty values, or if you are using auto_now or auto_now_add. If so, you will also want to set `null=True`.
`ForeignKey`, `ManyToManyField`, `OneToOneField`	*Okay* if you want to be able to set the value to `NULL` in the database.	*Okay* if you want the corresponding form widget (e.g. the select box) to accept empty values.
`GenericIPAddressField`	*Okay* if you want to be able to set the value to `NULL` in the database.	*Okay* if you want to make the corresponding field widget accept empty values.
`IPAddressField`	*Not recommended for use.* See warning below.	*Not recommended for use.* See warning below.

Table 6.2: When to Use Null and Blank by Field

TIP: Use GenericIPAddressField Instead of IPAddressField

For a variety of reasons including support for both IPv4 and IPv6, GenericIPAddress-Field is a much better field to use than IPAddressField. Furthermore, using Generic-IPAddressField future-proofs your project because IPAddressField was deprecated in Django 1.7.

Figure 6.2: A common source of confusion.

6.2.5 When to Use BinaryField

Added in Django 1.8, this field allows for the storage of raw binary data, or **bytes**. We can't perform filters, excludes, or other SQL actions on the field, but there are use cases for it. For example we could store:

- MessagePack-formatted content.
- Raw sensor data.
- Compressed data e.g. the type of data Sentry stores as a BLOB, but is required to base64-encode due to legacy issues.

The possibilities are endless, but remember that binary data can come in huge chunks, which can slow down databases. If this occurs and becomes a bottleneck, the solution might be to save the binary data in a file and reference it with a `FileField`.

WARNING: Don't Serve Files From BinaryField!

Storing files in a database field should never happen. If it's being considered as a solution to a problem, find a certified database expert and ask for a second opinion.

To summarize PostgreSQL expert Frank Wiles on the problems with using a database as a file store:

- 'read/write to a DB is always slower than a filesystem'
- 'your DB backups grow to be huge and more time consuming'
- 'access to the files now requires going through your app (Django) and DB layers'

See http://2scoops.co/three-things-not-to-put-in-database

When someone thinks there is a good use case for serving files from a database, and quotes a success like https://npmjs.org (stored files in CouchDB), it's time to do your research. The truth is that https://npmjs.org, migrated its database-as-file-store system to a more traditional file serving method (see https://scalenpm.org).

6.2.6 Try to Avoid Using Generic Relations

In general we advocate against **generic relations** and use of `models.field.GenericForeignKey`. They are usually more trouble than they are worth. Using them is often a sign that troublesome shortcuts are being taken, that the wrong solution is being explored.

The idea of a generic relations is that we are binding one table to another by way of an unconstrained foreign key (`GenericForeignKey`). Using it is akin to using a NoSQL datastore that lacks foreign key constraints as the basis for projects that could really use foreign key constraints. This causes the following:

- Reduction in speed of queries due to lack of indexing between models.
- Danger of data corruption as a table can refer to another against a non-existent record.

The upside of this lack of constraints is that generic relations makes it easier to build apps for things that need to interact with numerous model types we might have created. Specifically things like favorites, ratings, voting, messages, and tagging apps. Indeed, there are a number of existing apps that are built this way. While we hesitate to use them, we are comforted by the fact that the good ones are focused on a single task (for example, tagging).

Over time, we've found that we can build favorites, ratings, voting, messages, and tagging apps built off `ForeignKey` and `ManyToMany` field. For a little more development work, by avoiding the use of `GenericForeignKey` we get the benefit of speed and integrity.

Where the `GenericForeignKey` becomes really troublesome is when its unconstrained feature becomes the method by which a project's primary data is defined. For example, if we built an Ice Cream themed project where the relationships between toppings, flavors, containers, orders, and sales were all tracked via `GenericForeignKey`, we would have the problems described in the bullets above. In short:

- Try to avoid generic relations and `GenericForeignKey`.
- If you think you need generic relations, see if the problem can be solved through better model design or the new PostgreSQL fields.
- If usage can't be avoided, try to use an existing third-party app. The isolation a third-party app provides will help keep data cleaner.

6.2.7 PostgreSQL-Specific Fields: When to Use Null and Blank

Field Type	Setting null=True	Setting blank=True
`ArrayField`	*Okay.*	*Okay.*
`HStoreField`	*Okay.*	*Okay.*
`IntegerRangeField`, `BigIntegerRangeField`, and `FloatRangeField`	*Okay* if you want to be able to set the value to `NULL` in the database.	*Okay* if you want the corresponding form widget to accept empty values. If so, you will also want to set `null=True`.

Field Type	Setting null=True	Setting blank=True
`DatetimeRangeField` and `DateRangeField`	*Okay* if you want to be able to set the value to `NULL` in the database.	*Okay* if you want the corresponding form widget to accept empty values, or if you are using auto_now or auto_now_add. If so, you will also want to set `null=True`.

Table 6.3: When to Use Null and Blank for Postgres Fields

6.3 The Model `_meta` API

Before Django 1.8, the model `_meta` API was unofficial and purposely undocumented, as is normal with any API subject to change without notice. The original purpose of `_meta` was simply for Django to store extra info about models for its own use. However, it has proven so useful that it is now a documented API.

For most projects you shouldn't need `_meta`. The main uses for it are when you need to:

- Get a list of a model's fields.
- Get the class of a particular field for a model (or its inheritance chain or other info derived from such).
- Ensure that how you get this information remains constant across future Django versions.

Examples of these sorts of situations:

- Building a Django model introspection tool.
- Building your own custom specialized Django form library.
- Creating admin-like tools to edit or interact with Django model data.
- Writing visualization or analysis libraries, e.g. analyzing info only about fields that start with "foo".

Further reading:

- Model `_meta` docs: https://docs.djangoproject.com/en/1.8/ref/models/meta/

- Django 1.8 release notes about model _meta:
  https://docs.djangoproject.com/en/1.8/releases/1.8/#model-meta-api

6.4 Model Managers

Every time we use the Django ORM to query a model, we are using an interface called a **model manager** to interact with the database. Model managers are said to act on the full set of all possible instances of this model class (all the data in the table) to restrict the ones you want to work with. Django provides a default model manager for each model class, but we can define our own.

Here's a simple example of a custom model manager:

Example 6.4

```
from django.db import models
from django.utils import timezone

class PublishedManager(models.Manager):

    use_for_related_fields = True

    def published(self, **kwargs):
        return self.filter(pub_date__lte=timezone.now(), **kwargs)

class FlavorReview(models.Model):
    review = models.CharField(max_length=255)
    pub_date = models.DateTimeField()

    # add our custom model manager
    objects = PublishedManager()
```

Now, if we first want to display a count of all of the ice cream flavor reviews, and then a count of just the published ones, we can do the following:

Example 6.5

```
>>> from reviews.models import FlavorReview
>>> FlavorReview.objects.count()
```

```
35
>>> FlavorReview.objects.published().count()
31
```

Easy, right? Yet wouldn't it make more sense if you just added a second model manager? That way you could have something like:

Bad Example 6.1

```
>>> from reviews.models import FlavorReview
>>> FlavorReview.objects.filter().count()
35
>>> FlavorReview.published.filter().count()
31
```

On the surface, replacing the default model manager seems like the obvious thing to do. Unfortunately, our experiences in real project development makes us very careful when we use this method. Why?

First, when using model inheritance, children of abstract base classes receive their parent's model manager, and children of concrete base classes do not.

Second, the first manager applied to a model class is the one that Django treats as the default. This breaks significantly with the normal Python pattern, causing what can appear to be unpredictable results from QuerySets.

With this knowledge in mind, in your model class, `objects = models.Manager()` should be defined manually above any custom model manager.

WARNING: Know the Model Manager Order of Operations

Always set `objects = models.Manager()` above any custom model manager that has a new name.

Additional reading:

- https://docs.djangoproject.com/en/1.8/topics/db/managers/

6.5 Understanding Fat Models

The concept of **fat models** is that rather than putting data-related code in views and templates, instead we encapsulate the logic in model methods, classmethods, properties, even manager methods. That way, any view or task can use the same logic. For example, if we have a model that represents Ice Cream reviews we might attach to it the following methods:

- `Review.create_review(cls, user, rating, title, description)` A `classmethod` for creating reviews. Called on the model class itself from HTML and REST views, as well as an import tool that accepts spreadsheets.
- `review.product_average` A review instance property that returns the reviewed project's average rating. Used on review detail views so the reader can get a feel for the overall opinion without leaving the page.
- `review.found_useful(self, user, yes)` A method that sets whether or not readers found the review useful or not. Used in detail and list views, for both HTML and REST implementations.

As can be inferred from this list, fat models are a great way to improve reuse of code across a project. In fact, the practice of moving logic from views and templates to models has been growing across projects, frameworks and languages for years. This is a good thing, right?

Not necessarily.

The problem with putting all logic into models is it can cause models to explode in size of code, becoming what is called a **'god object'**. This anti-pattern results in model classes that are hundreds, thousands, even tens of thousands of lines of code. Because of their size and complexity, god objects are hard to understand, hence hard to test and maintain.

When moving logic into models, we try to remember one of the basic ideas of object-oriented programming, that big problems are easier to resolve when broken up into smaller problems. If a model starts to become unwieldy in size, we begin isolating code that is prime for reuse across other models, or whose complexity requires better management. The methods, classmethods, and properties are kept, but the logic they contain is moved into *Model Behaviors* or *Stateless Helper Functions*. Let's cover both techniques in the following subsections:

6.5.1 Model Behaviors a.k.a Mixins

Model behaviors embrace the idea of composition and encapsulation via the use of mixins. Models inherit logic from abstract models. For more information, see the following resources:

- `http://blog.kevinastone.com/django-model-behaviors.html` Kevin Stone's article on using composition to reduce replication of code.
- section 10.2, 'Using Mixins With CBVs'.

6.5.2 Stateless Helper Functions

By moving logic out of models and into utility functions, it becomes more isolated. This isolation makes it easier to write tests for the logic. The downside is that the functions are stateless, hence all arguments have to be passed.

We cover this in chapter 29, 'What About Those Random Utilities?'.

6.5.3 Model Behaviors vs Helper Functions

In our opinion, alone neither of these techniques are perfect. However, when both are used judiciously, they can make projects shine. Understanding when to use either isn't a static science, it is an evolving process. This kind of evolution is tricky, prompting our suggestion to have tests for the components of fat models.

6.6 Summary

Models are the foundation for most Django projects, so take the time to design them thoughtfully.

Start normalized, and only denormalize if you've already explored other options thoroughly. You may be able to simplify slow, complex queries by dropping down to raw SQL, or you may be able to address your performance issues with caching in the right places.

Don't forget to use indexes. Add indexes when you have a better feel for how you're using data throughout your project.

If you decide to use model inheritance, inherit from abstract base classes rather than concrete models. You'll save yourself from the confusion of dealing with implicit, unneeded joins.

Watch out for the "gotchas" when using the `null=True` and `blank=True` model field options. Refer to our handy table for guidance.

You may find django-model-utils and django-extensions pretty handy.

Finally, fat models are a way to encapsulate logic in models, but can all too readily turn into god objects.

Our next chapter is where we begin talking about queries and the database layer.

7 Queries and the Database Layer

Like any ORM, Django converts data from different types into objects that we can use pretty consistently across supported databases. Then it provides a set of methods for interacting with those objects. For the most part, Django's does a pretty good job at what its designed to do. However, it does have quirks, and understanding those quirks is part of learning how to use Django. Let's go over some of them, shall we?

7.1 Use get_object_or_404() for Single Objects

In views such as detail pages where you want to retrieve a single object and do something with it, use `get_object_or_404()` instead of `get()`.

WARNING: `get_object_or_404()` Is for Views Only

- Only use it in views.
- Don't use it in helper functions, forms, model methods or anything that is not a view or directly view related.

Many years ago a certain Python coder who we won't list by name, but likes to do cartwheels, was deploying his first Django project. So entranced was he by Django's `get_object_or_404()` function that he used it everywhere, in views, in models, in forms, everywhere. In development this worked great and passed tests. Unfortunately, this unconstrained use meant that when certain records were deleted by the admin staff, the entire site broke.

Keep `get_object_or_404()` in your views!

7.2 Be Careful With Queries That Might Throw Exceptions

When you're getting a single Django model instance with the `get_object_or_404()` shortcut, you don't need to wrap it in a try-except block. That's because `get_object_or_404()` already does that for you.

However, in most other situations you need to use a try-except block. Some tips:

7.2.1 ObjectDoesNotExist vs. DoesNotExist

`ObjectDoesNotExist` can be applied to any model object, whereas `DoesNotExist` is for a specific model.

Example 7.1

```python
from django.core.exceptions import ObjectDoesNotExist

from flavors.models import Flavor
from store.exceptions import OutOfStock

def list_flavor_line_item(sku):
    try:
        return Flavor.objects.get(sku=sku, quantity__gt=0)
    except Flavor.DoesNotExist:
        msg = "We are out of {0}".format(sku)
        raise OutOfStock(msg)

def list_any_line_item(model, sku):
    try:
        return model.objects.get(sku=sku, quantity__gt=0)
    except ObjectDoesNotExist:
        msg = "We are out of {0}".format(sku)
        raise OutOfStock(msg)
```

7.2.2 When You Just Want One Object but Get Three Back

If it's possible that your query may return more than one object, check for a `MultipleObjectsReturned` exception. Then in the except clause, you can do whatever makes sense, e.g. raise a special exception or log the error.

Example 7.2

```
from flavors.models import Flavor
from store.exceptions import OutOfStock, CorruptedDatabase

def list_flavor_line_item(sku):
    try:
        return Flavor.objects.get(sku=sku, quantity__gt=0)
    except Flavor.DoesNotExist:
        msg = "We are out of {}".format(sku)
        raise OutOfStock(msg)
    except Flavor.MultipleObjectsReturned:
        msg = "Multiple items have SKU {}. Please fix!".format(sku)
        raise CorruptedDatabase(msg)
```

7.3 Use Lazy Evaluation to Make Queries Legible

Django's ORM is very powerful. And with such power comes the responsibility to make code legible, hence maintainable. With complex queries, attempt to avoid chaining too much functionality on a small set of lines:

Bad Example 7.1

```
# Don't do this!
from django.models import Q

from promos.models import Promo

def fun_function(**kwargs):
    """Find working ice cream promo"""
    # Too much query chaining makes code go off the screen or page. Not go
    return Promo.objects.active().filter(Q(name__startswith=name)|Q(descri
```

This is unpleasant, right? Yet if we add in advanced Django ORM tools, then it will go from unpleasant to as terrible as a sriracha-based ice cream topping. To mitigate this unpleasantness, we can use the lazy evaluation feature of Django queries to keep our ORM code clean.

By lazy evaluation, we mean that the Django ORM doesn't make the SQL calls until the data is actually needed. We can chain ORM methods and functions as much as we want, and until we try to loop through the result, Django doesn't touch the database. Instead of being forced to chain many methods and advanced database features on a single line, we can break them up over as many lines as needed. This increases readability, which improves the ease of maintenance, which increases time for getting ice cream.

Here we take the code from *bad example 7.1* and break it up into more legible code:

Example 7.3

```
# Do this!
from django.models import Q

from promos.models import Promo

def fun_function(**kwargs):
    """Find working ice cream promo"""
    results = Promo.objects.active()
    results = results.filter(
                Q(name__startswith=name) |
                Q(description__icontains=name)
            )
    results = results.exclude(status='melted')
    results = results.select_related('flavors')
    return results
```

As can be seen in the corrected code, we can more easily tell what the end result will be. Even better, by breaking up the query statement we can comment on specific lines of code.

7.4 Lean on Advanced Query Tools

Django's ORM is easy to learn, intuitive, and covers many use cases. Yet there are a number of things it does not do well. What happens then is after the queryset is returned we begin processing more and more data in Python. This is a shame, because every database manages and transforms data faster than Python (or Ruby, JavaScript, Go, Java, et al).

Instead of managing data with Python, we always try to use Django's advanced query tools to do the lifting. In doing so we not only benefit from increased performance, we also enjoy using code that was more tested (Django and most databases are constantly-tested) than any Python-based workarounds we create.

7.4.1 Query Expressions

When performing reads on a database, query expressions can be used to create values or computations during that read. If that sounds confusing, don't feel alone, we're confused too. Since a code example is worth a thousand words, let's provide an example of how they can benefit us. In our case, we're trying to list all the customers who have on average ordered more than one scoop per visit to an ice cream store.

First, how this might be done, albeit dangerously, without query expressions:

Bad Example 7.2

```
from models.customers import Customer

customers = []
for customer in Customer.objects.iterate():
    if customer.scoops_ordered > customer.store_visits:
        customers.append(customer)
```

This example makes us shudder with fear. Why?

- It uses Python to loop through all the Customer records in the database, one by one. This is slow and memory consuming.
- Under any volume of use, it will generate race conditions. This is where while we're running the script, customers are interacting with the data. While probably not an issue in this simple 'READ' example, in real-world code combining that with an 'UPDATE' it can lead to loss of data.

Fortunately, through query expressions Django provides a way to make this more efficient and race-condition free:

Example 7.4

```
from django.db.models import F

from models.customers import Customer

customers = Customer.objects.filter(scoops_ordered__gt=F('store_visits'))
```

What this does is use the database itself to perform the comparison. Under the hood, Django is running something that probably looks like:

Example 7.5

```
SELECT * from customers_customer where scoops_ordered > store_visits
```

Query Expressions should be in your toolkit. They increase the performance and stability of projects.

➤ https://docs.djangoproject.com/en/1.8/ref/models/expressions/

7.4.2 Database Functions

In Django 1.8 we were given the ability to easily use common database functions such as `UPPER()`, `LOWER()`, `COALESCE()`, `CONCAT()`, `LENGTH()`, and `SUBSTR()`. Of all the advanced query tools provided by Django, these are our favorites. For that matter, it's one of our favorite things about the 1.8 release. Why?

1. Very easy to use, either on new projects or existing projects.
2. Database functions allow us to move some of the logic from Python to the database. This can be a performance booster, as processing data in Python is not as fast as processing data in a database.
3. Database functions are implemented differently per database, but Django's ORM abstracts this away. Code we write using them on PostgreSQL will work on MySQL or SQLite3.
4. They are also query expressions, which means they follow a common pattern already established by another nice part of the Django ORM.

Reference:

- https://docs.djangoproject.com/en/1.8/ref/models/database-functions/

7.5 Don't Drop Down to Raw SQL Until It's Necessary

Most of the queries we write are simple. The **Object-Relational Model** or **ORM** provides a great productivity shortcut: not only generating decent SQL queries for common use cases, but providing model access/update functionality that comes complete with validation and security. If you can write your query easily with the ORM, then take advantage of it!

It's also good to keep in mind that if you ever release one of your Django apps as a third-party package, using raw SQL will decrease the portability of the work.

Finally, in the rare event that the data has to be migrated from one database to another, any database-specific features that you use in your SQL queries will complicate the migration.

So when should you actually write raw SQL? If expressing your query as raw SQL would drastically simplify your Python code or the SQL generated by the ORM, then go ahead and do it. For example, if you're chaining a number of QuerySet operations that each operate on a large data set, there may be a more efficient way to write it as raw SQL.

TIP: Malcolm Tredinnick's Advice on Writing SQL in Django

Django core developer Malcolm Tredinnick said (paraphrased):

> "The ORM can do many wonderful things, but sometimes SQL is the right answer. The rough policy for the Django ORM is that it's a storage layer that happens to use SQL to implement functionality. If you need to write advanced SQL you should write it. I would balance that by cautioning against overuse of the `raw()` and `extra()` methods."

TIP: Jacob Kaplan-Moss' Advice on Writing SQL in Django

Django project co-leader Jacob Kaplan-Moss says (paraphrased):

> "If it's easier to write a query using SQL than Django, then do it. `extra()` is nasty and should be avoided; `raw()` is great and should be used where appropriate."

Figure 7.1: This flavor of ice cream contains raw SQL. It's a bit chewy.

7.6 Add Indexes as Needed

While adding `db_index=True` to any model field is easy, understanding when it should be done takes a bit of judgment. Our preference is to start without indexes and add them as needed.

When to consider adding indexes:

- The index is used frequently, as in 10-25% of all queries.
- There is real data, or something that approximates real data, so we can analyze the results of indexing.

- We can run tests to determine if indexing generates an improvement in results.

When using PostgreSQL, `pg_stat_activity` tells us what indexes are actually being used.

Once a project goes live, chapter 24, *Finding and Reducing Bottlenecks*, has information on index analysis.

7.7 Transactions

As of Django 1.8, the default behavior of the ORM is to autocommit every query when it is called. In the case of data modification, this means that every time a `.create()` or `.update()` is called, it immediately modifies data in the SQL database. The advantage of this is that it makes it easier for beginning developers to understand the ORM. The disadvantage is that if a view (or some other operation) requires two or more database modifications to occur, if one modification succeeds and the other fails, the database is at risk of corruption.

The way to resolve the risk of database corruption is through the use of database transactions. A database transaction is where two or more database updates are contained in a single **unit of work**. If a single update fails, all the updates in the transaction are rolled back. To make this work, a database transaction, by definition, must be **atomic**, **consistent**, **isolated** and **durable**. Database practitioners often refer to these properties of database transactions using the acronym **ACID**.

Django has a powerful and relatively easy-to-use transaction mechanism that was overhauled and modernized with the release of 1.8. This makes it much easier to lock down database integrity on a project, using decorators and context managers in a rather intuitive pattern.

7.7.1 Wrapping Each HTTP Request in a Transaction

Example 7.6

```
# settings/base.py

DATABASES = {
    'default': {
        # ...
        'ATOMIC_REQUESTS': True,
```

```
    },
}
```

Django makes it easy to handle all web requests inside of a transaction with the ATOMIC_REQUESTS setting. By setting it to True as show above, all requests are wrapped in transactions, including those that only read data. The advantage of this approach is safety: all database queries in views are protected, the disadvantage is performance can suffer. We can't tell you just how much this will affect performance, as it depends on individual database design and how well various database engines handle locking.

When using Django 1.8, we've found that this is a great way to ensure at the start that a write-heavy project's database maintains integrity. With lots of traffic, however, we've had to go back and change things to a more focused approach. Depending on the size this can be a small or monumental task.

Another thing to remember when using ATOMIC_REQUESTS, is that only the database state is rolled back on errors. It's quite embarrassing to send out a confirmation email and then have the transaction that wraps a request rolled back. This problem may crop up with any "write" to anything other than the database: sending email or SMS, calling a third-party API, writing to the filesystem, etc. Therefore, when writing views that create/update/delete records but interact with non-database items, you may choose to decorate the view with transaction.non_atomic_requests().

WARNING: Aymeric Augustin on non_atomic_requests()

Core Django developer and main implementer of the new transaction system, Aymeric Augustin says, "This decorator requires tight coupling between views and models, which will make a code base harder to maintain. We might have come up with a better design if we hadn't had to provide for backwards-compatibility."

Then you can use the more explicit declaration as described below in this super-simple API-style function-based view:

Example 7.7

```python
# flavors/views.py

from django.db import transaction
from django.http import HttpResponse
from django.shortcuts import get_object_or_404
from django.utils import timezone

from .models import Flavor

@transaction.non_atomic_requests
def posting_flavor_status(request, pk, status):
    flavor = get_object_or_404(Flavor, pk=pk)

    # This will execute in autocommit mode (Django's default).
    flavor.latest_status_change_attempt = timezone.now()
    flavor.save()

    with transaction.atomic():
        # This code executes inside a transaction.
        flavor.status = status
        flavor.latest_status_change_success = timezone.now()
        flavor.save()
        return HttpResponse("Hooray")

    # If the transaction fails, return the appropriate status
    return HttpResponse("Sadness", status_code=400)
```

If you are using `ATOMIC_REQUESTS=True` and want to switch to a more focused approach described in the following section, we recommend an understanding of *bottleneck analysis* (chapter 24), *good test coverage* (chapter 22), and *continuous integration* (chapter 32) before you undertake this effort.

TIP: Projects Touching Medical or Financial Data

For these kinds of projects, engineer systems for eventual consistency rather than for transactional integrity. In other words, be prepared for transactions to fail and rollbacks to occur. Fortunately, because of transactions, even with a rollback, the data will remain accurate and clean.

7.7.2 Explicit Transaction Declaration

Explicit transaction declaration is one way to increase site performance. In other words, specifying which views and business logic are wrapped in transactions and which are not. The downside to this approach is that it increases development time.

TIP: Aymeric Augustin on ATOMIC_REQUESTS vs. Explicit Transaction Declaration

Aymeric Augustin says, 'Use ATOMIC_REQUESTS as long as the performance overhead is bearable. That means "forever" on most sites.'

When it comes to transactions, here are some good guidelines to live by:

- Database operations that do not modify the database *should not be* wrapped in transactions.
- Database operations that modify the database *should be* wrapped in a transaction.
- Special cases including database modifications that require database reads and performance considerations can affect the previous two guidelines.

If that's not clear enough, here is a table explaining when different Django ORM calls should be wrapped in transactions.

Purpose	ORM method	Generally Use Transactions?
Create Data	.create(), .bulk_create(), .get_or_create(),	✓
Retrieve Data	.get(), .filter(), .count(), .iterate(), .exists(), .exclude(), .in_bulk, etc.	

Modify Data	.update()	✓
Delete Data	.delete()	✓

Table 7.1: When to Use Transactions

Figure 7.2: Because no one loves ice cream quite like a database.

We also cover this in chapter 24, *Finding and Reducing Bottlenecks*, specifically subsection subsection 24.2.4, 'Switch ATOMIC_REQUESTS to False.'

> **TIP: Never Wrap Individual ORM Method Calls**
>
> Django's ORM actually relies on transactions internally to ensure consistency of data. For instance, if an update affects multiple tables because of concrete inheritance, Django has that wrapped up in transactions.
>
> Therefore, it is never useful to wrap an individual ORM method [`.create()`, `.update()`, `.delete()`] call in a transaction. Instead, use transactions when you are calling several ORM methods in a view, function, or method.

7.7.3 django.http.StreamingHttpResponse and Transactions

If a view is returning `django.http.StreamingHttpResponse`, it's impossible to handle transaction errors once the response has begun. If your project uses this response method then `ATOMIC_REQUESTS` should do one of the following:

❶ Set `ATOMIC_REQUESTS` to Django's default, which is `False`. Then you can use the techniques explored in subsection 7.7.2. Or...

❷ Wrap the view in the `django.db.transaction.non_atomic_requests` decorator.

Keep in mind that you can use `ATOMIC_REQUESTS` with a streaming response, but the transaction will only apply to the view itself. If the generation of the response stream triggers additional SQL queries, they will be made in autocommit mode. Hopefully generating a response doesn't trigger database writes...

7.7.4 Transactions in MySQL

If the database being used is **MySQL**, transactions may not be supported depending on your choice of table type such as **InnoDB** or **MyISAM**. If transactions are not supported, Django will always function in autocommit mode, regardless of `ATOMIC_REQUESTS` or code written to support transactions. For more information, we recommend reading the following articles:

- http://2scoops.co/1.8-transactions-in-mysql
- http://dev.mysql.com/doc/refman/5.0/en/sql-syntax-transactions.html

7.7.5 Django ORM Transaction Resources

- https://docs.djangoproject.com/en/1.8/topics/db/transactions/
  Django's documentation on transactions.
- Real Python has a great tutorial on the subject of transactions.
  https://realpython.com/blog/python/transaction-management-with-django-1-6/

7.8 Summary

In this chapter we went over different ways to query a project's persistent data. Now that we know how to store data, let's begin to display it. Starting with the next chapter we're diving into views!

8 Function- and Class-Based Views

Both function-based views (FBVs) and class-based views (CBVs) are in Django 1.8. We recommend that you understand how to use both types of views.

> **TIP: Historical Note**
>
> During the release of Django 1.5, there was a bit of confusion about FBVs due to the wording of the release notes and incorrect information on some blog posts. However, no plans ever existed for removing function-based views from Django and function-based views are still in Django.

8.1 When to Use FBVs or CBVs

Whenever you implement a view, think about whether it would make more sense to implement as a FBV or as a CBV. Some views are best implemented as CBVs, and others are best implemented as FBVs.

If you aren't sure which method to choose, on the next page we've included a flow chart that might be of assistance.

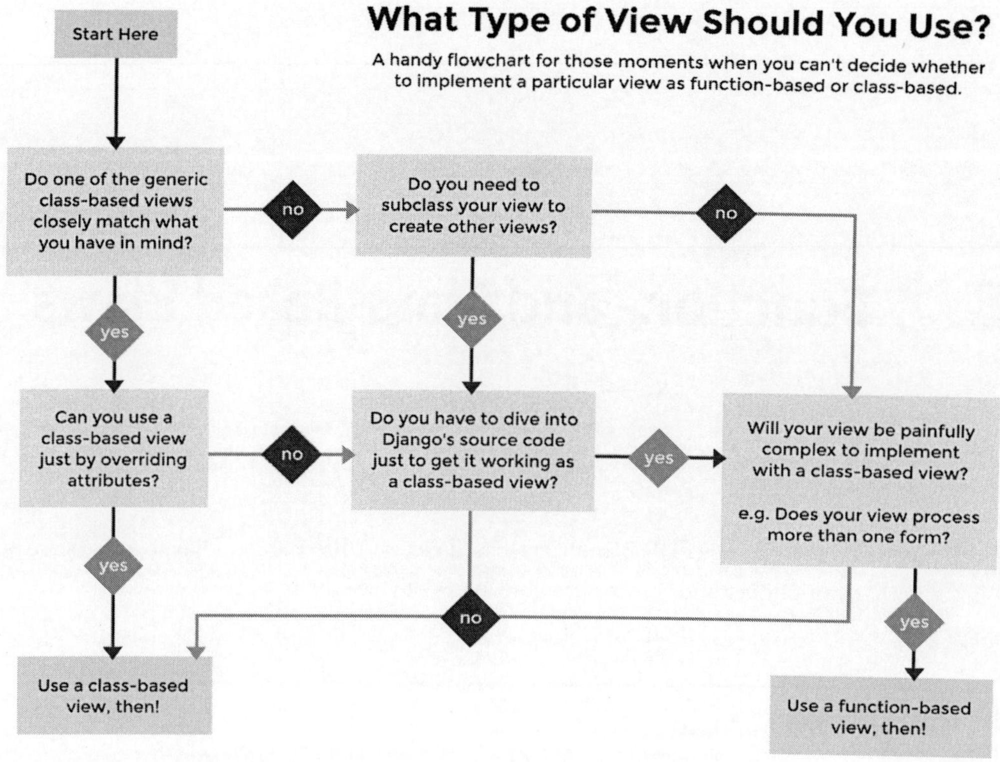

Figure 8.1: Should you use a FBV or a CBV? flow chart.

This flowchart follows our preference for using CBVs over FBVs. We prefer to use CBVs for most views, using FBVs to implement only the custom error views or complicated ones that would be a pain to implement with CBVs.

> **TIP: Alternative Approach - Staying With FBVs**
>
> Some developers prefer to err on the side of using FBVs for most views and CBVs only for views that need to be subclassed. That strategy is fine as well.

8.2 Keep View Logic Out of URLConfs

Requests are routed to views via **URLConfs**, in a module that is normally named *urls.py*. Per Django's URL design philosophy (`http://2scoops.co/1.8-url-design`), the coupling of views with urls is loose, allows for infinite flexibility, and encourages best practices.

And yet, this is what Daniel feels like yelling every time he sees complex ***urls.py*** files:

> *"I didn't write J2EE XML and Zope ZCML configuration files back in the day just so you darn kids could stick logic into Django url modules!"*

Remember that Django has a wonderfully simple way of defining URL routes. Like everything else we bring up in this book, that simplicity is to be honored and respected. The rules of thumb are obvious:

1. The views modules should contain view logic.
2. The URL modules should contain URL logic.

Ever see code like this? Perhaps in the official Django tutorial?

Bad Example 8.1

```
from django.conf.urls import url
from django.views.generic import DetailView

from tastings.models import Tasting

urlpatterns = [
    url(r"^(?P<pk>\d+)/$",
        DetailView.as_view(
            model=Tasting,
            template_name="tastings/detail.html"),
        name="detail"),
    url(r"^(?P<pk>\d+)/results/$",
        DetailView.as_view(
            model=Tasting,
            template_name="tastings/results.html"),
        name="results"),
]
```

At a glance this code might seem okay, but we argue that it violates the Django design philosophies:

- **Loose coupling** between views, urls, and models has been replaced with tight coupling, meaning you can never reuse the view definitions.

- **Don't Repeat Yourself** is violated by using the same/similar arguments repeatedly between CBVs.
- Infinite flexibility (for URLs) is destroyed. Class inheritance, the primary advantage of Class Based Views, is impossible using this anti-pattern.
- Lots of other issues: What happens when you have to add in authentication? And what about authorization? Are you going to wrap each URLConf view with two or more decorators? Putting your view code into your URLConfs quickly turns your URLConfs into an unmaintainable mess.

In fact, we've heard from developers that seeing CBVs defined in URLConfs this way was part of why they steered clear of using them.

Alright, enough griping. We'll show our preferences in the next section.

8.3 Stick to Loose Coupling in URLConfs

Figure 8.2: Loose coupling of chocolate chip cookie dough ice cream.

Here is how to create URLconfs that avoid the problems we mentioned on the previous page. First, we write the views:

Example 8.1

```
# tastings/views.py
from django.views.generic import ListView, DetailView, UpdateView
from django.core.urlresolvers import reverse

from .models import Tasting
```

```
class TasteListView(ListView):
    model = Tasting

class TasteDetailView(DetailView):
    model = Tasting

class TasteResultsView(TasteDetailView):
    template_name = "tastings/results.html"

class TasteUpdateView(UpdateView):
    model = Tasting

    def get_success_url(self):
        return reverse("tastings:detail",
            kwargs={"pk": self.object.pk})
```

Then we define the urls:

Example 8.2

```
# tastings/urls.py
from django.conf.urls import url

from . import views

urlpatterns = [
    url(
        regex=r"^$",
        view=views.TasteListView.as_view(),
        name="list"
    ),
    url(
        regex=r"^(?P<pk>\d+)/$",
        view=views.TasteDetailView.as_view(),
        name="detail"
    ),
    url(
```

```
        regex=r"^(?P<pk>\d+)/results/$",
        view=views.TasteResultsView.as_view(),
        name="results"
    ),
    url(
        regex=r"^(?P<pk>\d+)/update/$",
        view=views.TasteUpdateView.as_view(),
        name="update"
    )
]
```

Your first response to our version of this should go something like, *"Are you sure this is a good idea? You changed things to use two files AND more lines of code! How is this better?"*

Well, this is the way we do it. Here are some of the reasons we find it so useful:

- **Don't Repeat Yourself**: No argument or attribute is repeated between views.
- **Loose coupling**: We've removed the model and template names from the URLConf because views should be views and URLConfs should be URLConfs. We should be able to call our views from one or more URLConfs, and our approach lets us do just that.
- **URLConfs should do one thing and do it well**: Related to our previous bullet, our URLConf is now focused primarily on just one thing: URL routing. We aren't tracking down view logic across both views and URLConfs, we just look in our views.
- **Our views benefit from being class-based**: Our views, by having a formal definition in the views module, can inherit from other classes. This means adding authentication, authorization, new content formats, or any other business requirement tossed our way is much easier to handle.
- **Infinite flexibility**: Our views, by having a formal definition in the views module, can implement their own custom logic.

8.3.1 What if We Aren't Using CBVs?

The same rules apply.

We've encountered debugging nightmares of projects using FBVs with extensive URLConf hackery, such as elaborate tricks with the __file__ attribute of Python modules combined with directory walking and regular expressions to automagically create URLConfs. If that sounds painful, it was.

Keep logic out of URLConfs!

8.4 Use URL Namespaces

What URL namespaces do is provide an identifier for app-level and instance level namespaces. URL namespaces are one of those things where on the surface they seem like they might not help much, but once a developer begins using them they wonder why they didn't use them already. We'll sum up using URL namespaces as follows:

Instead of writing URL names like `tastings_detail` write them like `tastings:detail`.

Before we explain why this is so useful, we'll provide an example of usage based on the app-level URLConf code from example 8.2. In the root URLConf we would add:

Example 8.3

```
# urls.py at root of project
urlpatterns += [
    url(r'^tastings/', include('tastings.urls', namespace='tastings')),
]
```

To see this in action in a view, let's take a look at a snippet of code from example 8.1:

Example 8.4

```
# tastings/views.py snippet
class TasteUpdateView(UpdateView):
    model = Tasting

    def get_success_url(self):
        return reverse("tastings:detail",
            kwargs={"pk": self.object.pk})
```

See this in action in an HTML template:

Example 8.5

```
{% extends "base.html" %}

{% block title %}Tastings{% endblock title %}

{% block content %}
<ul>
  {% for taste in tastings %}
    <li>
      <a href="{% url "tastings:detail" taste.pk %}">{{ taste.title }}</a>
      <small>
        (<a href="{% url "tastings:update" taste.pk %}">update</a>)
      </small>
    </li>
  {% endfor %}
</ul>
{% endblock content %}
```

Now that we understand how to implement URL namespaces, let's cover why they are useful.

8.4.1 Makes for Shorter, More Obvious and Don't Repeat Yourself URL Names

In example 8.2 what we don't see are URL names like "`tastings_detail`" and "`tastings_results`" that copy the model or app name. Instead there are simple, obvious names like "*detail*" and "*results*". This greatly increases the legibility of apps, especially to newer Django developers.

Also, who wants to type "tastings" or whatever an app is called so many extra times?

8.4.2 Increases Interoperability With Third-Party Libraries

One of the problems of writing URL names things like `<myapp>_detail` is when app names collide. While this might not be a problem with things like our *tastings* app, it's certainly happened to the authors with blog and contact applications. Fortunately, URL namespaces makes this easy to resolve. Assuming that we have an existing contact app, but needed to add a second one, using URL namespaces we could integrate them to our root URLConf like so:

Example 8.6

```
# urls.py at root of project
urlpatterns += [
    url(r'^contact/', include('contactmonger.urls',
                                    namespace='contactmonger')),
    url(r'^report-problem/', include('contactapp.urls',
                                    namespace='contactapp')),
]
```

Then work them into our templates doing the following:

Example 8.7

```
{% extends "base.html" %}
{% block title %}Contact{% endblock title %}
{% block content %}
<p>
  <a href="{% url "contactmonger:create" %}">Contact Us</a>
</p>
<p>
  <a href="{% url "contactapp:report" %}">Report a Problem</a>
</p>
{% endblock content %}
```

8.4.3 Easier Searches, Upgrades, and Refactors

Considering the prevalence of underscores in names for PEP 8-friendly frameworks like Django, searching code or names like "`tastings_detail`" can be challenging. When a result comes up, is that for a view name, a URL name, or something else?

On the other hand, searching for "`tastings:detail`" makes for obvious search result responses. This can and has made upgrades and refactoring of apps and projects easier, including when interacting with new third-party libraries.

8.4.4 Allows for More App and Template Reverse Tricks

We're not going to cover any tricks here, because we feel such things are almost never justified. In fact, they usually just add to the complexity of a project without adding any tangible benefit. However, there are a couple use cases worth mentioning:

- Development tools like django-debug-toolbar that perform debug-level introspection.
- Projects that allow end-users to add "modules" to change or alter the behavior of their account.

While developers can use either of these to justify the use of creative URL namespaces tricks, as always, we recommend trying the simplest approach first.

8.5 Don't Reference Views as Strings in URLConfs

Before release 1.8 Django tutorials often instructed that referencing views in *urls.py* should be done with strings:

Bad Example 8.2

```
# DON'T DO THIS!
# polls/urls.py
from django.conf.urls import patterns, url

urlpatterns = patterns('',
    # Defining the view as a string
    url(r'^$', 'polls.views.index', name='index'),
```

```
)
```

There are a couple problems with this approach.

1. Django magically adds the view function/class. The problem with magic features like this is that when a view has an error, the abstraction required to perform said magic makes the error harder to debug.
2. Instructors have to explain to beginners the need for an empty string at the beginning of the `urlpatterns` variable.

Here is the correct way to define views in ***urls.py***:

Example 8.8

```
# polls/urls.py
from django.conf.urls import url

from . import views

urlpatterns = [
    # Defining the views explicitly
    url(r'^$', views.index, name='index'),
]
```

References:

- Old Way: http://www.2scoops.co/7E/info/
- New Way: http://www.2scoops.co/1.8-django-conf-urls-patterns/

8.6 Try to Keep Business Logic Out of Views

In the past, we've placed an amazing amount of sophisticated business logic into our views. Unfortunately, when it became time to generate PDFs, add a REST API, or serve out other formats, placing so much logic in our views made it much harder to deliver new formats.

This is where our preferred approach of model methods, manager methods, or general utility helper functions come into play. When business logic is placed into easily reusable components, and called from within views, it makes extending components of the project to do more things much easier.

Since it's not always possible to do this at the beginning of a project, our rule of thumb has become whenever we find ourselves duplicating business logic instead of Django boilerplate between views, it's time to move code out of the view.

8.7 Django Views Are Functions

When it comes down to it, every Django view is a function. This function takes an HTTP request object and turns it into a HTTP response object. If you know anything about basic mathematical functions, this process of change should look very familiar.

Example 8.9

```
# Django FBV as a function
HttpResponse = view(HttpRequest)

# Deciphered into basic math (remember functions from algebra?)
y = f(x)

# ... and then translated into a CBV example
HttpResponse = View.as_view()(HttpRequest)
```

This concept of change serves as a foundation for all sorts of things you can do with Django views, be they function- or class-based.

TIP: Class-Based Views Are Actually Called as Functions

Django's CBVs appear to be very different than FBVs. However, the `View.as_view()` classmethod called in URLConfs is actually returning a callable instance of the view. In other words, a callback function that handles the request/response cycle in exactly the same manner as a function-based view!

8.7.1 The Simplest Views

With this in mind, it's good to remember the simplest possible views that can be created with Django:

Example 8.10

```
# simplest_views.py
from django.http import HttpResponse
from django.views.generic import View

# The simplest FBV
def simplest_view(request):
    # Business logic goes here
    return HttpResponse("FBV")

# The simplest CBV
class SimplestView(View):
    def get(self, request, *args, **kwargs):
        # Business logic goes here
        return HttpResponse("CBV")
```

Why is this useful to know?

- Sometimes we need one-off views that do tiny things.
- Understanding the simplest Django views means we better understand what they are really doing.
- Illustrates how Django FBVs are HTTP method neutral, but Django CBVs require specific HTTP method declaration.

8.8 Don't Use `locals()` as Views Context

Returning `locals()` from any callable is an anti-pattern. While it seems like a handy shortcut, in fact it is a time consuming nightmare. Let's use an example to explore why. Here is a view following this anti-pattern:

Bad Example 8.3

```python
def ice_cream_store_display(request, store_id):
    store = get_object_or_404(Store, id=store_id)
    date = timezone.now()
    return render(request, 'melted_ice_cream_report.html', locals())
```

On the surface everything *seems* fine.

However, as we've gone from an explicit design to implicit anti-pattern has made this simple view annoying to maintain. Specifically that we don't know what the view is supposed to return. This becomes an issue because changing any of the variables returned by the view is not immediately apparent:

Bad Example 8.4

```python
def ice_cream_store_display(request, store_id):
    store = get_object_or_404(Store, id=store_id)
    now = timezone.now()
    return render(request, 'melted_ice_cream_report.html', locals())
```

How long did it take you to spot the different between Bad Example 8.3 and Bad Example 8.4? This was a simple example, imagine a more complicated one with a large template. This is why we strongly advocate use of explicit context in views:

Example 8.11

```python
def ice_cream_store_display(request, store_id):
    return render(request, 'melted_ice_cream_report.html', dict{
        'store': get_object_or_404(Store, id=store_id),
        'now': timezone.now()
    })
```

- Martin Aspelli's Reasoning: 2scoops.co/django-views-and-locals-antipattern

8.9 Summary

This chapter started with discussing when to use either FBVs or CBVs, and matched our own preference for the latter. In fact, in the next chapter we'll start to dig deep into the functionality that can be exploited when using FBVs, followed up by a chapter on CBVs.

We also discussed keeping view logic out of the URLConfs. We feel view code belongs in the apps' ***views.py*** modules, and URLConf code belongs in the apps' ***urls.py*** modules. Adhering to this practice allows for object inheritance when used with class-based views, easier code reuse, and greater flexibility of design.

9 Best Practices for Function-Based Views

In Django since the beginning of the project, **function-based views** are in frequent use by developers around the world. While class-based views have risen in usage, the simplicity of using a function is appealing to both new and experienced developers alike. While the authors are in the camp of preferring CBVs, we work on projects that use FBVs and here are some patterns we've grown to enjoy.

9.1 Advantages of FBVs

The simplicity of FBVs comes at the expense of code reuse: FBVs don't have the same ability to inherit from superclasses the way that CBVs do. They do have the advantage of being more obviously functional in nature, which lends itself to a number of interesting strategies.

We follow these guidelines when writing FBVs:

- Less view code is better.
- Never repeat code in views.
- Views should handle presentation logic. Try to keep business logic in models when possible, or in forms if you must.
- Keep your views simple.
- Use them to write custom 403, 404, and 500 error handlers.
- Complex nested-if blocks are to be avoided.

9.2 Passing the HttpRequest Object

There are times where we want to reuse code in views, but not tie it into global actions such as **middleware** or **context processors**. Starting in the introduction of this book, we advised creating utility functions that can be used across the project.

For many utility functions, we are taking an attribute or attributes from the `django.http.HttpRequest` (or `HttpRequest` for short) object and gathering data or performing operations. What we've found, is by having the request object itself as a primary argument, we have simpler arguments on more methods. This means less cognitive overload of managing function/method arguments: just pass in the `HttpRequest` object!

Example 9.1

```
# sprinkles/utils.py

from django.core.exceptions import PermissionDenied

def check_sprinkle_rights(request):
    if request.user.can_sprinkle or request.user.is_staff:
        return request

    # Return a HTTP 403 back to the user
    raise PermissionDenied
```

The `check_sprinkle_rights()` function does a quick check against the rights of the user, raising a `django.core.exceptions.PermissionDenied` exception, which triggers a custom HTTP 403 view as we describe in subsection 29.4.3.

You'll note that we return back a `HttpRequest` object rather than an arbitrary value or even a `None` object. We do this because as Python is a dynamically typed language, we can attach additional attributes to the `HttpRequest`. For example:

Example 9.2

```
# sprinkles/utils.py

from django.core.exceptions import PermissionDenied
```

```
def check_sprinkles(request):
    if request.user.can_sprinkle or request.user.is_staff:
        # By adding this value here it means our display templates
        #   can be more generic. We don't need to have
        #   {% if request.user.can_sprinkle or request.user.is_staff %}
        #   instead just using
        #   {% if request.can_sprinkle %}
        request.can_sprinkle = True
        return request

    # Return a HTTP 403 back to the user
    raise PermissionDenied
```

There's another reason, which we'll cover shortly. In the meantime, let's demonstrate this code in action:

Example 9.3

```
# sprinkles/views.py

from django.shortcuts import get_object_or_404
from django.shortcuts import render

from .utils import check_sprinkles
from .models import Sprinkle

def sprinkle_list(request):
    """Standard list view"""

    request = check_sprinkles(request)

    return render(request,
        "sprinkles/sprinkle_list.html",
        {"sprinkles": Sprinkle.objects.all()})

def sprinkle_detail(request, pk):
    """Standard detail view"""
```

```
    request = check_sprinkles(request)

    sprinkle = get_object_or_404(Sprinkle, pk=pk)

    return render(request, "sprinkles/sprinkle_detail.html",
        {"sprinkle": sprinkle})

def sprinkle_preview(request):
    """"preview of new sprinkle, but without the
            check_sprinkles function being used.
    """
    sprinkle = Sprinkle.objects.all()
    return render(request,
        "sprinkles/sprinkle_preview.html",
        {"sprinkle": sprinkle})
```

Another good feature about this approach is that it's trivial to integrate into class-based views:

Example 9.4

```
# sprinkles/views.py
from django.views.generic import DetailView

from .utils import check_sprinkles
from .models import Sprinkle

class SprinkleDetail(DetailView):
    """Standard detail view"""

    model = Sprinkle

    def dispatch(self, request, *args, **kwargs):
        request = check_sprinkles(request)
        return super(SprinkleDetail, self).dispatch(
                                request, *args, **kwargs)
```

TIP: Specific Function Arguments Have Their Place

The downside to single argument functions is that specific function arguments like 'pk', 'flavor' or 'text' make it easier to understand the purpose of a function at a glance. In other words, try to use this technique for actions that are as generic as possible.

Since we're repeatedly reusing functions inside functions, wouldn't it be nice to easily recognize when this is being done? This is when we bring decorators into play.

9.3 Decorators Are Sweet

For once, this isn't about ice cream, it's about code! In computer science parlance, **syntactic sugar** is a syntax added to a programming language in order to make things easier to read or to express. In Python, decorators are a feature added not out of necessity, but in order to make code cleaner and *sweeter* for humans to read. So yes, Decorators Are Sweet.

When we combine the power of simple functions with the syntactic sugar of decorators, we get handy, reusable tools like the extremely useful to the point of being ubiquitous `django.contrib.auth.decorators.login_required` decorator.

Here's a sample decorator template for use in function-based views:

Example 9.5

```
# simple decorator template
import functools

def decorator(view_func):
    @functools.wraps(view_func)
    def new_view_func(request, *args, **kwargs):
        # You can modify the request (HttpRequest) object here.
        response = view_func(request, *args, **kwargs)
        # You can modify the response (HttpResponse) object here.
        return response
    return new_view_func
```

That might not make too much sense, so we'll go through it step-by-step, using in-line code comments to clarify what we are doing. First, let's modify the decorator template from the previous example to match our needs:

Example 9.6

```
# sprinkles/decorators.py
from functools import wraps

from . import utils

# based off the decorator template from Example 8.5
def check_sprinkles(view_func):
    """Check if a user can add sprinkles"""
    @wraps(view_func)
    def new_view_func(request, *args, **kwargs):
        # Act on the request object with utils.can_sprinkle()
        request = utils.can_sprinkle(request)

        # Call the view function
        response = view_func(request, *args, **kwargs)

        # Return the HttpResponse object
        return response
    return new_view_func
```

Then we attach it to the function thus:

Example 9.7

```
# views.py
from django.shortcuts import get_object_or_404, render

from .decorators import check_sprinkles
from .models import Sprinkle

# Attach the decorator to the view
@check_sprinkles
def sprinkle_detail(request, pk):
    """Standard detail view"""
```

```
sprinkle = get_object_or_404(Sprinkle, pk=pk)

return render(request, "sprinkles/sprinkle_detail.html",
    {"sprinkle": sprinkle})
```

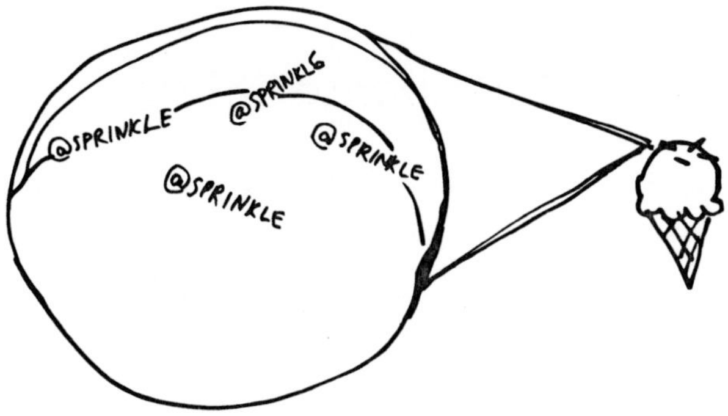

Figure 9.1: If you look at sprinkles closely, you'll see that they're Python decorators.

TIP: What About functools.wraps()?

Astute readers may have noticed that our decorator examples used the `functools.wraps()` decorator function from the Python standard library. This is a convenience tool that copies over metadata including critical data like docstrings to the newly decorated function. It's not necessary, but it makes project maintenance much easier.

9.3.1 Be Conservative With Decorators

As with any powerful tool, decorators can be used the wrong way. Too many decorators can create their own form of obfuscation, making even complex class-based view hierarchies seem simple in comparison. When using decorators, establish a limit of how many decorators can be set on a view and stick with it.

Video on the subject: http://www.2scoops.co/how-to-write-obfuscated-python/

9.3.2 Additional Resources on Decorators

- Decorators Explained: http://2scoops.co/decorators-explained
- Decorators and Functional Python: http://2scoops.co/decorators-functional-python
- Decorator Cheat Sheet by author Daniel Roy Greenfeld http://2scoops.co/decorator-cheatsheet
- "Appendix C: Useful Resources", specifically the section on "Useful Python Material"

9.4 Passing the HttpResponse Object

Just as with the `HttpRequest` object, we can also pass around the `HttpResponse` object from function to function. Think of this as a selective `Middleware.process_request()` method (see http://2scoops.co/1.8-process-response).

Yes, this technique can be leveraged with decorators. See Example 8.5 which gives a hint as to how this can be accomplished.

9.5 Summary

Function-based views are still alive and well in the Django world. If we remember that every function accepts a `HttpRequest` object and returns an `HttpResponse` object, we can use that to our advantage. We can leverage in generic `HttpRequest` and `HttpResponse` altering functions, which can also be used to construct decorator functions.

We'll close this chapter by acknowledging that every lesson we've learned about function-based views can be applied to what we begin to discuss next chapter, class-based views.

10 Best Practices for Class-Based Views

Django provides a standard way to write class-based views (CBVs). In fact, as we mentioned in previous chapters, a Django view is just a callable that accepts a request object and returns a response. For function-based views (FBVs), the view function is that callable. For CBVs, the view class provides an `as_view()` class method that returns the callable. This mechanism is implemented in `django.views.generic.View`. All CBVs should inherit from that class, directly or indirectly.

Django also provides a series of generic class-based views (GCBVs) that implement common patterns found in most web projects and illustrate the power of CBVs.

Shortly after the release of Django 1.3, due to the placement of all views, there was some confusion between the general concept of CBVs because of the placement of all CBVs, including non-generic views in `django.views.generic`. These early problems have been addressed almost entirely, thanks to improvements in the documentation, resources such as Marc Tamlyn and Charles Denton's `ccbv.co.uk` code inspector, and the advent of third party packages designed to expedite CBV development.

PACKAGE TIP: Filling the Missing Parts of Django GCBVs

Out of the box, Django does not provide critically important mixins for GCBVs, including authentication. The **django-braces** library addresses most of these issues. It provides a set of clearly coded mixins that make Django GCBVs much easier and faster to implement. The next few chapters will demonstrate its mixins in various code examples.

10.1 Guidelines When Working With CBVs

- Less view code is better.
- Never repeat code in views.
- Views should handle presentation logic. Try to keep business logic in models when possible, or in forms if you must.
- Keep your views simple.
- Don't use CBVs to write custom 403, 404, and 500 error handlers. Use FBVs instead.
- Keep your **mixins** simpler.

10.2 Using Mixins With CBVs

Think of mixins in programming along the lines of mixins in ice cream: you can enhance any ice cream flavor by mixing in crunchy candy bits, sliced fruit, or even bacon.

Figure 10.1: Popular and unpopular mixins used in ice cream.

Soft serve ice cream greatly benefits from mixins: ordinary vanilla soft serve turns into birthday cake ice cream when sprinkles, blue buttercream icing, and chunks of yellow cake are mixed in.

In programming, a mixin is a class that provides functionality to be inherited, but isn't meant for instantiation on its own. In programming languages with multiple inheritance, mixins can be used to add enhanced functionality and behavior to classes.

We can use the power of mixins to compose our own view classes for our Django apps.

When using mixins to compose our own view classes, we recommend these rules of inheritance provided by Kenneth Love. The rules follow Python's **method resolution order**, which in the most simplistic definition possible, proceeds from left to right:

1. The base view classes provided by Django *always* go to the right.
2. Mixins go to the left of the base view.
3. Mixins should inherit from Python's built-in object type.

Example of the rules in action:

Example 10.1

```
from django.views.generic import TemplateView

class FreshFruitMixin(object):

    def get_context_data(self, **kwargs):
        context = super(FreshFruitMixin,
                    self).get_context_data(**kwargs)
        context["has_fresh_fruit"] = True
        return context

class FruityFlavorView(FreshFruitMixin, TemplateView):
    template_name = "fruity_flavor.html"
```

In our rather silly example, the `FruityFlavorView` class inherits from both `FreshFruitMixin` and `TemplateView`.

Since `TemplateView` is the base view class provided by Django, it goes on the far right (rule 1), and to its left we place the `FreshFruitMixin` (rule 2). This way we know that our methods and properties will execute correctly.

Finally, `FreshFruitMixin` inherits from `object` (rule 3).

10.3 Which Django GCBV Should Be Used for What Task?

The power of generic class-based views comes at the expense of simplicity: GCBVs come with a complex inheritance chain that can have up to eight superclasses on import. Trying to work out exactly which view to use or which method to customize can be very challenging at times.

To mitigate this challenge, here's a handy chart listing the name and purpose of each Django CBV. All views listed here are assumed to be prefixed with `django.views.generic`.

Name	Purpose	Two Scoops Example

Name	Purpose	Two Scoops Example
`View`	Base view or handy view that can be used for anything.	See section 10.6, `Using Just django.views.generic.View'.
`RedirectView`	Redirect user to another URL	Send users who visit `/log-in/' to `/login/'.
`TemplateView`	Display a Django HTML template.	The `/about/' page of our site.
`ListView`	List objects	List of ice cream flavors.
`DetailView`	Display an object	Details on an ice cream flavor.
`FormView`	Submit a form	The site's contact or email form.
`CreateView`	Create an object	Create a new ice cream flavor.
`UpdateView`	Update an object	Update an existing ice cream flavor.
`DeleteView`	Delete an object	Delete an unpleasant ice cream flavor like Vanilla Steak.
Generic date views	For display of objects that occur over a range of time.	Blogs are a common reason to use them. For Two Scoops, we could create a public history of when flavors have been added to the database.

Table 10.1: Django CBV Usage Table

TIP: The Three Schools of Django CBV/GCBV Usage

We've found that there are three major schools of thought around CBV and GCBV usage. They are:

The School of "Use all the generic views"!
This school of thought is based on the idea that since Django provides functionality to reduce your workload, why not use that functionality? We tend to belong to this school of thought, and have used it to great success, rapidly building and then maintaining a number of projects.

The School of "Just use django.views.generic.View"
This school of thought is based on the idea that the base Django CBV does just enough and is 'the True CBV, everything else is a Generic CBV'. In the past year, we've found this can be a really useful approach for tricky tasks for which the resource-based approach of "Use all the views" breaks down. We'll cover some use cases for it in this chapter.

The School of "Avoid them unless you're actually subclassing views"
Jacob Kaplan-Moss says, "My general advice is to start with function views since they're easier to read and understand, and only use CBVs where you need them. Where do you need them? Any place where you need a fair chunk of code to be reused among multiple views."

We generally belong to the first school, but it's good for you to know that there's no real consensus on best practices here.

10.4 General Tips for Django CBVs

This section covers useful tips for all or many Django CBV and GCBV implementations. We've found they expedite writing of views, templates, and their their tests. These techniques will work with Class-Based Views, Generic Class-Based Views, and even the views provided by **django-vanilla-views**.

10.4.1 Constraining Django CBV/GCBV Access to Authenticated Users

While the Django CBV documentation gives a helpful working example of using the `django.contrib.auth.decorators.login_required` decorator with a CBV, the example contains a lot of boilerplate cruft: http://2scoops.co/1.8-login-required-cbv

Fortunately, django-braces provides a ready implementation of a `LoginRequiredMixin` that you can attach in moments. For example, we could do the following in all of the Django GCBVs that we've written so far:

Example 10.2

```
# flavors/views.py
from django.views.generic import DetailView

from braces.views import LoginRequiredMixin

from .models import Flavor

class FlavorDetailView(LoginRequiredMixin, DetailView):
    model = Flavor
```

TIP: Don't Forget the GCBV Mixin Order!

Remember that:

- `LoginRequiredMixin` must always go on the far left side.
- The base view class must always go on the far right side.

If you forget and switch the order, you will get broken or unpredictable results.

10.4.2 Performing Custom Actions on Views With Valid Forms

When you need to perform a custom action on a view with a **valid** form, the `form_valid()` method is where the GCBV workflow sends the request.

Example 10.3

```python
from django.views.generic import CreateView

from braces.views import LoginRequiredMixin

from .models import Flavor

class FlavorCreateView(LoginRequiredMixin, CreateView):
    model = Flavor
    fields = ('title', 'slug', 'scoops_remaining')

    def form_valid(self, form):
        # Do custom logic here
        return super(FlavorCreateView, self).form_valid(form)
```

To perform custom logic on form data that has already been validated, simply add the logic to `form_valid()`. The return value of `form_valid()` should be a `django.http.HttpResponseRedirect`.

10.4.3 Performing Custom Actions on Views With Invalid Forms

When you need to perform a custom action on a view with an **invalid** form, the `form_invalid()` method is where the Django GCBV workflow sends the request. This method should return a `django.http.HttpResponse`.

Example 10.4

```python
from django.views.generic import CreateView

from braces.views import LoginRequiredMixin

from .models import Flavor

class FlavorCreateView(LoginRequiredMixin, CreateView):
    model = Flavor
```

```python
    def form_invalid(self, form):
        # Do custom logic here
        return super(FlavorCreateView, self).form_invalid(form)
```

Just as you can add logic to `form_valid()`, you can also add logic to `form_invalid()`.

You'll see an example of overriding both of these methods in chapter 11, *Form Fundamentals*, subsection 11.5.1, 'ModelForm Data Is Saved to the Form, Then the Model Instance.'

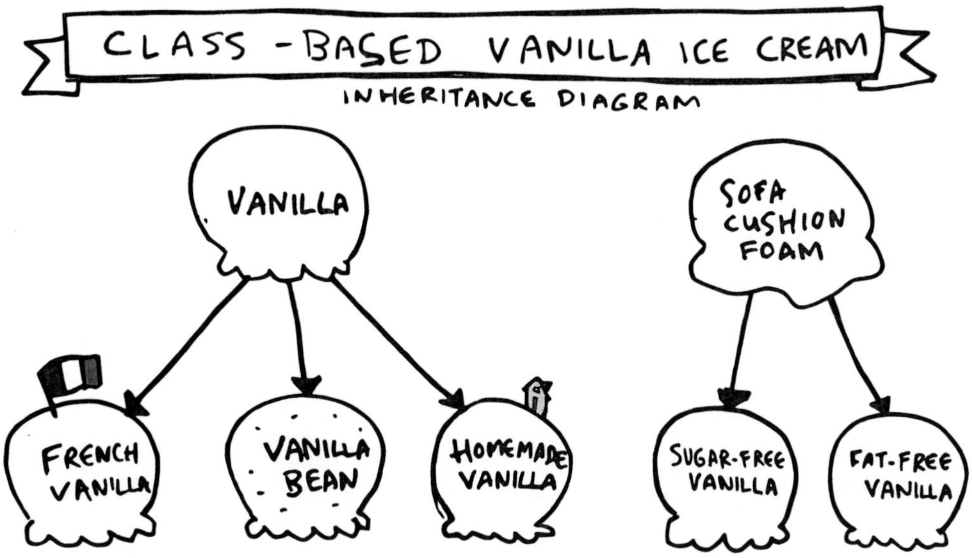

Figure 10.2: The other CBV: class-based vanilla ice cream.

10.4.4 Using the View Object

If you are using class-based views for rendering content, consider using the view object itself to provide access to properties and methods that can be called by other method and properties. They can also be called from templates. For example:

Example 10.5

```python
from django.utils.functional import cached_property
from django.views.generic import UpdateView, TemplateView

from braces.views import LoginRequiredMixin

from .models import Flavor
from .tasks import update_users_who_favorited

class FavoriteMixin(object):

    @cached_property
    def likes_and_favorites(self):
        """Returns a dictionary of likes and favorites"""
        likes = self.object.likes()
        favorites = self.object.favorites()
        return {
            "likes": likes,
            "favorites": favorites,
            "favorites_count": favorites.count(),

        }

class FlavorUpdateView(LoginRequiredMixin, FavoriteMixin, UpdateView):
    model = Flavor
    fields = ('title', 'slug', 'scoops_remaining')

    def form_valid(self, form):
        update_users_who_favorited(
            instance=self.object,
            favorites=self.likes_and_favorites['favorites']
        )
        return super(FlavorCreateView, self).form_valid(form)

class FlavorDetailView(LoginRequiredMixin, FavoriteMixin, TemplateView):
    model = Flavor
```

The nice thing about this is the various *flavors/* app templates can now access this property:

Example 10.6

```
{# flavors/base.html #}
{% extends "base.html" %}

{% block likes_and_favorites %}
<ul>
  <li>Likes: {{ view.likes_and_favorites.likes }}</li>
  <li>Favorites: {{ view.likes_and_favorites.favorites_count }}</li>
</ul>
{% endblock likes_and_favorites %}
```

10.5 How GCBVs and Forms Fit Together

A common source of confusion with GCBVs is their usage with Django forms.

Using our favorite example of the ice cream flavor tracking app, let's chart out a couple of examples of how form-related views might fit together.

First, let's define a flavor model to use in this section's view examples:

Example 10.7

```
# flavors/models.py
from django.core.urlresolvers import reverse
from django.db import models

STATUS = (
    (0, "zero"),
    (1, "one"),
)

class Flavor(models.Model):
    title = models.CharField(max_length=255)
    slug = models.SlugField(unique=True)
    scoops_remaining = models.IntegerField(default=0, choices=STATUS)

    def get_absolute_url(self):
```

```
        return reverse("flavors:detail", kwargs={"slug": self.slug})
```

Now, let's explore some common Django form scenarios that most Django users run into at one point or another.

10.5.1 Views + ModelForm Example

This is the simplest and most common Django form scenario. Typically when you create a model, you want to be able to add new records and update existing records that correspond to the model.

In this example, we'll show you how to construct a set of views that will create, update and display Flavor records. We'll also demonstrate how to provide confirmation of changes.

Here we have the following views:

1. **FlavorCreateView** corresponds to a form for adding new flavors.
2. **FlavorUpdateView** corresponds to a form for editing existing flavors.
3. **FlavorDetailView** corresponds to the confirmation page for both flavor creation and flavor updates.

To visualize our views:

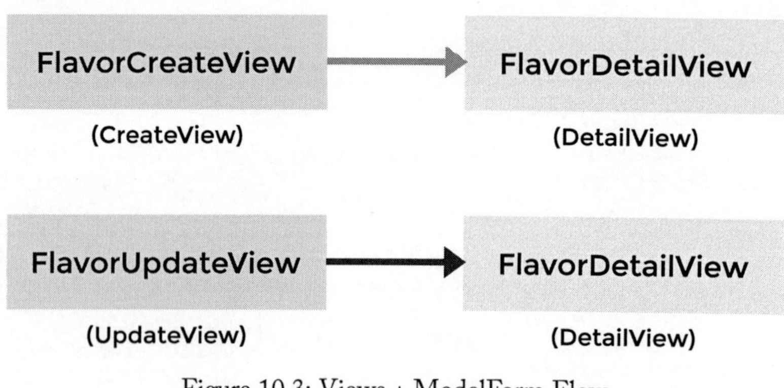

Figure 10.3: Views + ModelForm Flow

Note that we stick as closely as possible to Django naming conventions. `FlavorCreateView` subclasses Django's `CreateView`, `FlavorUpdateView` subclasses Django's `UpdateView`, and `FlavorDetailView` subclasses Django's `DetailView`.

Writing these views is easy, since it's mostly a matter of using what Django gives us:

Example 10.8

```python
# flavors/views.py
from django.views.generic import CreateView, UpdateView, DetailView

from braces.views import LoginRequiredMixin

from .models import Flavor

class FlavorCreateView(LoginRequiredMixin, CreateView):
    model = Flavor
    fields = ('title', 'slug', 'scoops_remaining')

class FlavorUpdateView(LoginRequiredMixin, UpdateView):
    model = Flavor
    fields = ('title', 'slug', 'scoops_remaining')

class FlavorDetailView(DetailView):
    model = Flavor
```

Simple at first glance, right? We accomplish so much with just a little bit of code!

But wait, there's a catch. If we wire these views into a ***urls.py*** module and create the necessary templates, we'll uncover a problem:

The FlavorDetailView is not a confirmation page.

For now, that statement is correct. Fortunately, we can fix it quickly with a few modifications to existing views and templates.

The first step in the fix is to use `django.contrib.messages` to inform the user visiting the `FlavorDetailView` that they just added or updated the flavor.

We'll need to override the `FlavorCreateView.form_valid()` and `FlavorUpdateView.form_valid()` methods. We can do this conveniently for both views with a `FlavorActionMixin`.

For the confirmation page fix, we change *flavors/views.py* to contain the following:

Example 10.9

```
# flavors/views.py

from django.contrib import messages
from django.views.generic import CreateView, UpdateView, DetailView

from braces.views import LoginRequiredMixin

from .models import Flavor

class FlavorActionMixin(object):

    fields = ('title', 'slug', 'scoops_remaining')

    @property
    def success_msg(self):
        return NotImplemented

    def form_valid(self, form):
        messages.info(self.request, self.success_msg)
        return super(FlavorActionMixin, self).form_valid(form)

class FlavorCreateView(LoginRequiredMixin, FlavorActionMixin,
                        CreateView):
    model = Flavor
    success_msg = "Flavor created!"

class FlavorUpdateView(LoginRequiredMixin, FlavorActionMixin,
                        UpdateView):
    model = Flavor
    success_msg = "Flavor updated!"

class FlavorDetailView(DetailView):
```

```
model = Flavor
```

Earlier in this chapter, we covered a simpler example of how to override `form_valid()` within a GCBV. Here, we reuse a similar `form_valid()` override method by creating a mixin to inherit from in multiple views.

Now we're using Django's **messages** framework to display confirmation messages to the user upon every successful add or edit. We define a `FlavorActionMixin` whose job is to queue up a confirmation message corresponding to the action performed in a view.

TIP: Mixins Should Inherit From Object

Please take notice that the `FlavorActionMixin` inherits from Python's object type rather than a pre-existing mixin or view. It's important that mixins have as shallow inheritance chain as possible. Simplicity is a virtue!

After a flavor is created or updated, a list of messages is passed to the context of the `FlavorDetailView`. We can see these messages if we add the following code to the views' template and then create or update a flavor:

EXAMPLE 10.10

```
{# templates/flavors/flavor_detail.html #}
{% if messages %}
    <ul class="messages">
        {% for message in messages %}
        <li id="message_{{ forloop.counter }}"
            {% if message.tags %} class="{{ message.tags }}"
                {% endif %}>
            {{ message }}
        </li>
        {% endfor %}
    </ul>
{% endif %}
```

> **TIP: Reuse the Messages Template Code!**
>
> It is common practice to put the above code into your project's base HTML template. Doing this allows message support for templates in your project.

To recap, this example demonstrated yet again how to override the `form_valid()` method, incorporate this into a mixin, how to incorporate multiple mixins into a view, and gave a quick introduction to the very useful `django.contrib.messages` framework.

10.5.2 Views + Form Example

Sometimes you want to use a Django `Form` rather than a `ModelForm`. Search forms are a particularly good use case for this, but you'll run into other scenarios where this is true as well.

In this example, we'll create a simple flavor search form. This involves creating a HTML form that doesn't modify any flavor data. The form's action will query the ORM, and the records found will be listed on a search results page.

Our intention is that when using our flavor search page, if users do a flavor search for "Dough", they should be sent to a page listing ice cream flavors like "Chocolate Chip Cookie Dough," "Fudge Brownie Dough," "Peanut Butter Cookie Dough," and other flavors containing the string "Dough" in their title. Mmm, we definitely want this feature in our web application.

There are more complex ways to implement this, but for our simple use case, all we need is a single view. We'll use a `FlavorListView` for both the search page and the search results page.

Here's an overview of our implementation:

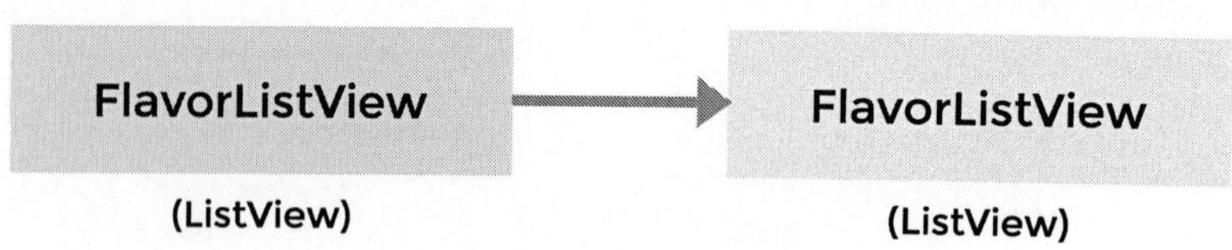

Figure 10.4: Views + Form Flow

In this scenario, we want to follow the standard internet convention for search pages, where 'q' is used for the search query parameter. We also want to accept a GET request rather than a POST request, which is unusual for forms but perfectly fine for this use case. Remember, this form doesn't add, edit, or delete objects, so we don't need a POST request here.

To return matching search results based on the search query, we need to modify the standard queryset supplied by the `ListView`. To do this, we override the `ListView's` `get_queryset()` method. We add the following code to *flavors/views.py*:

Example 10.11

```
from django.views.generic import ListView

from .models import Flavor

class FlavorListView(ListView):
    model = Flavor

    def get_queryset(self):
        # Fetch the queryset from the parent get_queryset
        queryset = super(FlavorListView, self).get_queryset()

        # Get the q GET parameter
        q = self.request.GET.get("q")
        if q:
            # Return a filtered queryset
            return queryset.filter(title__icontains=q)
        # Return the base queryset
        return queryset
```

Now, instead of listing all of the flavors, we list only the flavors whose titles contain the search string.

As we mentioned, search forms are unusual in that unlike nearly every other HTML form they specify a GET request in the HTML form. This is because search forms are not changing data, but simply retrieving information from the server. The search form should look something like this:

Example 10.12

```
{# templates/flavors/_flavor_search.html #}
{% comment %}
    Usage: {% include "flavors/_flavor_search.html" %}
{% endcomment %}
<form action="{% url "flavor_list" %}" method="GET">
    <input type="text" name="q" />
    <button type="submit">search</button>
</form>
```

TIP: Specify the Form Target in Search Forms

We also take care to specify the URL in the form action, because we've found that search forms are often included in several pages. This is why we prefix them with '_' and create them in such a way as to be included in other templates.

Once we get past overriding the `ListView's get_queryset()` method, the rest of this example is just a simple HTML form. We like this kind of simplicity.

10.6 Using Just django.views.generic.View

It's entirely possible to build a project just using `django.views.generic.View` for all the views. It's not as extreme as one might think. For example, if we look at the official Django documentation's introduction to class-based views (http://2scoops.co/1.8-using-cbvs), we can see the approach is very close to how function-based views are written. In fact, we highlighted this two chapters ago in subsection 8.7.1 'The Simplest Views' because it's important.

Imagine instead of writing function-based views with nested-ifs representing different HTTP methods or class-based views where the HTTP methods are hidden behind `get_context_data()` and `form_valid()` methods, they are readily accessible to developers. Imagine something like:

EXAMPLE 10.13

```
from django.shortcuts import get_object_or_404
from django.shortcuts import render, redirect
from django.views.generic import View

from braces.views import LoginRequiredMixin

from .forms import FlavorForm
from .models import Flavor

class FlavorView(LoginRequiredMixin, View):

    def get(self, request, *args, **kwargs):
        # Handles display of the Flavor object
        flavor = get_object_or_404(Flavor, slug=kwargs['slug'])
        return render(request,
            "flavors/flavor_detail.html",
                {"flavor": flavor}
            )

    def post(self, request, *args, **kwargs):
        # Handles updates of the Flavor object
        flavor = get_object_or_404(Flavor, slug=kwargs['slug'])
        form = FlavorForm(request.POST)
        if form.is_valid():
            form.save()
        return redirect("flavors:detail", flavor.slug)
```

While we can do this in a function-based view, it can be argued that the GET/POST method declarations within the `FlavorView` are easier to read than the traditional "`if request.method == ...`" conditions. In addition, since the inheritance chain is so shallow, it means using mixins doesn't threaten us with cognitive overload.

What we find really useful, even on projects which use a lot of generic class-based views, is using the `django.views.generic.View` class with a GET method for displaying JSON, PDF or other non-HTML content. All the tricks that we've used for rendering CSV, Excel, and PDF files in function-based views apply when using the GET method. For example:

Example 10.14

```
from django.http import HttpResponse
from django.shortcuts import get_object_or_404
from django.views.generic import View

from braces.views import LoginRequiredMixin

from .models import Flavor
from .reports import make_flavor_pdf

class PDFFlavorView(LoginRequiredMixin, View):

    def get(self, request, *args, **kwargs):
        # Get the flavor
        flavor = get_object_or_404(Flavor, slug=kwargs['slug'])

        # create the response
        response = HttpResponse(content_type='application/pdf')

        # generate the PDF stream and attach to the response
        response = make_flavor_pdf(response, flavor)

        return response
```

This is a pretty straight-forward example, but if we have to leverage more mixins and deal with more custom logic, the simplicity of `django.views.generic.View` makes it much easier than the more heavyweight views. In essence, we get all the advantages of function-based views combined with the object-oriented power that CBVs gave us starting with Django 1.3.

10.7 Additional Resources

- http://2scoops.co/1.8-topics-class-based-views
- http://2scoops.co/1.8-cbv-generic-display
- http://2scoops.co/1.8-cbv-generic-editing
- http://2scoops.co/1.8-cbv-mixins
- http://2scoops.co/1.8-ref-class-based-views

- The GCBV inspector at `http://ccbv.co.uk`
- `www.python.org/download/releases/2.3/mro/`
- `http://pydanny.com/tag/class-based-views.html`

PACKAGE TIP: Other Useful CBV Libraries

- **django-extra-views** Another great CBV library, django-extra-views covers the cases that django-braces does not.
- **django-vanilla-views** A very interesting library that provides all the power of classic Django GCBVs in a vastly simplified, easier-to-use package. Works great in combination with django-braces.

10.8 Summary

This chapter covered:

- Using mixins with CBVs
- Which Django CBV should be used for which task
- General tips for CBV usage
- Connecting CBVs to forms
- Using the base `django.views.generic.View`

The next chapter explores common CBV/form patterns. Knowledge of these are helpful to have in your developer toolbox.

11 Form Fundamentals

100% of Django projects should use Forms.
95% of Django projects should use ModelForms.
91% of all Django projects use ModelForms.
80% of ModelForms require trivial logic.
20% of ModelForms require complicated logic.

– pydanny made-up statistics™

Django's forms are really powerful, and a knowing how to use them anytime data is coming from outside your application is part of keeping your data clean.

There are edge cases that can cause a bit of anguish. If you understand the structure of how forms are composed and how to call them, most edge cases can be readily overcome.

The most important thing to remember about Django Forms is they should be used to validate all incoming data.

11.1 Validate All Incoming Data With Django Forms

Django's forms are a wonderful framework designed to validate Python dictionaries. While most of the time we use them to validate incoming HTTP requests containing POST, there is nothing limiting them to be used just in this manner.

For example, let's say we have a Django app that updates its model via CSV files fetched from another project. To handle this sort of thing, it's not uncommon to see code like this (albeit in not as simplistic an example):

Bad Example 11.1

```python
import csv
import StringIO

from .models import Purchase

def add_csv_purchases(rows):

    rows = StringIO.StringIO(rows)
    records_added = 0

    # Generate a dict per row, with the first CSV row being the keys
    for row in csv.DictReader(rows, delimiter=","):
        # DON'T DO THIS: Tossing unvalidated data into your model.
        Purchase.objects.create(**row)
        records_added += 1
    return records_added
```

In fact, what you don't see is that we're not checking to see if sellers, stored as a string in the `Purchase` model, are actually valid sellers. We could add validation code to our `add_csv_purchases()` function, but let's face it, keeping complex validation code understandable as requirements and data changes over time is hard.

A better approach is to validate the incoming data with a Django `Form` like so:

Example 11.1

```python
import csv
import StringIO

from django import forms

from .models import Purchase, Seller

class PurchaseForm(forms.ModelForm):

    class Meta:
        model = Purchase
```

```
    def clean_seller(self):
        seller = self.cleaned_data["seller"]
        try:
            Seller.objects.get(name=seller)
        except Seller.DoesNotExist:
            msg = "{0} does not exist in purchase #{1}.".format(
                seller,
                self.cleaned_data["purchase_number"]
            )
            raise forms.ValidationError(msg)
        return seller

def add_csv_purchases(rows):

    rows = StringIO.StringIO(rows)

    records_added = 0
    errors = []
    # Generate a dict per row, with the first CSV row being the keys.
    for row in csv.DictReader(rows, delimiter=","):

        # Bind the row data to the PurchaseForm.
        form = PurchaseForm(row)
        # Check to see if the row data is valid.
        if form.is_valid():
            # Row data is valid so save the record.
            form.save()
            records_added += 1
        else:
            errors.append(form.errors)

    return records_added, errors
```

What's really nice about this practice is that rather than cooking up our own validation system for incoming data, we're using the well-proven data testing framework built into Django.

TIP: What about the `code` parameter?

Arnaud Limbourg pointed out that the official Django docs recommend passing a `code` parameter to `ValidationError` as follows:

Example 11.2

```
ValidationError(_('Invalid value'), code='invalid')
```

In our example we don't include one, but you can use it in your code if you want.

Django core developer Marc Tamlyn says, "On a personal note, I feel that Django's docs are maybe a little heavy handed with recommending they use of code as a best practice everywhere, although it should be encouraged in third party applications. It is however definitely the best practice for any situation where you wish to check the nature of the errors - it's much better than checking the message of the validation error as this is subject to copy changes."

Reference:

- http://www.2scoops.co/1.8-raising-validationerror/

11.2 Use the POST Method in HTML Forms

Every HTML form that alters data must submit its data via the POST method:

Example 11.3

```
<form action="{% url "flavor_add" %}" method="POST">
```

The only exception you'll ever see to using POST in forms is with search forms, which typically submit queries that don't result in any alteration of data. Search forms that are idempotent should use the GET method.

11.3 Always Use CSRF Protection With HTTP Forms That Modify Data

Django comes with cross-site request forgery protection (CSRF) built in, and usage of it is introduced in Part 4 of the Django introductory tutorial. It's easy to use, and Django even throws a friendly warning during development when you forget to use it. This is a critical security issue, and here and in our security chapter we recommend always using Django's CSRF protection capabilities.

In our experience, the only use case for turning off CSRF protection across a site is for creating machine-accessible APIs. API frameworks such as django-tastypie and django-rest-framework do this for you. Since API requests should be signed/authenticated on a per-request basis, these two frameworks don't normally rely on HTTP cookies for authentication. Therefore, CSRF isn't always a problem when using these frameworks.

If you are writing an API from scratch that accepts data changes, it's a good idea to become familiar with Django's CSRF documentation at
`https://docs.djangoproject.com/en/1.8/ref/csrf/`.

> **TIP: HTML Search Forms**
>
> Since HTML search forms don't change data, they use the HTTP GET method and do not trigger Django's CSRF protection.

You should use Django's `CsrfViewMiddleware` as blanket protection across your site rather than manually decorating views with `csrf_protect`. To ensure that CSRF works in Jinja2 templates, see section 15.3, 'CSRF and Jinja2'.

11.3.1 Posting Data via AJAX

You should use Django's CSRF protection even when posting data via AJAX. Do not make your AJAX views CSRF-exempt.

Instead, when posting via AJAX, you'll need to set an HTTP header called **X-CSRFToken**.

The official Django documentation includes a snippet that shows how to set this header for only POST requests, in conjunction with jQuery 1.5 or higher's cross-domain checking: https://docs.djangoproject.com/en/1.8/ref/csrf/#ajax

See our complete example of how to use this snippet in practice in section 17.6, AJAX and the CSRF Token, in chapter 16, *Building REST APIs*.

Recommended reading: https://docs.djangoproject.com/en/1.8/ref/csrf/

11.4 Understand How to Add Django Form Instance Attributes

Sometimes in the `clean()`, `clean_FOO()` or `save()` methods of a Django form, we need to have additional form instance attributes available. A sample case for this is having the `request.user` object available. Here is a simple taster-driven example.

First, the form:

EXAMPLE 11.4

```python
from django import forms

from .models import Taster

class TasterForm(forms.ModelForm):

    class Meta:
        model = Taster

    def __init__(self, *args, **kwargs):
        # set the user as an attribute of the form
        self.user = kwargs.pop('user')
        super(TasterForm, self).__init__(*args, **kwargs)
```

See how we set `self.user` before calling `super()`, and calls it from `kwargs`? Pointed out to us by Christopher Lambacher, this makes our form more robust, especially when using multiple inheritence. Now the view:

Example 11.5

```
from django.views.generic import UpdateView

from braces.views import LoginRequiredMixin

from .forms import TasterForm
from .models import Taster

class TasterUpdateView(LoginRequiredMixin, UpdateView):
    model = Taster
    form_class = TasterForm
    success_url = "/someplace/"

    def get_form_kwargs(self):
        """This method is what injects forms with keyword arguments."""
        # grab the current set of form #kwargs
        kwargs = super(TasterUpdateView, self).get_form_kwargs()
        # Update the kwargs with the user_id
        kwargs['user'] = self.request.user
        return kwargs
```

PACKAGE TIP: django-braces's ModelForm Mixins

Inserting the `request.user` object into forms is so frequently done that **django-braces** can do it for us. Nevertheless, knowing how it works is useful for when what you need to add is not the `request.user` object.

- http://www.2scoops.co/django-braces-user-form-kwargs-mixin/
- http://www.2scoops.co/django-braces-user-kwarg-model-form-mixin/

11.5 Know How Form Validation Works

Form validation is one of those areas of Django where knowing the inner workings will drastically improve your code. Let's take a moment to dig into form validation and cover some of the key points.

When you call form.is_valid(), a lot of things happen behind the scenes. The following things occur according to this workflow:

1. If the form has bound data, form.is_valid() calls the form.full_clean() method.
2. form.full_clean() iterates through the form fields and each field validates itself:
   a. Data coming into the field is coerced into Python via the to_python() method or raises a ValidationError.
   b. Data is validated against field-specific rules, including custom validators. Failure raises a ValidationError.
   c. If there are any custom clean_<field>() methods in the form, they are called at this time.
3. form.full_clean() executes the form.clean() method.
4. If it's a ModelForm instance, form._post_clean() does the following:
   a. Sets ModelForm data to the Model instance, regardless of whether form.is_valid() is True or False.
   b. Calls the model's clean() method. For reference, saving a model instance through the ORM does not call the model's clean() method.

If this seems complicated, just remember that it gets simpler in practice, and that all of this functionality lets us really understand what's going on with incoming data. The example in the next section should help to explain this further.

Figure 11.1: When ice cream validation fails.

11.5.1 ModelForm Data Is Saved to the Form, Then the Model Instance

We like to call this the *WHAT?!?* of form validation. At first glance, form data being set to the form instance might seem like a bug. But it's not a bug. It's intended behavior.

In a `ModelForm`, form data is saved in two distinct steps:

1. First, form data is saved to the form instance.
2. Later, form data is saved to the model instance.

Since `ModelForms` don't save to the model instance until they are activated by the `form.save()` method, we can take advantage of this separation as a useful feature.

For example, perhaps you need to catch the details of failed submission attempts for a form, saving both the user-supplied form data as well as the intended model instance changes.

A simple, perhaps simplistic, way of capturing that data is as follows. First, we create a form failure history model in *core/models.py* as shown on the next page:

Example 11.6

```
# core/models.py
from django.db import models


class ModelFormFailureHistory(models.Model):
    form_data = models.TextField()
    model_data = models.TextField()
```

Second, we add the following to the `FlavorActionMixin` in *flavors/views.py*:

Example 11.7

```
# flavors/views.py
import json

from django.contrib import messages
from django.core import serializers
```

```
from core.models import ModelFormFailureHistory

class FlavorActionMixin(object):

    @property
    def success_msg(self):
        return NotImplemented

    def form_valid(self, form):
        messages.info(self.request, self.success_msg)
        return super(FlavorActionMixin, self).form_valid(form)

    def form_invalid(self, form):
        """Save invalid form and model data for later reference."""
        form_data = json.dumps(form.cleaned_data)
        model_data = serializers.serialize("json",
                    [form.instance])[1:-1]
        ModelFormFailureHistory.objects.create(
            form_data=form_data,
            model_data=model_data
        )
        return super(FlavorActionMixin,
                    self).form_invalid(form)
```

If you recall, `form_invalid()` is called after failed validation of a form with bad data. When it is called here in this example, both the cleaned form data and the final data saved to the database are saved as a `ModelFormFailureHistory` record.

11.6 Add Errors to Forms with `Form.add_error()`

Shared with us by Michael Barr, as of Django 1.7 we can streamline `Form.clean()` with the `Form.add_error()` method.

Example 11.8

```
from django import forms
```

```
class IceCreamReviewForm(forms.Form):
    # Rest of tester form goes here
    ...

    def clean(self):
        cleaned_data = super(TasterForm, self).clean()
        flavor = cleaned_data.get("flavor")
        age = cleaned_data.get("age")

        if flavor == 'coffee' and age < 3:
            # Record errors that will be displayed later.
            msg = u"Coffee Ice Cream is not for Babies."
            self.add_error('flavor', msg)
            self.add_error('age', msg)

        # Always return the full collection of cleaned data.
        return cleaned_data
```

11.6.1 Other Useful Form Methods

Here are other form validation methods worth exploring:

- http://www.2scoops.co/1.8-form.errors.as_data/
- http://www.2scoops.co/1.8-form.errors.as_json/
- http://www.2scoops.co/1.8-form.has_error/
- http://www.2scoops.co/1.8-form.non_field_errors/

11.7 Fields Without Pre-Made Widgets

Two of the new `django.contrib.postgres` fields, (`ArrayField` and `HStoreField`) don't work well with existing Django HTML fields. They don't come with corresponding widgets at all. Nevertheless, you should still be using forms with these fields.

As in the previous section this topic is covered in section 11.1, "Validate All Incoming Data With Django Forms".

11.8 Additional Resources

- Author Daniel Roy Greenfeld's blog series on forms expands upon concepts touched in this book http://www.pydanny.com/tag/forms.html
- Brad Montgomery's article on how to create a widget for the ArrayField. http://www.2scoops.co/bradmontgomery-nice-arrayfield/
- Miguel Araujo's tutorial on creating custom widgets and fields. http://www.2scoops.co/django-forms-i-custom-fields-and-widgets-in/

11.9 Summary

Once you dig into forms, keep yourself focused on clarity of code and testability. Forms are one of the primary validation tools in your Django project, an important defense against attacks and accidental data corruption.

In the next chapter we'll dig into using Forms, CBVs, and models together.

12 Common Patterns for Forms

Django forms are powerful, flexible, extensible, and robust. For this reason, the Django admin and CBVs use them extensively. In fact, all the major Django API frameworks use ModelForms or a similar implementation as part of their validation.

Combining forms, models, and views allows us to get a lot of work done for little effort. The learning curve is worth it: once you learn to work fluently with these components, you'll find that Django provides the ability to create an amazing amount of useful, stable functionality at an amazing pace.

> **PACKAGE TIP: Useful Form-Related Packages**
>
> - **django-floppyforms** for rendering Django inputs in HTML5.
> - **django-crispy-forms** for advanced form layout controls. By default, forms are rendered with Twitter Bootstrap form elements and styles. This package plays well with django-floppyforms, so they are often used together.
> - **django-forms-bootstrap** is a simple tool for rendering Django forms using Twitter Bootstrap styles. This package plays well with django-floppyforms but conflicts with django-crispy-forms.

This chapter goes explicitly into one of the best parts of Django: forms, models, and CBVs working in concert. This chapter covers five common form patterns that should be in every Django developer's toolbox.

12.1 Pattern 1: Simple ModelForm With Default Validators

The simplest data-changing form that we can make is a `ModelForm` using several default validators as-is, without modification. In fact, we already relied on default validators in chapter 10, *Best Practices for Class-Based Views*, subsection 10.5.1, "Views + ModelForm Example."

If you recall, using `ModelForms` with CBVs to implement add/edit forms can be done in just a few lines of code:

Example 12.1

```
# flavors/views.py
from django.views.generic import CreateView, UpdateView

from braces.views import LoginRequiredMixin

from .models import Flavor

class FlavorCreateView(LoginRequiredMixin, CreateView):
    model = Flavor
    fields = ('title', 'slug', 'scoops_remaining')

class FlavorUpdateView(LoginRequiredMixin, UpdateView):
    model = Flavor
    fields = ('title', 'slug', 'scoops_remaining')
```

To summarize how we use default validation as-is here:

- `FlavorCreateView` and `FlavorUpdateView` are assigned `Flavor` as their model.
- Both views auto-generate a `ModelForm` based on the Flavor model.
- Those `ModelForms` rely on the default field validation rules of the Flavor model.

Yes, Django gives us a lot of great defaults for data validation, but in practice, the defaults are never enough. We recognize this, so as a first step, the next pattern will demonstrate how to create a custom field validator.

12.2 Pattern 2: Custom Form Field Validators in ModelForms

What if we wanted to be certain that every use of the `title` field across our project's dessert apps started with the word 'Tasty'?

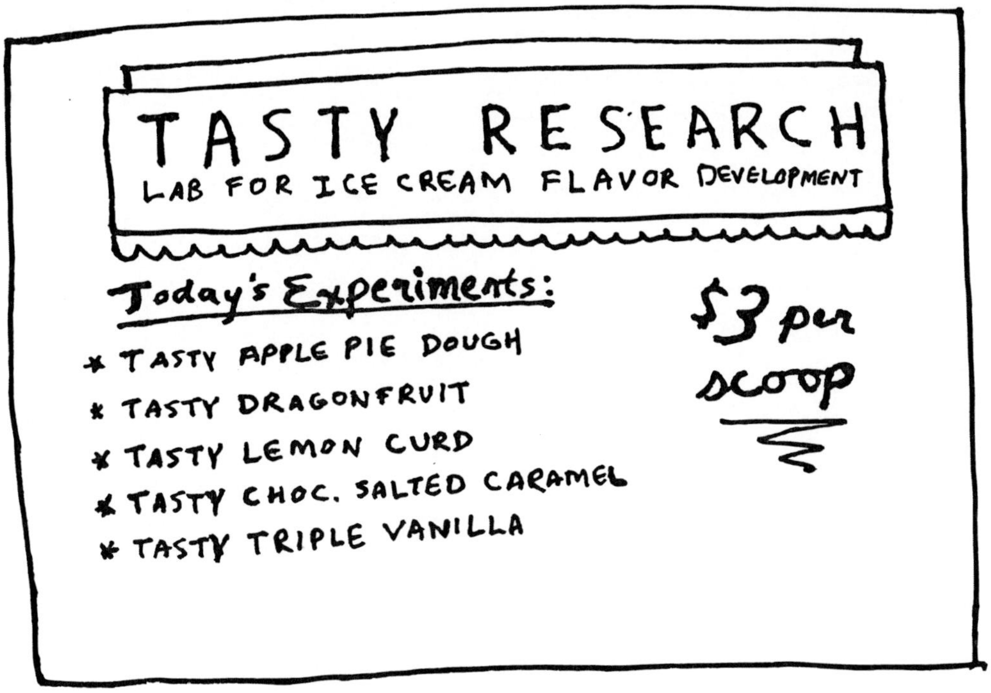

Figure 12.1: At Tasty Research, every flavor must begin with "Tasty".

This is a string validation problem that can be solved with a simple **custom field validator**.

In this pattern, we cover how to create custom single-field validators and demonstrate how to add them to both abstract models and forms.

Imagine for the purpose of this example that we have a project with two different dessert-related models: a `Flavor` model for ice cream flavors, and a `Milkshake` model for different types of milkshakes. Assume that both of our example models have `title` fields.

To validate all editable model titles, we start by creating a *validators.py* module:

Example 12.2

```python
# core/validators.py
from django.core.exceptions import ValidationError

def validate_tasty(value):
    """Raise a ValidationError if the value doesn't start with the
        word 'Tasty'.
    """
    if not value.startswith(u"Tasty"):
        msg = u"Must start with Tasty"
        raise ValidationError(msg)
```

In Django, a custom field validator is simply a function that raises an error if the submitted argument doesn't pass its test.

Of course, while our `validate_tasty()` validator function just does a simple string check for the sake of example, it's good to keep in mind that form field validators can become quite complex in practice.

TIP: Test Your Validators Carefully

Since validators are critical in keeping corruption out of Django project databases, it's especially important to write detailed tests for them.

These tests should include thoughtful edge case tests for every condition related to your validators' custom logic.

In order to use our `validate_tasty()` validator function across different dessert models, we're going to first add it to an abstract model called `TastyTitleAbstractModel`, which we plan to use across our project.

Assuming that our `Flavor` and `Milkshake` models are in separate apps, it doesn't make sense to put our validator in one app or the other. Instead, we create a ***core/models.py*** module and place the `TastyTitleAbstractModel` there.

EXAMPLE 12.3

```
# core/models.py
from django.db import models

from .validators import validate_tasty

class TastyTitleAbstractModel(models.Model):

    title = models.CharField(max_length=255, validators=[validate_tasty])

    class Meta:
        abstract = True
```

The last two lines of the above example code for ***core/models.py*** make `TastyTitleAbstractModel` an abstract model, which is what we want.

Let's alter the original ***flavors/models.py*** `Flavor` code to use `TastyTitleAbstractModel` as the parent class:

EXAMPLE 12.4

```
# flavors/models.py
from django.core.urlresolvers import reverse
from django.db import models

from core.models import TastyTitleAbstractModel

class Flavor(TastyTitleAbstractModel):
    slug = models.SlugField()
    scoops_remaining = models.IntegerField(default=0)

    def get_absolute_url(self):
        return reverse("flavors:detail", kwargs={"slug": self.slug})
```

This works with the `Flavor` model, and it will work with any other tasty food-based model such as a `WaffleCone` or `Cake` model. Any model that inherits from the `TastyTitleAbstractModel` class will throw a validation error if anyone attempts to save a model with a title that doesn't start with 'Tasty'.

Now, let's explore a couple of questions that might be forming in your head:

- What if we wanted to use `validate_tasty()` in just forms?
- What if we wanted to assign it to other fields besides the title?

To support these behaviors, we need to create a custom `FlavorForm` that utilizes our custom field validator:

Example 12.5

```
# flavors/forms.py
from django import forms

from core.validators import validate_tasty
from .models import Flavor

class FlavorForm(forms.ModelForm):
    def __init__(self, *args, **kwargs):
        super(FlavorForm, self).__init__(*args, **kwargs)
        self.fields["title"].validators.append(validate_tasty)
        self.fields["slug"].validators.append(validate_tasty)

    class Meta:
        model = Flavor
```

A nice thing about both examples of validator usage in this pattern is that we haven't had to change the `validate_tasty()` code at all. Instead, we just import and use it in new places.

Attaching the custom form to the views is our next step. The default behavior of Django model-based edit views is to auto-generate the ModelForm based on the view's model attribute. We are going to override that default and pass in our custom `FlavorForm`. This occurs in the ***flavors/views.py*** module, where we alter the create and update forms as demonstrated below:

Example 12.6

```
# flavors/views.py
from django.contrib import messages
```

```
from django.views.generic import CreateView, UpdateView, DetailView

from braces.views import LoginRequiredMixin

from .models import Flavor
from .forms import FlavorForm

class FlavorActionMixin(object):

    model = Flavor
    fields = ('title', 'slug', 'scoops_remaining')

    @property
    def success_msg(self):
        return NotImplemented

    def form_valid(self, form):
        messages.info(self.request, self.success_msg)
        return super(FlavorActionMixin, self).form_valid(form)

class FlavorCreateView(LoginRequiredMixin, FlavorActionMixin,
                            CreateView):
    success_msg = "created"
    # Explicitly attach the FlavorForm class
    form_class = FlavorForm

class FlavorUpdateView(LoginRequiredMixin, FlavorActionMixin,
                            UpdateView):
    success_msg = "updated"
    # Explicitly attach the FlavorForm class
    form_class = FlavorForm

class FlavorDetailView(DetailView):
    model = Flavor
```

The `FlavorCreateView` and `FlavorUpdateView` views now use the new `FlavorForm` to validate incoming data.

Note that with these modifications, the `Flavor` model can either be identical to the one at the start of this chapter, or it can be an altered one that inherits from `TastyTitleAbstractModel`.

12.3 Pattern 3: Overriding the Clean Stage of Validation

Let's discuss some interesting validation use cases:

- Multi-field validation
- Validation involving existing data from the database that has already been validated

Both of these are great scenarios for overriding the `clean()` and `clean_<field_name>()` methods with custom validation logic.

After the default and custom field validators are run, Django provides a second stage and process for validating incoming data, this time via the `clean()` method and `clean_<field_name>()` methods. You might wonder why Django provides more hooks for validation, so here are our two favorite arguments:

1. The `clean()` method is the place to validate two or more fields against each other, since it's not specific to any one particular field.
2. The clean validation stage is a better place to attach validation against persistent data. Since the data already has some validation, you won't waste as many database cycles on needless queries.

Let's explore this with another validation example. Perhaps we want to implement an ice cream ordering form, where users could specify the flavor desired, add toppings, and then come to our store and pick them up.

Since we want to prevent users from ordering flavors that are out of stock, we'll put in a `clean_slug()` method. With our flavor validation, our form might look like:

Example 12.7

```
# flavors/forms.py
from django import forms
from flavors.models import Flavor
```

```python
class IceCreamOrderForm(forms.Form):
    """Normally done with forms.ModelForm. But we use forms.Form here
        to demonstrate that these sorts of techniques work on every
        type of form.
    """

    slug = forms.ChoiceField("Flavor")
    toppings = forms.CharField()

    def __init__(self, *args, **kwargs):
        super(IceCreamOrderForm, self).__init__(*args,
                    **kwargs)
        # We dynamically set the choices here rather than
        # in the flavor field definition. Setting them in
        # the field definition means status updates won't
        # be reflected in the form without server restarts.
        self.fields["slug"].choices = [
            (x.slug, x.title) for x in Flavor.objects.all()
        ]
        # NOTE: We could filter by whether or not a flavor
        #       has any scoops, but this is an example of
        #       how to use clean_slug, not filter().

    def clean_slug(self):
        slug = self.cleaned_data["slug"]
        if Flavor.objects.get(slug=slug).scoops_remaining <= 0:
            msg = u"Sorry, we are out of that flavor."
            raise forms.ValidationError(msg)
        return slug
```

For HTML-powered views, the `clean_slug()` method in our example, upon throwing an error, will attach a "Sorry, we are out of that flavor" message to the flavor HTML input field. This is a great shortcut for writing HTML forms!

Now imagine if we get common customer complaints about orders with too much chocolate. Yes, it's silly and quite impossible, but we're just using 'too much chocolate' as a completely mythical example for the sake of making a point.

In any case, let's use the `clean()` method to validate the flavor and toppings fields against each other.

EXAMPLE 12.8

```python
# attach this code to the previous example (12.7)
def clean(self):
    cleaned_data = super(IceCreamOrderForm, self).clean()
    slug = cleaned_data.get("slug", "")
    toppings = cleaned_data.get("toppings", "")

    # Silly "too much chocolate" validation example
    if u"chocolate" in slug.lower() and \
            u"chocolate" in toppings.lower():
        msg = u"Your order has too much chocolate."
        raise forms.ValidationError(msg)
    return cleaned_data
```

There we go, an implementation against the impossible condition of too much chocolate!

TIP: Common Fields Used in Multi-Field Validation

It is common practice for user account forms involved with email and password entry to force the user to enter the same data twice. Other things to check for against those fields include:

- Strength of the submitted password.
- If the email model field isn't set to `unique=True`, whether or not the email is unique.

Figure 12.2: Why would they do this to us?

12.4 Pattern 4: Hacking Form Fields (2 CBVs, 2 Forms, 1 Model)

This is where we start to get fancy. We're going to cover a situation where two views/forms correspond to one model. We'll hack Django forms to produce a form with custom behavior.

It's not uncommon to have users create a record that contains a few empty fields which need additional data later. An example might be a list of stores, where we want each store entered into the system as fast as possible, but want to add more data such as phone number and description later. Here's our `IceCreamStore` model:

Example 12.9

```
# stores/models.py
```

```python
from django.core.urlresolvers import reverse
from django.db import models

class IceCreamStore(models.Model):
    title = models.CharField(max_length=100)
    block_address = models.TextField()
    phone = models.CharField(max_length=20, blank=True)
    description = models.TextField(blank=True)

    def get_absolute_url(self):
        return reverse("store_detail", kwargs={"pk": self.pk})
```

The default `ModelForm` for this model forces the user to enter the `title` and `block_address` field but allows the user to skip the phone and `description` fields. That's great for initial data entry, but as mentioned earlier, we want to have future updates of the data to require the phone and description fields.

The way we implemented this in the past before we began to delve into their construction was to override the phone and description fields in the edit form. This resulted in heavily-duplicated code that looked like this:

Bad Example 12.1

```python
# stores/forms.py
from django import forms

from .models import IceCreamStore

class IceCreamStoreUpdateForm(forms.ModelForm):
    # Don't do this! Duplication of the model field!
    phone = forms.CharField(required=True)
    # Don't do this! Duplication of the model field!
    description = forms.TextField(required=True)

    class Meta:
        model = IceCreamStore
```

This form should look very familiar. Why is that?

Well, we're nearly copying the `IceCreamStore` model!

This is just a simple example, but when dealing with a lot of fields on a model, the duplication becomes extremely challenging to manage. In fact, what tends to happen is copy-pasting of code from models right into forms, which is a gross violation of **Don't Repeat Yourself**.

Want to know how gross? Using the above approach, if we add a simple `help_text` attribute to the `description` field in the model, it will not show up in the template until we also modify the `description` field definition in the form. If that sounds confusing, that's because it is.

A better way is to rely on a useful little detail that's good to remember about Django forms: instantiated form objects store fields in a dict-like attribute called `fields`.

Instead of copy-pasting field definitions from models to forms, we can simply apply new attributes to each field in the `__init__()` method of the `ModelForm`:

Example 12.10

```
# stores/forms.py
# Call phone and description from the self.fields dict-like object
from django import forms

from .models import IceCreamStore

class IceCreamStoreUpdateForm(forms.ModelForm):

    class Meta:
        model = IceCreamStore

    def __init__(self, *args, **kwargs):
        # Call the original __init__ method before assigning
        # field overloads
        super(IceCreamStoreUpdateForm, self).__init__(*args,
                            **kwargs)
        self.fields["phone"].required = True
        self.fields["description"].required = True
```

This improved approach allows us to stop copy-pasting code and instead focus on just the field-specific settings.

An important point to remember is that when it comes down to it, Django forms are just Python classes. They get instantiated as objects, they can inherit from other classes, and they can act as superclasses.

Therefore, we can rely on inheritance to trim the line count in our ice cream store forms:

Example 12.11

```
# stores/forms.py
from django import forms

from .models import IceCreamStore

class IceCreamStoreCreateForm(forms.ModelForm):

    class Meta:
        model = IceCreamStore
        fields = ("title", "block_address", )

class IceCreamStoreUpdateForm(IceCreamStoreCreateForm):

    def __init__(self, *args, **kwargs):
        super(IceCreamStoreUpdateForm,
                self).__init__(*args, **kwargs)
        self.fields["phone"].required = True
        self.fields["description"].required = True

    class Meta(IceCreamStoreCreateForm.Meta):
        # show all the fields!
        fields = ("title", "block_address", "phone",
                "description", )
```

WARNING: Use Meta.fields and Never Use Meta.exclude

We use `Meta.fields` instead of `Meta.exclude` so that we know exactly what fields we are exposing. See chapter 26, *Security Best Practices*, section 26.13, 'Don't use ModelForms.Meta.exclude'.

Finally, now we have what we need to define the corresponding CBVs. We've got our form classes, so let's use them in the `IceCreamStore` create and update views:

Example 12.12

```
# stores/views
from django.views.generic import CreateView, UpdateView

from .forms import IceCreamStoreCreateForm
from .forms import IceCreamStoreUpdateForm
from .models import IceCreamStore

class IceCreamCreateView(CreateView):
    model = IceCreamStore
    form_class = IceCreamStoreCreateForm

class IceCreamUpdateView(UpdateView):
    model = IceCreamStore
    form_class = IceCreamStoreUpdateForm
```

We now have two views and two forms that work with one model.

12.5 Pattern 5: Reusable Search Mixin View

In this example, we're going to cover how to reuse a search form in two views that correspond to two different models.

Assume that both models have a field called `title` (this pattern also demonstrates why naming standards in projects is a good thing). This example will demonstrate how a single CBV can be used to provide simple search functionality on both the `Flavor` and `IceCreamStore` models.

We'll start by creating a simple search mixin for our view:

Example 12.13

```
# core/views.py
class TitleSearchMixin(object):

    def get_queryset(self):
        # Fetch the queryset from the parent's get_queryset
        queryset = super(TitleSearchMixin, self).get_queryset()

        # Get the q GET parameter
        q = self.request.GET.get("q")
        if q:
            # return a filtered queryset
            return queryset.filter(title__icontains=q)
        # No q is specified so we return queryset
        return queryset
```

The above code should look very familiar as we used it almost verbatim in the Forms + View example. Here's how you make it work with both the `Flavor` and `IceCreamStore` views. First the flavor views:

Example 12.14

```
# add to flavors/views.py
from django.views.generic import ListView

from core.views import TitleSearchMixin
from .models import Flavor

class FlavorListView(TitleSearchMixin, ListView):
    model = Flavor
```

And we'll add it to the ice cream store views:

Example 12.15

```
# add to stores/views.py
from django.views.generic import ListView
```

```python
from core.views import TitleSearchMixin
from .models import Store

class IceCreamStoreListView(TitleSearchMixin, ListView):
    model = Store
```

As for the form? We just define it in HTML for each `ListView`:

Example 12.16

```html
{# form to go into stores/store_list.html template #}
<form action="" method="GET">
    <input type="text" name="q" />
    <button type="submit">search</button>
</form>
```

and

Example 12.17

```html
{# form to go into flavors/flavor_list.html template #}
<form action="" method="GET">
    <input type="text" name="q" />
    <button type="submit">search</button>
</form>
```

Now we have the same mixin in both views. Mixins are a good way to reuse code, but using too many mixins in a single class makes for very hard-to-maintain code. As always, try to keep your code as simple as possible.

12.6 Summary

We began this chapter with the simplest form pattern, using a `ModelForm`, CBV, and default validators. We iterated on that with an example of a custom validator.

Next, we explored more complex validation. We covered an example overriding the clean methods. We also closely examined a scenario involving two views and their corresponding forms that were tied to a single model.

Finally, we covered an example of creating a reusable search mixin to add the same form to two different apps.

13 Templates: Best Practices

One of Django's early design decisions was to limit the functionality of the template language. This heavily constrains what can be done with Django templates, which we often think is a very good thing since it forces us to keep business logic in the Python side of things.

Think about it: the limitations of Django templates force us to put the most critical, complex and detailed parts of our project into `.py` files rather than into template files. Python happens to be one of the most clear, concise, elegant programming languages of the planet, so why would we want things any other way?

> **TIP: Using Jinja2 With Django**
>
> Starting with 1.8 Django natively supports Jinja2, as well as providing an interface for including other template languages. We cover this topic in chapter 15, *Using Alternate Template Systems.*

13.1 Keep Templates Mostly in `templates/`

In our projects, we keep the majority of our templates in the main 'templates/' directory. We put subdirectories in 'templates/' to correspond to each of our apps, as shown here:

Example 13.1

```
templates/
    base.html
    ... (other sitewide templates in here)
```

```
    freezers/
        ("freezers" app templates in here)
```

However, some tutorials advocate putting templates within a subdirectory of each app. We find that the extra nesting is a pain to deal with, as shown here:

Bad Example 13.1

```
freezers/
    templates/
        freezers/
            ... ("freezers" app templates in here)
templates/
    base.html
    ... (other sitewide templates in here)
```

That said, some people like to do it the second way, and that's alright.

The exception to all of this is when we work with Django apps that are installed as pluggable packages. A Django package usually contains its own in-app 'templates/' directory. Then we override those templates anyway from our project's main 'templates/' directory in order to add design and styling.

13.2 Template Architecture Patterns

We've found that for our purposes, simple 2-tier or 3-tier template architectures are ideal. The difference in tiers is how many levels of template extending needs to occur before content in apps is displayed. See the examples below:

13.2.1 2-Tier Template Architecture Example

With a 2-tier template architecture, all templates inherit from a single root ***base.html*** file.

Example 13.2

```
templates/
    base.html
    dashboard.html # extends base.html
    profiles/
        profile_detail.html # extends base.html
        profile_form.html # extends base.html
```

This is best for sites with a consistent overall layout from app to app.

13.2.2 3-Tier Template Architecture Example

With a 3-tier template architecture:

- Each app has a ***base_<app_name>.html*** template. App-level base templates share a common parent ***base.html*** template.
- Templates within apps share a common parent ***base_<app_name>.html*** template.
- Any template at the same level as ***base.html*** inherits ***base.html***.

Example 13.3

```
templates/
    base.html
    dashboard.html # extends base.html
    profiles/
        base_profiles.html # extends base.html
        profile_detail.html # extends base_profiles.html
        profile_form.html # extends base_profiles.html
```

The 3-tier architecture is best for websites where each section requires a distinctive layout. For example, a news site might have a local news section, a classified ads section, and an events section. Each of these sections requires its own custom layout.

This is extremely useful when we want HTML to look or behave differently for a particular section of the site that groups functionality.

13.2.3 Flat Is Better Than Nested

Figure 13.1: An excerpt from the Zen of Ice Cream.

Complex template hierarchies make it exceedingly difficult to debug, modify, and extend HTML pages and tie in CSS styles. When template block layouts become unnecessarily nested, you end up digging through file after file just to change, say, the width of a box.

Giving your template blocks as shallow an inheritance structure as possible will make your templates easier to work with and more maintainable. If you're working with a designer, your designer will thank you.

That being said, there's a difference between excessively-complex template block hierarchies and templates that use blocks wisely for code reuse. When you have large, multi-line chunks of the same or very similar code in separate templates, refactoring that code into reusable blocks will make your code more maintainable.

The *Zen of Python* includes the aphorism "*Flat is better than nested*" for good reason. Each level of nesting adds mental overhead. Keep that in mind when architecting your Django templates.

TIP: The Zen of Python

At the command line, do the following:

```
python -c `import this'
```

What you'll see is the *Zen of Python*, an eloquently-expressed set of guiding principles for the design of the Python programming language.

13.3 Limit Processing in Templates

The less processing you try to do in your templates, the better. This is particularly a problem when it comes to queries and iteration performed in the template layer.

Whenever you iterate over a queryset in a template, ask yourself the following questions:

1. How large is the queryset? Looping over gigantic querysets in your templates is almost always a bad idea.
2. How large are the objects being retrieved? Are all the fields needed in this template?
3. During each iteration of the loop, how much processing occurs?

If any warning bells go off in your head, then there's probably a better way to rewrite your template code.

WARNING: Why Not Just Cache?

Sometimes you can just cache away your template inefficiencies. That's fine, but before you cache, you should first try to attack the root of the problem.
You can save yourself a lot of work by mentally tracing through your template code, doing some quick run time analysis, and refactoring.

Let's now explore some examples of template code that can be rewritten more efficiently.

Suspend your disbelief for a moment and pretend that the nutty duo behind Two Scoops ran a 30-second commercial during the Super Bowl. "Free pints of ice cream for the first million developers who request them! All you have to do is fill out a form to get a voucher redeemable in stores!"

Figure 13.2: Two Scoops, official halftime sponsor of the Super Bowl.

Naturally, we have a "vouchers" app to track the names and email addresses of everyone who requested a free pint voucher. Here's what the model for this app looks like:

Example 13.4

```
# vouchers/models.py
from django.core.urlresolvers import reverse
from django.db import models
from .managers import VoucherManager

class Voucher(models.Model):
    """Vouchers for free pints of ice cream."""
    name = models.CharField(max_length=100)
    email = models.EmailField()
    address = models.TextField()
    birth_date = models.DateField(blank=True)
    sent = models.BooleanField(default=False)
```

```
    redeemed = models.BooleanField(default=False)

    objects = VoucherManager()
```

This model will be used in the following examples to illustrate a few "gotchas" that you should avoid.

13.3.1 Gotcha 1: Aggregation in Templates

Since we have birth date information, it would be interesting to display a rough breakdown by age range of voucher requests and redemptions.

A very bad way to implement this would be to do all the processing at the template level. To be more specific in the context of this example:

- Don't iterate over the entire voucher list in your template's JavaScript section, using JavaScript variables to hold age range counts.
- Don't use the `add` template filter to sum up the voucher counts.

Those implementations are ways of getting around Django's limitations of logic in templates, but they'll slow down your pages drastically.

The better way is to move this processing out of your template and into your Python code. Sticking to our minimal approach of using templates only to *display* data that has already been processed, our template looks like this:

Example 13.5

```
{# templates/vouchers/ages.html #}
{% extends "base.html" %}

{% block content %}
<table>
    <thead>
        <tr>
            <th>Age Bracket</th>
```

```
            <th>Number of Vouchers Issued</th>
        </tr>
    </thead>
    <tbody>
        {% for age_bracket in age_brackets %}
        <tr>
            <td>{{ age_bracket.title }}</td>
            <td>{{ age_bracket.count }}</td>
        </tr>
        {% endfor %}
    </tbody>
</table>
{% endblock content %}
```

In this example, we can do the processing with a model manager, using the Django ORM's aggregation methods and the handy *dateutil* library described in Appendix A: *Packages Mentioned In This Book*:

Example 13.6

```
# vouchers/managers.py
from django.utils import timezone

from dateutil.relativedelta import relativedelta

from django.db import models

class VoucherManager(models.Manager):
    def age_breakdown(self):
        """Returns a dict of age brackets/counts."""
        age_brackets = []
        now = timezone.now()

        delta = now - relativedelta(years=18)
        count = self.model.objects.filter(birth_date__gt=delta).count()
        age_brackets.append(
            {"title": "0-17", "count": count}
```

```
    )
    count = self.model.objects.filter(birth_date__lte=delta).count()
    age_brackets.append(
        {"title": "18+", "count": count}
    )
    return age_brackets
```

This method would be called from a view, and the results would be passed to the template as a context variable.

13.3.2 Gotcha 2: Filtering With Conditionals in Templates

Suppose we want to display a list of all the Greenfelds and the Roys who requested free pint vouchers, so that we could invite them to our family reunion. We want to filter our records on the name field. A very bad way to implement this would be with giant loops and if statements at the template level.

Bad Example 13.2

```
<h2>Greenfelds Who Want Ice Cream</h2>
<ul>
{% for voucher in voucher_list %}
    {# Don't do this: conditional filtering in templates #}
    {% if "greenfeld" in voucher.name.lower %}
        <li>{{ voucher.name }}</li>
    {% endif %}
{% endfor %}
</ul>

<h2>Roys Who Want Ice Cream</h2>
<ul>
{% for voucher in voucher_list %}
    {# Don't do this: conditional filtering in templates #}
    {% if "roy" in voucher.name.lower %}
        <li>{{ voucher.name }}</li>
    {% endif %}
```

```
{% endfor %}
</ul>
```

In this bad snippet, we're looping and checking for various "if" conditions. That's filtering a potentially gigantic list of records in templates, which is not designed for this kind of work, and will cause performance bottlenecks. On the other hand, databases like PostgreSQL and MySQL are great at filtering records, so this should be done at the database layer. The Django ORM can help us with this as demonstrated in the next example.

Example 13.7

```python
# vouchers/views.py
from django.views.generic import TemplateView

from .models import Voucher

class GreenfeldRoyView(TemplateView):
    template_name = "vouchers/views_conditional.html"

    def get_context_data(self, **kwargs):
        context = super(GreenfeldRoyView, self).get_context_data(**kwargs)
        context["greenfelds"] = \
                Voucher.objects.filter(name__icontains="greenfeld")
        context["roys"] = Voucher.objects.filter(name__icontains="roy")
        return context
```

Then to call the results, we use the following, simpler template:

Example 13.8

```
<h2>Greenfelds Who Want Ice Cream</h2>
<ul>
{% for voucher in greenfelds %}
    <li>{{ voucher.name }}</li>
{% endfor %}
</ul>
```

```
<h2>Roys Who Want Ice Cream</h2>
<ul>
{% for voucher in roys %}
    <li>{{ voucher.name }}</li>
{% endfor %}
</ul>
```

It's easy to speed up this template by moving the filtering to a model manager. With this change, we now simply use the template to display the already-filtered data. The above template now follows our preferred minimalist approach.

13.3.3 Gotcha 3: Complex Implied Queries in Templates

Despite the limitations on logic allowed in Django templates, it's all too easy to find ourselves calling unnecessary queries repeatedly in a view. For example, if we list users of our site and all their flavors this way:

Bad Example 13.3

```
{# list generated via User.object.all() #}
<h1>Ice Cream Fans and their favorite flavors.</h1>
<ul>
{% for user in user_list %}
    <li>
        {{ user.name }}:
        {# DON'T DO THIS: Generated implicit query per user #}
        {{ user.flavor.title }}
        {# DON'T DO THIS: Second implicit query per user!!! #}
        {{ user.flavor.scoops_remaining }}
    </li>
{% endfor %}
</ul>
```

Then calling each user generates a second query. While that might not seem like much, we are certain that if we had enough users and made this mistake frequently enough, our site would have a lot of trouble.

One quick correction is to use the Django ORM's `select_related()` method:

Example 13.9

```
{% comment %}
List generated via User.object.all().select_related("flavors")
{% endcomment %}
<h1>Ice Cream Fans and their favorite flavors.</h1>
<ul>
{% for user in user_list %}
    <li>
        {{ user.name }}:
        {{ user.flavor.title }}
        {{ user.flavor.scoops_remaining }}
    </li>
{% endfor %}
</ul>
```

One more thing: If you've embraced using model methods, the same applies. Be cautious putting too much query logic in the model methods called from templates.

13.3.4 Gotcha 4: Hidden CPU Load in Templates

Watch out for innocent-looking calls in templates that result in intensive CPU processing. Although a template might look simple and contain very little code, a single line could be invoking an object method that does a lot of processing.

Figure 13.3: Bubble gum ice cream looks easy to eat but requires a lot of processing.

Common examples are template tags that manipulate images, such as the template tags provided by libraries like **sorl-thumbnail**. In many cases tools like this work great, but we've had some issues. Specifically, the manipulation and the saving of image data to file systems (often across networks) inside a template means there is a choke point within templates.

This is why projects that handle a lot of image or data processing increase the performance of their site by taking the image processing out of templates and into views, models, helper methods, or asynchronous messages queues like Celery.

13.3.5 Gotcha 5: Hidden REST API Calls in Templates

You saw in the previous gotcha how easy it is to introduce template loading delays by accessing object method calls. This is true not just with high-load methods, but also with methods that contain REST API calls. A good example is querying an unfortunately slow maps API hosted by a third-party service that your project absolutely requires. Don't do this in the template code by calling a method attached to an object passed into the view's context.

Where should actual REST API consumption occur? We recommend doing this in:

- JavaScript code so after your project serves out its content, the client's browser handles the work. This way you can entertain or distract the client while they wait for data to load.
- The view's Python code where slow processes might be handled in a variety of ways including message queues, additional threads, multiprocesses, or more.

13.4 Don't Bother Making Your Generated HTML Pretty

Bluntly put, no one cares if the HTML generated by your Django project is attractive. In fact, if someone were to look at your rendered HTML, they'd do so through the lens of a browser inspector, which would realign the HTML spacing anyway. Therefore, if you shuffle up the code in your Django templates to render pretty HTML, you are wasting time obfuscating your code for an audience of yourself.

And yet, we've seen code like the following. This evil code snippet generates nicely formatted HTML but itself is an illegible, unmaintainable template mess:

BAD EXAMPLE 13.4

```
{% comment %}Don't do this! This code bunches everything
together to generate pretty HTML.
{% endcomment %}
{% if list_type=="unordered" %}<ul>{% else %}<ol>{% endif %}{% for
syrup in syrup_list %}<li class="{{ syrup.temperature_type|roomtemp
}}"><a href="{% url 'syrup_detail' syrup.slug %}">{% syrup.title %}
</a></li>{% endfor %}{% if list_type=="unordered" %}</ul>{% else %}
</ol>{% endif %}
```

A better way of writing the above snippet is to use indentation and one operation per line to create a readable, maintainable template:

EXAMPLE 13.10

```
{# Use indentation/comments to ensure code quality #}
{# start of list elements #}
{% if list_type=="unordered" %}
    <ul>
{% else %}
    <ol>
{% endif %}

{% for syrup in syrup_list %}
    <li class="{{ syrup.temperature_type|roomtemp }}">
        <a href="{% url 'syrup_detail' syrup.slug %}">
            {% syrup.title %}
        </a>
    </li>
{% endfor %}
{# end of list elements #}
{% if list_type=="unordered" %}
    </ul>
{% else %}
    </ol>
{% endif %}
```

Are you worried about the volume of whitespace generated? Don't be. First of all, experienced developers favor readability of code over obfuscation for the sake of optimization. Second, there are compression and minification tools that can help more than anything you can do manually here. See chapter 24, *Finding and Reducing Bottlenecks*, for more details.

13.5 Exploring Template Inheritance

Let's begin with a simple ***base.html*** file that we'll inherit from another template:

Example 13.11

```
{# simple base.html #}
{% load staticfiles %}
<html>
<head>
    <title>
        {% block title %}Two Scoops of Django{% endblock title %}
    </title>
    {% block stylesheets %}
        <link rel="stylesheet" type="text/css"
                href="{% static "css/project.css" %}">
    {% endblock stylesheets %}
</head>
<body>
    <div class="content">
        {% block content %}
            <h1>Two Scoops</h1>
        {% endblock content %}
    </div>
</body>
</html>
```

The ***base.html*** file contains the following features:

- A `title` block containing "`Two Scoops of Django`".
- A `stylesheets` block containing a link to a *project.css* file used across our site.
- A `content` block containing "`<h1>Two Scoops</h1>`".

Our example relies on just three template tags, which are summarized below:

Template Tag	Purpose
`{% load %}`	Loads the staticfiles built-in template tag library
`{% block %}`	Since *base.html* is a parent template, these define which child blocks can be filled in by child templates. We place links and scripts inside them so we can override if necessary.
`{% static %}`	Resolves the named static media argument to the static media server.

Table 13.1: Template Tags in base.html

To demonstrate ***base.html*** in use, we'll have a simple ***about.html*** inherit the following from it:

- A custom title.
- The original stylesheet and an additional stylesheet.
- The original header, a sub header, and paragraph content.
- The use of child blocks.
- The use of the `{{ block.super }}` template variable.

Example 13.12

```
{% extends "base.html" %}
{% load staticfiles %}
{% block title %}About Audrey and Daniel{% endblock title %}
{% block stylesheets %}
    {{ block.super }}
    <link rel="stylesheet" type="text/css"
            href="{% static "css/about.css" %}">
{% endblock stylesheets %}
{% block content %}
    {{ block.super }}
    <h2>About Audrey and Daniel</h2>
    <p>They enjoy eating ice cream</p>
{% endblock content %}
```

When we render this template in a view, it generates the following HTML:

Example 13.13

```
<html>
<head>
    <title>
        About Audrey and Daniel
    </title>
        <link rel="stylesheet" type="text/css"
                href="/static/css/project.css">
        <link rel="stylesheet" type="text/css"
                href="/static/css/about.css">
</head>
<body>
    <div class="content">
            <h1>Two Scoops</h1>
            <h2>About Audrey and Daniel</h2>
            <p>They enjoy eating ice cream</p>
    </div>
</body>
</html>
```

Notice how the rendered HTML has our custom title, the additional stylesheet link, and more material in the body? We'll use the table below to review the template tags and variables in the ***about.html*** template.

Template Object	Purpose
`{% extends %}`	Informs Django that about.html is inheriting or extending from base.html
`{% block %}`	Since about.html is a child template, block overrides the content provided by base.html. This means our title will render as <title>Audrey and Daniel</title>.
`{{ block.super }}`	When placed in a child template's block, it ensures that the parent's content is also included in the block. In the content block of the about.html template, this will render <h1>Two Scoops</h1>.

Table 13.2: Template Objects in about.html

Note that the {% block %} tag is used differently in ***about.html*** than in ***base.html***, serving to override content. In blocks where we want to preserve the ***base.html*** content, we use {{ block.super }} variable to display the content from the parent block. This brings us to the next topic, {{ block.super }}.

13.6 block.super Gives the Power of Control

Let's imagine that we have a template which inherits everything from the ***base.html*** but replaces the project's link to the ***project.css*** file with a link to ***dashboard.css***. This use case might occur when you have a project with one design for normal users, and a dashboard with a different design for staff.

If we aren't using {{ block.super }}, this often involves writing a whole new base file, often named something like ***base_dashboard.html***. For better or for worse, we now have two template architectures to maintain.

If we are using {{ block.super }}, we don't need a second (or third or fourth) base template. Assuming all templates extend from base.html we use {{ block.super }} to assume control of our templates. Here are three examples:

Template using both ***project.css*** and a custom link:

Example 13.14

```
{% extends "base.html" %}
{% block stylesheets %}
    {{ block.super }} {# this brings in project.css #}
    <link rel="stylesheet" type="text/css"
        href="{% static "css/custom.css" %}" />
{% endblock %}
```

Dashboard template that excludes the ***project.css*** link:

Example 13.15

```
{% extends "base.html" %}
{% block stylesheets %}
    <link rel="stylesheet" type="text/css"
        href="{% static "css/dashboard.css" %}" />
```

```
    {% comment %}
        By not using {{ block.super }}, this block overrides the
        stylesheet block of base.html
    {% endcomment %}
{% endblock %}
```

Template just linking the *project.css* file:

Example 13.16

```
{% extends "base.html" %}
{% comment %}
    By not using {% block stylesheets %}, this template inherits the
    stylesheets block from the base.html parent, in this case the
    default project.css link.
{% endcomment %}
```

These three examples demonstrate the amount of control that `{{ block.super }}` provides. The variable serves a good way to reduce template complexity, but can take a little bit of effort to fully comprehend.

> **TIP: block.super Is Similar but Not the Same as super()**
>
> For those coming from an object oriented programming background, it might help to think of the behavior of the `{{ block.super }}` variable to be like a very limited version of the Python built-in function, `super()`. In essence, the `{{ block.super }}` variable and the `super()` function both provide access to the parent.
> Just remember that they aren't the same. For example, the `{{ block.super }}` variable doesn't accept arguments. It's just a nice mnemonic that some developers might find useful.

13.7 Useful Things to Consider

The following are a series of smaller things we keep in mind during template development.

13.7.1 Avoid Coupling Styles Too Tightly to Python Code

Aim to control the styling of all rendered templates entirely via CSS and JS.

Use CSS for styling whenever possible. Never hardcode things like menu bar widths and color choices into your Python code. Avoid even putting that type of styling into your Django templates.

Here are some tips:

- If you have magic constants in your Python code that are entirely related to visual design layout, you should probably move them to a CSS file.
- The same applies to JavaScript.

13.7.2 Common Conventions

Here are some naming and style conventions that we recommend:

- We prefer underscores over dashes in template names, block names, and other names in templates. Most Django users seem to follow this convention. Why? Well, because underscores are allowed in names of Python objects but dashes are forbidden.
- We rely on clear, intuitive names for blocks. `{% block javascript %}` is good.
- We include the name of the block tag in the endblock. Never write just `{% endblock %}`, include the whole `{% endblock javascript %}`.
- Templates called by other templates are prefixed with '_'. This applies to templates called via `{% include %}` or custom template tags. It does not apply to templates inheritance controls such as `{% extends %}` or `{% block %}`.

13.7.3 Location, Location, Location!

Templates should usually go into the root of the Django project, at the same level as the apps. This is the most common convention, and it's an intuitive, easy pattern to follow.

The only exception is when you bundle up an app into a third-party package. That packages template directory should go into app directly. We'll explore this in section 21.9, 'How to Release Your Own Django Packages.'

13.7.4 Use Named Context Objects

When you use generic display CBVs, you have the option of using the generic `{{ object_list }}` and `{{ object }}` in your template. Another option is to use the ones that are named after your model.

For example, if you have a Topping model, you can use `{{ topping_list }}` and `{{ topping }}` in your templates, instead of `{{ object_list }}` and `{{ object }}`. This means both of the following template examples will work:

Example 13.17

```
{# toppings/topping_list.html #}
{# Using implicit names #}
<ol>
{% for object in object_list %}
    <li>{{ object }} </li>
{% endfor %}
</ol>

{# Using explicit names #}
<ol>
{% for topping in topping_list %}
   <li>{{ topping }} </li>
{% endfor %}
</ol>
```

13.7.5 Use URL Names Instead of Hardcoded Paths

A common developer mistake is to hardcode URLs in templates like this:

Bad Example 13.5

```
<a href="/flavors/">
```

The problem with this is that if the URL patterns of the site need to change, all the URLs across the site need to be addressed. This impacts HTML, JavaScript, and even RESTful APIs.

Instead, we use the `{% url %}` tag and references the names in our **URLConf** files:

Example 13.18

```
<a href="{% url 'flavors_list' %}">
```

13.7.6 Debugging Complex Templates

A trick recommended by Lennart Regebro is that when templates are complex and it becomes difficult to determine where a variable is failing, you can force more verbose errors through the use of the `string_if_invalid` option in `OPTIONS` of your `TEMPLATES` setting:

Example 13.19

```
# settings/local.py
TEMPLATES = [
    {
        'BACKEND': 'django.template.backends.django.DjangoTemplates',
        'APP_DIRS': True,
        'OPTIONS':
            'string_if_invalid': 'INVALID EXPRESSION: %s'
    },
]
```

13.8 Error Page Templates

Even the most tested and analyzed site will have a few problems now and then, and that's okay. The problem lies in how you handle those errors. The last thing that you want to do is show an ugly response or a blank web server page back to the end user.

It's standard practice to create at least ***404.html*** and ***500.html*** templates. See the GitHub HTML Styleguide link at the end of this section for other types of error pages that you may want to consider.

We suggest serving your error pages from a static file server (e.g. Nginx or Apache) as entirely self-contained static HTML files. That way, if your entire Django site goes down but your static file server is still up, then your error pages can still be served.

If you're on a PaaS, check the documentation on error pages. For example, Heroku allows users to upload a custom static HTML page to be used for 500 errors.

WARNING: Resist the Temptation to Overcomplicate Your Error Pages

Interesting or amusing error pages can be a draw to your site, but don't get carried away. It's embarrassing when your 404 page has a broken layout or your 500 page can't load the CSS and JavaScript. Worse yet is dynamic 500 error pages that break in the event of a database failure.

GitHub's 404 and 500 error pages are great examples of fancy but entirely static, self-contained error pages:

- `https://github.com/404`
- `https://github.com/500`

View the source of either of them and you'll notice that:

- All CSS styles are inline in the head of the same HTML page, eliminating the need for a separate stylesheet.
- All images are entirely contained as data within the HTML page. There are no `<img>` links to external URLs.
- All JavaScript needed for the page is contained within the HTML page. There are no external links to JavaScript assets.

For more information, see the Github HTML Styleguide:

- `https://github.com/styleguide`

13.9 Follow a Minimalist Approach

We recommend taking a minimalist approach to your template code. Treat the so-called limitations of Django templates as a blessing in disguise. Use those constraints as inspiration to find simple, elegant ways to put more of your business logic into Python code rather than into templates.

Taking a minimalist approach to templates also makes it much easier to adapt your Django apps to changing format types. When your templates are bulky and full of nested looping, complex conditionals, and data processing, it becomes harder to reuse business logic code in templates, not to mention impossible to use the same business logic in template-less views such as API views. Structuring your Django apps for code reuse is especially important as we move forward into the era of increased API development, since APIs and web pages often need to expose identical data with different formatting.

To this day, HTML remains a standard expression of content, providing the practices and patterns for this chapter.

13.10 Summary

In this chapter, we covered the following:

- Template inheritance, including the use of {{ `block.super` }}.
- Writing legible, maintainable templates.
- Easy methods to optimize template performance.
- Issues with limitations of template processing.
- Error page templates.
- Many other helpful little details about templates.

In the next chapter we'll examine template tags and filters.

14 Template Tags and Filters

Django provides dozens of default template tags and filters, all of which share the following common traits:

- All of the defaults have clear, obvious names.
- All of the defaults do just one thing.
- None of the defaults alter any sort of persistent data.

These traits serve as very good best practices when you have to write your own template tags. Let's now dive a bit deeper into practices and recommendations when writing custom filters and template tags.

14.1 Filters Are Functions

Filters are functions that accept just one or two arguments, and that don't give developers the ability to add behavior controls in Django templates.

We feel that this simplicity makes filters less prone to abuse, since they are essentially just functions with decorators that make Python usable inside of Django templates. This means that they can be called as normal functions (although we prefer to have our filters call functions imported from utility modules).

In fact, a quick scan of the source code of Django's default filters at `http://2scoops.co/1.8-slugify-source` shows that the `slugify()` template filter simply calls the `django.utils.text.slugify` function.

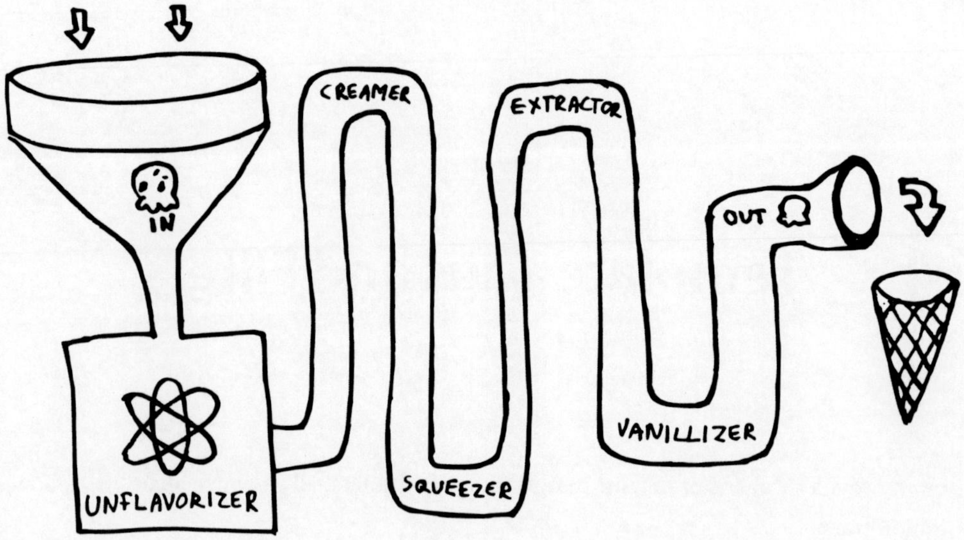

Figure 14.1: This filter transforms 1-2 flavors of ice cream into vanilla, outputting to a cone.

14.1.1 Filters Are Easy to Test

Testing a filter is just a matter of testing a function, which we cover in chapter 22, *Testing Stinks and Is a Waste of Money!*

14.1.2 Filters and Code Reuse

As can be seen in the Django 1.8 ***defaultfilter.py*** source code, most of the filter logic is imported from other libraries. For example, it's not necessary to import `django.template.defaultfilters.slugify`. Instead we can use `django.utils.text.slugify`. While it might seem to be perfectly acceptable to import the filter, it adds a level of code abstraction that can make debugging a problem a little more difficult.

Since filters are just functions, we advocate that anything but the simplest logic for them be moved to more reusable utility functions, perhaps stored in a ***utils.py*** module. Doing this makes it easier to introspect code bases and test, and can mean dramatically fewer imports. Over time core Django has followed this pattern more and more.

14.1.3 When to Write Filters

Filters are good for modifying the presentation of data, and they can be readily reused in REST APIs and other output formats. Being constrained to two arguments limits the functionality so it's harder (but not impossible) to make them unbearably complex.

14.2 Custom Template Tags

> "*Please stop writing so many template tags. They are a pain to debug.*"
>
> – Audrey Roy Greenfeld, while debugging Daniel Roy Greenfeld's code.

While template tags are great tools when developers have the discipline to keep them in check, in practice they tend to get abused. This section covers the problems that you run into when you put too much of your logic into template tags and filters.

14.2.1 Template Tags Are Harder to Debug

Template tags of any complexity can be challenging to debug. When they include opening and closing elements, they become even harder to handle. We've found liberal use of log statements and tests are very helpful when they become hard to inspect and correct.

14.2.2 Template Tags Make Code Reuse Harder

It can be difficult to consistently apply the same effect as a template tag on alternative output formats used by REST APIs, RSS feeds, or in PDF/CSV generation. If you do need to generate alternate formats, it's worth considering putting all logic for template tags into ***utils.py***, for easy access from other views.

14.2.3 The Performance Cost of Template Tags

Template tags can have a significant performance cost, especially when they load other templates. While templates run much faster than they did in previous versions of Django, it's easy to lose those performance benefits if you don't have a deep understanding of how templates are loaded in Django.

If your custom template tags are loading a lot of templates, you might want to consider caching the loaded templates. See `http://2scoops.co/1.8-template-cached-loader` for more details.

14.2.4 When to Write Template Tags

These days, we're very cautious about adding new template tags. We consider two things before writing them:

- Anything that causes a read/write of data might be better placed in a model or object method.
- Since we implement a consistent naming standard across our projects, we can add an abstract base class model to our `core.models` module. Can a method or property in our project's abstract base class model do the same work as a custom template tag?

When should you write new template tags? We recommend writing them in situations where they are only responsible for rendering of HTML. For example, projects with very complex HTML layouts with many different models or data types might use them to create a more flexible, understandable template architecture.

PACKAGE TIP: We Do Use Custom Template Tags

It sounds like we stay away from custom template tags, but that's not the case. We're just cautious. Interestingly enough, Daniel has been involved with at least three prominent libraries that make extensive use of template tags.

- django-crispy-forms
- django-wysiwyg
- django-uni-form (deprecated, use django-crispy-forms instead)

14.3 Naming Your Template Tag Libraries

The convention we follow is *<app_name>_tags.py*. Using the twoscoops example, we would have files named thus:

- *flavors_tags.py*
- *blog_tags.py*
- *events_tags.py*
- *tickets_tags.py*

This makes determining the source of a template tag library trivial to discover.

WARNING: Don't Name Your Template Tag Libraries With the Same Name as Your App

For example, naming the ***events*** app's templatetag library ***events.py*** is problematic. This will cause all sorts of problems because of the way that Django loads template tags. If you do this, expect things to break.

WARNING: Don't Use Your IDE's Features as an Excuse to Obfuscate Your Code

Do not rely on your text editor or IDE's powers of introspection to determine the name of your templatetag library.

14.4 Loading Your Template Tag Modules

In your template, right after `{% extends "base.html" %}` (or any other parent template besides ***base.html***) is where you load your template tags:

Example 14.1

```
{% extends "base.html" %}

{% load flavors_tags %}
```

Simplicity itself! Explicit loading of functionality! Hooray!

14.4.1 Watch Out for This Crazy Anti-Pattern

Unfortunately, there is an obscure anti-pattern that will drive you mad with fury each and every time you encounter it:

Bad Example 14.1

```
# Don't use this code!
# It's an evil anti-pattern!
from django import template
template.add_to_builtins(
    "flavors.templatetags.flavors_tags"
)
```

The anti-pattern replaces the explicit load method described above with an implicit behavior which supposedly fixes a "Don't Repeat Yourself" (DRY) issue. However, any DRY "improvements" it creates are destroyed by the following:

- It will add some overhead due to the fact this literally loads the template tag library into each and every template loaded by `django.template.Template`. This means every inherited template, template `{% include %}`, `inclusion_tag`, and more will be impacted. While we have cautioned against premature optimization, we are also not in favor of adding this much unneeded extra computational work into our code when better alternatives exist.
- Because the template tag library is implicitly loaded, it immensely adds to the difficulty in introspection and debugging. Per the **Zen of Python**, "Explicit is better than Implicit."
- The `add_to_builtins` method has no convention for placement. To our chagrin, we often find it placed in an `__init__` module or the template tag library itself, either of which can cause unexpected problems.

Fortunately, this is obscure because beginning Django developers don't know enough to make this mistake and experienced Django developers get really angry when they have to deal with it.

14.5 Summary

It is our contention that template tags and filters should concern themselves only with the manipulation of presentable data. So long as we remember this when we write or use them, our projects run faster and are easier to maintain.

In the next chapter we explore the use of Django templates and Jinja2.

15 Django Templates and Jinja2

With Django 1.8 comes support for multiple template engines. As of now, the only available backends for the Django template system are the **Django template language (DTL)** and **Jinja2**, both of which are built into Django itself.

15.1 What's the Syntactical Difference?

At the syntax level, DTL and Jinja2 are very similar. In fact, Jinja2 was inspired by DTL. Here are the most significant syntax differences:

Subject	DTL	Jinja2
Method Calls	`{{ user.get_favorites }}`	`{{ user.get_favorites() }}`
Filter Arguments	`{{ toppings|join:", " }}`	`{{ toppings|join(", ") }}`
Loop Empty Argument	`{% empty %}`	`{% else %}`
Loop Variable	`{{ forloop }}`	`{{ loop }}`
Cycle	`{% cycle "odd" "even" %}`	`{{ loop.cycle("odd", "even") }}`

Table 15.1: DTL vs Jinja2 Syntax Differences

Please note that over time DTL has evolved to have syntax much closer to Jinja2 than is described in `http://jinja.pocoo.org/docs/dev/switching/#django`. Similarities that contradict the Jinja2 Documentation:

Subject	DTL	Jinja2
Conditions	`{% if topping=="sprinkles" %}`	`{% if topping=="sprinkles" %}`
Conditions	`{% elif topping=="fudge" %}`	`{% elif topping=="fudge" %}`
Conditions	`{% else %}`	`{% else %}`
`is` operator	`{% customer is happy %}`	`{% customer is happy %}`

Table 15.2: DTL vs Jinja2 Syntax Similarities

15.2 Should I Switch?

First off, with the advent of Django 1.8 we don't have to choose between DTL or Jinja2. We can set `settings.TEMPLATES` to use DTL for some template directories and Jinja2 for others. If we have a lot of templates in our codebase, we can hold onto our existing templates and leverage the benefits of Jinja2 where we need it. This allows for the best of both worlds: Access to the vast Django ecosystem of third-party packages and the features of alternatives to DTL.

In short, we can use multiple template languages together harmoniously.

For example, most of a site can be rendered using DTL, with the larger pages rendered content done with Jinja2. A good example of this behavior are the `djangopackages.com/grids`. Because of their size and complexity, in the near future these pages will be refactored to be powered by Jinja2 rather than DTL.

15.2.1 Advantages of DTL

Here are reasons to use the Django template language:

- It's batteries-included with all the functionality clearly documented within the Django docs. The official Django documentation on DTL is very extensive and easy to follow. The template code examples in the Django docs use DTL.
- The DTL+Django combination is much more tried and mature than the Jinja2+Django combination.
- Most third-party Django packages use DTL. Converting them to Jinja2 is extra work.
- Converting a large codebase from DTL to Jinja2 is a lot of work.

15.2.2 Advantages of Jinja2

Here are reasons to use Jinja2:

- Can be used independently of Django.
- As Jinja2's syntax is closer to Python's syntax, many find it more intuitive.
- Jinja2 is generally more explicit, e.g. function calls in the template use parentheses.
- Jinja2 has less arbitrary restrictions on logic, e.g. you can pass unlimited arguments to a filter with Jinja2 vs. only 1 argument with DTL.
- According to the benchmarks online and our own experiments, Jinja2 is generally faster. That said, templates are always a much smaller performance bottleneck than database optimization. See chapter 24 'Finding and Reducing Bottlenecks'.

15.2.3 Which One Wins?

It depends on your situation:

- New users should always stick with DTL.
- Existing projects with large codebases will want to stick with DTL except for those few pages that need performance improvements.
- Experienced Djangonauts should try both, weigh the benefits of DTL and Jinja, and make their own decision.

TIP: Choose a Primary Template Language

While we can mix multiple template languages across a project, doing so risks adding dramatically to the mental overload of a project. To mitigate this risk, choose a single, primary template language.

15.3 Considerations When Using Jinja2 With Django

Here are some things to keep in mind when using Jinja2 templates with Django:

15.3.1 CSRF and Jinja2

Jinja2 accesses Django's **CSRF** mechanism differently than DTL. To incorporate CSRF into Jinja2 templates, when rendering forms make certain to include the necessary HTML:

Example 15.1

```
<div style="display:none">
    <input type="hidden" name="csrfmiddlewaretoken" value="{{ csrf_token }}">
</div>
```

15.3.2 Using Template Tags in Jinja2 Templates

At this time using Django-style Template Tags isn't possible in Jinja2. If we need the functionality of a particular template tag, depending on what we're trying to do we convert it using one of these techniques:

- Convert the functionality into a function.
- Create a Jinja2 Extension. See http://www.2scoops.co/writing-jinja2-extensions/

15.3.3 Using Django-Style Template Filters in Jinja2 Templates

One thing we've grown used to having around in DTL is Django's default template filters. Fortunately, as filters are functions (see section 14.1), we can easily specify a custom Jinja2 environment that includes the template filters:

EXAMPLE 15.2

```
# core/jinja2.py
from __future__ import absolute_import  # Python 2 only

from django.contrib.staticfiles.storage import staticfiles_storage
from django.core.urlresolvers import reverse
from django.template import defaultfilters

from jinja2 import Environment

def environment(**options):
    env = Environment(**options)
    env.globals.update({
        'static': staticfiles_storage.url,
        'url': reverse,
        'dj': defaultfilters
    })
    return env
```

Here is a an example of using Django template filters as functions in a Jinja2 template:

EXAMPLE 15.3

```
<table><tbody>
{% for purchase in purchase_list %}
    <tr>
        <a href="{{ url("purchase:detail", pk=purchase.pk) }}">
            {{ purchase.title }}
        </a>
    </tr>
    <tr>{{ dj.date(purchase.created, "SHORT_DATE_FORMAT") }}</tr>
    <tr>{{ dj.floatformat(purchase.amount, 2) }}</tr>
```

```
{% endfor %}
</tbody></table>
```

If you want a less global approach, we can use a technique explored in Figure 10.4.3, 'Using the View Object'. Here we create a mixin for attach the Django template filters as an attribute on views:

Example 15.4

```
# core/mixins.py
from django.template import defaultfilters

class DjFilterMixin(object):
    dj = defaultfilters
```

If a view inherits from our `core.mixins.DjFilterMixin` class, in its Jinja2 template we can do the following:

Example 15.5

```
<table><tbody>
{% for purchase in purchase_list %}
    <tr>
        <a href="{{ url("purchase:detail", pk=purchase.pk) }}">
            {{ purchase.title }}
        </a>
    </tr>
    <!-- Call the django.template.defaultfilters functions from the view -->
    <tr>{{ view.dj.date(purchase.created, "SHORT_DATE_FORMAT") }}</tr>
    <tr>{{ view.dj.floatformat(purchase.amount, 2) }}</tr>
{% endfor %}
</tbody></table>
```

15.3.4 Context Processors Aren't Called by Jinja2 Templates

If our project has heavily embraced the use of Django's **context processor** system, we might have a problem. For reference, context processors are a list of callables specified in the `context_processors` option of **settings.TEMPLATES** when using DTL that take in a request object and return a dictionary of items to be merged into the context.

Currently we're exploring the concept of moving what has previously been in context processors to **middleware** that modifies the request object. For example, if we had a context processor that added an ice cream themed advertisement to every template:

Example 15.6

```python
# advertisements/context_processors.py
import random

from advertisements.models import Advertisement as Ad

def advertisements(request):
    count = Advertisement.objects.filter(subject='ice-cream').count()
    ads = Advertisement.objects.filter(subject='ice-cream')
    return {'ad': ads[random.randrange(0, count)]}
```

Which we placed in our *base.html* file:

Example 15.7

```html
<!-- base.html -->
...
<div class="ice-cream-advertisement">
    <a href="{{ ad.url }}">
        <img src="{{ ad.image }}" />
    </a>
</div>
...
```

This HTML wouldn't render as desired in Jinja2 templates. However, we can create middleware that does something similar:

Example 15.8

```python
# advertisements/middleware.py
import random

from advertisements.models import Advertisement as Ad

def AdvertisementMiddleware(object):

    def process_request(request):
        count = Advertisement.objects.filter(subject='ice-cream').count()
        ads = Advertisement.objects.filter(subject='ice-cream')
        # If necessary, add a context variable to the request object.
        if not hasattr(request, 'context'):
            request.context = {}
        # Don't overwrite the context, instead we build on it.
        request.context.update({'ad': ads[random.randrange(0, count)]})
```

Then, in our ***base.html*** file we would call it thus:

Example 15.9

```
<!-- base.html -->
{% set ctx = request.context %}
...
<div class="ice-cream-advertisement">
    <a href="{{ ctx.ad.url }}">
        <img src="ctx.ad.image.url" />
    </a>
</div>
...
```

15.3.5 The Jinja2 Environment Object Should Be Considered Static

In example 15.1 we demonstrate the use of the core component of Jinja2, the `jinja2.Environment` class. This object is where Jinja2 shares configuration, filters, tests, globals, and more. When the first template in your project is loaded, Jinja2 instantiates this class as what is essentially a static object.

Example:

Example 15.10

```
# core/jinja2.py
from __future__ import absolute_import # Python 2 only
from jinja2 import Environment

import random

def environment(**options):
    env = Environment(**options)
    env.globals.update({
        # Runs only on the first template load! The three displays below
        #   will all present the same number.
        #   {{ random }} {{ random }} {{ random }}
        'random_once': random.randint(1, 5)
        # Can be called repeated as a function in templates. Each call
        #   returns a random number:
        #   {{ random() }} {{ random() }} {{ random() }}
        'random': lambda: random.randint(1, 5),
    })
    return env
```

WARNING: Don't Alter jinja.Environment After Instantiation

While possible, modifying the `jinja.Environment` object is dangerous. Per the Jinja2 API documentation, "Modifications on environments after the first template was loaded will lead to surprising effects and undefined behavior."

Reference: http://jinja.pocoo.org/docs/dev/api/#jinja2.Environment

15.4 Resources

- http://www.2scoops.co/1.8-jinja2-templates/ Django's documentation on using Jinja2.

- jinja.pocoo.org

15.5 Summary

In this chapter we covered the similarities and differences between DTL and Jinja2. We also explored some of the ramifications and workarounds for using Jinja2 in projects.

Starting in the next chapter we leave templates behind and explore the world of REST from both the server and client sides.

16 Building REST APIs

Today's internet is much more than HTML-powered websites. Developers need to support AJAX and native mobile apps. Having tools that support easy creation of **JSON, YAML, XML**, and other formats is important. By design, a **Representational State Transfer (REST) Application Programming Interface (API)** exposes application data to other concerns.

We'll go over the other side of REST APIs in chapter 17, *Consuming REST APIs*.

> ## PACKAGE TIP: Packages for Crafting APIs
>
> - **django-rest-framework** builds off of Django CBVs, adding a wonderful browsable API feature. It has a lot of features, follows elegant patterns, and is great to work with. This library has the definitive lead in functionality over other similar tools, providing powerful tools for building CBV and FBV powered REST APIs. As of the release of this book, it is the defacto Django tool for building APIs.
> - **django-tastypie** is a mature API framework that implements its own class-based view system. It's a feature-rich, mature, powerful, stable tool for creating APIs from Django models. It was created by Daniel Lindsley, the developer who started the django-haystack project, the most commonly used Django search library.
> - For super-quick, super-simple one-off REST API views **django-braces** (CBVs) and **django-jsonview** (FBVs) can prove really useful. The downside is that when you get into the full range of HTTP methods and more complex designs, they rapidly become a hindrance due to their lack of focus on building APIs.

Figure 16.1: A tasty pie is one filled with ice cream.

16.1 Fundamentals of Basic REST API Design

The Hypertext Transfer Protocol (HTTP) is a protocol for distributing content that provides a set of methods to declare actions. By convention, REST APIs rely on these methods, so use the appropriate HTTP method for each type of action:

Purpose of Request	HTTP Method	Rough SQL equivalent
Create a new resource	POST	INSERT
Read an existing resource	GET	SELECT
Request the metadata of an existing resource	HEAD	
Update an existing resource	PUT	UPDATE
Update part of an existing resource	PATCH	UPDATE
Delete an existing resource	DELETE	DELETE
Return the supported HTTP methods for the given URL	OPTIONS	
Echo back the request	TRACE	
Tunneling over TCP/IP (usually not implemented)	CONNECT	

Table 16.1: HTTP Methods

A couple of notes on the above:

- If you're implementing a read-only API, you might only need to implement GET methods.

- If you're implementing a read-write API you must at least also use POST, but should consider using PUT and DELETE.
- For simplicity, REST API architects sometimes prefer the use of just GET and POST.
- By definition, GET, PUT, and DELETE are idempotent. POST and PATCH are not.
- PATCH is often not implemented, but it's a good idea to implement it if your API supports PUT requests.
- django-rest-framework and django-tastypie handle all of this for you.

Here are some common HTTP status codes that should be considered when implementing a REST API. Note that this is a partial list; a much longer list of status codes can be found at `http://en.wikipedia.org/wiki/List_of_HTTP_status_codes`.

HTTP Status Code	Success/Failure	Meaning
200 OK	Success	GET - Return resource PUT - Provide status message or return resource
201 Created	Success	POST - Provide status message or return newly created resource
204 No Content	Success	DELETE - Response to successful delete request
304 Unchanged	Redirect	ALL - Indicates no changes since the last request. Used for checking Last-Modified and Etag headers to improve performance.
400 Bad Request	Failure	ALL - Return error messages, including form validation errors.
401 Unauthorized	Failure	ALL - Authentication required but user did not provide credentials.
403 Forbidden	Failure	ALL - User attempted to access restricted content
404 Not Found	Failure	ALL - Resource is not found
405 Method Not Allowed	Failure	ALL - An unallowed HTTP method was attempted.
410 Gone	Failure	ALL - A method was attempted that is no longer supported. Used when an API is shut down in favor of a newer version of an API. Mobile applications can test for this condition, and if it occurs, tell the user to upgrade.

HTTP Status Code	Success/Failure	Meaning
429 Too Many Requests	Failure	ALL - The user has sent too many requests in a given amount of time. Intended for use with rate limiting.

Table 16.2: HTTP Status Codes

16.2 Implementing a Simple JSON API

Let's use the *flavors* app example from previous chapters as our base, providing the capability to create, read, update, and delete flavors via HTTP requests using AJAX, python-requests, or some other library. We'll also use **django-rest-framework**, as it provides us with the capability to build a REST API quickly using patterns similar to the class-based views that we describe in previous chapters. We'll begin by listing the `Flavor` model again:

Example 16.1

```
# flavors/models.py
from django.core.urlresolvers import reverse
from django.db import models

class Flavor(models.Model):
    title = models.CharField(max_length=255)
    slug = models.SlugField(unique=True)
    scoops_remaining = models.IntegerField(default=0)

    def get_absolute_url(self):
        return reverse("flavors:detail", kwargs={"slug": self.slug})
```

Define the serializer class:

Example 16.2

```
from rest_framework import serializers

from .models import flavor
```

```
class FlavorSerializer(serializers.ModelSerializer):
    class Meta:
        model = flavor
        fields = ('title', 'slug', 'scoops_remaining')
```

Now let's add in some views:

Example 16.3

```
# flavors/views
from rest_framework.generics import ListCreateAPIView
from rest_framework.generics import RetrieveUpdateDestroyAPIView
from .models import Flavor
from .serializers import FlavorSerializer

class FlavorCreateReadView(ListCreateAPIView):
    queryset = Flavor.objects.all()
    serializer_class = FlavorSerializer
    lookup_field = 'slug'

class FlavorReadUpdateDeleteView(RetrieveUpdateDestroyAPIView):
    queryset = Flavor.objects.all()
    serializer_class = FlavorSerializer
    lookup_field = 'slug'
```

We're done! Wow, that was fast!

TIP: Classy Django REST Framework is a Useful Reference

For working with the Django Rest Framework, we've found that http://cdrf.co is a great cheat sheet. It is patterned after the famous http://ccbv.co.uk reference site, but tailored for Django Rest Framework.

Now we'll wire this into our *flavors/urls.py* module:

Example 16.4

```
# flavors/urls.py
from django.conf.urls import url

from flavors import views

urlpatterns = [
    url(
        regex=r"^api/$",
        view=views.FlavorCreateReadView.as_view(),
        name="flavor_rest_api"
    ),
    url(
        regex=r"^api/(?P<slug>[-\w]+)/$",
        view=views.FlavorReadUpdateDeleteView.as_view(),
        name="flavor_rest_api"
    )
]
```

What we are doing is reusing the same view and URLConf name, making it easier to manage when you have a need for a JavaScript-heavy front-end. All you need to do is access the Flavor resource via the `{% url %}` template tag.

In case it's not clear exactly what our URLConf is doing, let's review it with a table:

Url	View	Url Name (same)
/flavors/api/	FlavorCreateReadView	flavor_rest_api
/flavors/api/:slug/	FlavorReadUpdateDeleteView	flavor_rest_api

Table 16.3: URLConf for the Flavor REST APIs

WARNING: Our Simple API Does Not Use Permissions

If you implement an API using our example, don't forget to authenticate users and assign them permissions appropriately!

- http://www.django-rest-framework.org/api-guide/authentication/
- http://www.django-rest-framework.org/api-guide/permissions/

The end result is the traditional REST-style API definition:

Example 16.5

```
flavors/api/
flavors/api/:slug/
```

TIP: Common Syntax for Describing REST APIs

It's not uncommon to see syntax like what is described in Example 14.4. In this particular case, `/flavors/api/:slug/` includes a `:slug` value. This represents a variable, but in a manner suited for documentation across frameworks and languages, and you'll see it used in many third-party REST API descriptions.

We've shown you (if you didn't know already) how it's very easy to build REST APIs in Django, now let's go over some advice on maintaining and extending them.

16.3 REST API Architecture

Building quick APIs is easy with tools like django-rest-framework and django-tastypie, but extending and maintaining them to match your project's needs takes a bit more thought.

16.3.1 Code for a Project Should Be Neatly Organized

For projects with a lot of small, interconnecting apps, it can be hard to hunt down where a particular API view lives. In contrast to placing all API code within the each relevant app, sometimes it makes more sense to build an app specifically for the API. This is where all the serializers, renderers, and views are placed. Of course, the name of the app should reflect its API version (see subsection 16.3.6).

For example, we might place all our views, serializers, and other API components in an app titled *apiv4*.

The downside is the possibility for the API app to become too large and disconnected from the apps that power it. Hence why we consider an alternative in the next subsection.

16.3.2 Code for an App Should Remain in the App

When it comes down to it, REST APIs are just views. For simpler, smaller projects, REST API views should go into *views.py* or *viewsets.py* modules and follow the same guidelines we endorse when it comes to any other view. The same goes for app- or model-specific serializers and renderers. If we do have app-specific serializers or renderers, the same applies.

For larger projects with too many REST API view classes for a single *views.py/viewsets.py* module, we can break them up. In other words, move the view classes into a *viewset* package complete with *__init__.py* and Python modules containing a smaller number of REST API views.

The downside is that if there are too many small, interconnecting apps, it can be hard to keep track of the myriad of places API components are placed. Hence why we considered another approach in the previous subsection.

16.3.3 Try to Keep Business Logic Out of API Views

Regardless of which architectural approach you take, it's a good idea to try to keep as much logic as possible out of API views. If this sounds familiar, it should. We covered this in 'Try to Keep Business Logic out of Views,' chapter 8 *Function- and Class-Based Views*, and remember, API views are just another type of view, after all.

Figure 16.2: An Ice Cream as a Service API.

16.3.4 Grouping API URLs

If you have REST API views in multiple Django apps, how do you build a project-wide API that looks like this?

Example 16.6

```
api/flavors/ # GET, POST
api/flavors/:slug/ # GET, PUT, DELETE
api/users/ # GET, POST
api/users/:slug/ # GET, PUT, DELETE
```

In the past, we placed all API view code into a dedicated Django app called ***api*** or ***apiv1***, with custom logic in some of the REST views, serializers, and more. In theory it's a pretty good approach, but in practice it means we have logic for a particular app in more than just one location.

Our current approach is to lean on URL configuration. When building a project-wide API we write the REST views in the ***views.py*** or ***viewsets.py*** modules, wire them into a URL-Conf called something like ***core/api.py*** or ***core/apiv1.py*** and include that from the project root's ***urls.py*** module. This means that we might have something like the following code:

Example 16.7

```
# core/api.py
"""Called from the project root's urls.py URLConf thus:
        url(r"^api/", include("core.api", namespace="api")),
"""
from django.conf.urls import url

from flavors import views as flavor_views
from users import views as user_views

urlpatterns = [
    # {% url "api:flavors" %}
    url(
        regex=r"^flavors/$",
        view=flavor_views.FlavorCreateReadView.as_view(),
        name="flavors"
    ),
    # {% url "api:flavors" flavor.slug %}
    url(
        regex=r"^flavors/(?P<slug>[-\w]+)/$",
        view=flavor_views.FlavorReadUpdateDeleteView.as_view(),
        name="flavors"
    ),
    # {% url "api:users" %}
    url(
        regex=r"^users/$",
        view=user_views.UserCreateReadView.as_view(),
        name="users"
    ),
    # {% url "api:users" user.slug %}
    url(
```

```
        regex=r"^users/(?P<slug>[-\w]+)/$",
        view=user_views.UserReadUpdateDeleteView.as_view(),
        name="users"
    ),
]
```

16.3.5 Test Your API

We find that Django's test suite makes it really easy to test API implementations. It's certainly much easier than staring at `curl` results! Testing is covered at length in chapter 22, *Testing Stinks and Is a Waste of Money!*, and we even include in that chapter the tests we wrote for our simple JSON API (see subsection 22.3.1).

16.3.6 Version Your API

It's a good practice to abbreviate the urls of your API with the version number e.g. `/api/v1/flavors` or `/api/v1/users` and then as the API changes, `/api/v2/flavors` or `/api/v2/users`. When the version number changes, existing customers can continue to use the previous version without unknowingly breaking their calls to the API.

Also, in order to avoid angering API consumers, it's critical to maintain both the existing API and the predecessor API during and after upgrades. It's not uncommon for the deprecated API to remain in use for several months.

When you do implement an API, provide customers/users with a deprecation warning along with ample time so they can perform necessary upgrades and not break their own applications. From personal experience, the ability to send a deprecation warning to end users is an excellent reason to request email addresses from users of even free and open source API services.

16.4 Service-Oriented Architecture

In Service-Oriented Architecture, or SOA, a web application is broken up into isolated, independent components. Each component might run on its own server or cluster, with the components communicating with one another. For SOA-style Django projects, communication between components typically occurs via REST APIs.

The main reason to follow SOA is to make it easier for many engineers to work on different components of a web application without running into conflicts with one another. Instead of having a giant team of 100 engineers all working on the same codebase simultaneously, there might be 10 teams of 10 engineers, each team working on an isolated SOA component.

For smaller team projects, we've found that SOA tends to cause more trouble than it's worth. Having more moving parts causes greater complexity.

To implement an SOA-style web application, think about how to break your Django project into isolated web applications, each running independently. Each Django app might get split off into its own isolated Django project.

For example, if you're implementing the Airbnb of Ice Cream Truck Rentals, you might start with a single Django project containing 8 loosely-coupled apps: trucks, owners, renters, payments, receipts, reservations, scheduling, and reviews. As your company grows, you might refactor each app into its own REST API-powered Django project, maintained by its own team.

- `http://amzn.to/1KgRHG3` Domain-Driven Development by Eric Evans. Instructs on systematic approaches to domain-driven design.
- `http://en.wikipedia.org/wiki/Service-oriented_architecture`
- `http://steve-yegge.blogspot.com/2006/03/execution-in-kingdom-of-nouns.html`

16.5 Shutting Down an External API

When it's time to shut down an older version of an external API in favor of a new one, here are useful steps to follow:

16.5.1 Step #1: Notify Users of Pending Shut Down

Provide as much advanced notice as possible. Preferably six months, but as short as one month. Inform API users via email, blogs, and social media. We like to report the shutdown notification to the point that we worry people are getting tired of the message.

16.5.2 Step #2: Replace API With 410 Error View

When the API is finally shut down, we provide a simple 410 Error View. We include a very simple message that includes the following information:

- A link to the new API's endpoint.
- A link to the new API's documentation.
- A link to an article describing the details of the shut down.

Below is a sample shutdown view that works against any HTTP method:

Example 16.8

```
# core/apiv1_shutdown.py
from django.http import HttpResponseGone

apiv1_gone_msg = """APIv1 was removed on April 2, 2015. Please switch to APIv3:
<ul>
    <li>
        <a href="https://www.example.com/api/v3/">APIv3 Endpoint</a>
    </li>
    <li>
        <a href="https://example.com/apiv3_docs/">APIv3 Documentation</a>
    </li>
    <li>
        <a href="http://example.com/apiv1_shutdown/">APIv1 shut down notice</a>
    </li>
</ul>
"""

def apiv1_gone(request):
    return HttpResponseGone(apiv1_gone_msg)
```

16.6 Evaluating REST Frameworks

When you begin considering REST frameworks, it's worthwhile to consider the following:

16.6.1 Django Rest Framework Is the Defacto Package

The vast majority of Django projects being built at the time of the release of this book use Django Rest Framework. This popularity ensures that the package will be maintained in the future, and that finding other Django coders to work on the project will be easier than if we used an alternative.

16.6.2 How Much Boilerplate Do You Want to Write?

These days, most frameworks make an effort to reduce boilerplate when dealing with resources. In fact, usually when we hear grumbling on the lines of *'X framework has too much boilerplate!!!'* it is actually a matter of trying to figure out how to implement **Remote Procedure Calls** in a resource-driven system.

Speaking of Remote Procedure calls, let's move on to the next sub-section...

16.6.3 Are Remote Procedure Calls Easy to Implement?

The resource model used by REST frameworks to expose data is very powerful, but it doesn't cover every case. Specifically, resources don't always match the reality of application design. For example, it is easy to represent syrup and a sundae as two resources, but what about the action of pouring syrup? Using this analogy, we change the state of the sundae and decrease the syrup inventory by one. While we could have the API user change things individually, that can generate issues with database integrity. Therefore *in some cases it can be good idea to present a method* like `sundae.pour_syrup(syrup)` to the client as part of the RESTful API.

In computer science terms, `sundae.pour_syrup(syrup)` could be classified as a **Remote Procedure Call** or **RPC**.

Depending on the REST framework or system you chose, RPC calls can be easy or challenging to implement. This is an area that needs to be investigated early on, as it's painful to discover in the middle of a project that a framework of choice makes this a pain point.

Additional Reading:

- https://en.wikipedia.org/wiki/Remote_Procedure_Call
- https://en.wikipedia.org/wiki/Resource-oriented_architecture

16.6.4 CBVs or FBVs?

As mentioned in the previous chapters, the authors prefer CBVs, but other developers prefer FBVs. If this is a sticking point, then consider exploring options that support FBV-based implementations such as django-rest-framework.

16.7 Rate Limiting Your API

Rate limiting is when an API restricts how many requests can be made by a user of the API within a period of time. This is done for a number of reasons, which we'll explain below.

16.7.1 Unfettered API Access is Dangerous

In the ancient times (2010) we launched the Django Packages website. The project, started during the Django Dash contest, was an instant hit for the Django community. We sprinted on it constantly, and its feature set grew rapidly. Unfortunately, we quickly hit the rate limit of GitHub's first API. This meant that after a certain amount of API requests per hour, we weren't allowed to make any more until a new hour passed.

Fortunately at DjangoCon 2010 we had the opportunity to ask one of the founders of GitHub if we could have unlimited access to their API. He graciously said 'yes' and within a day we could get data from GitHub as much as we wanted.

We were delighted. Our users were delighted. Usage of the site increased, people were thirsty for data as to what were the most active projects. So desirous of data were we that every hour we requested the latest data from GitHub. And that caused a problem for GitHub.

You see, this was 2010 and GitHub was not the giant, powerful company it is today. At 17 minutes past each hour, Django Packages would send thousands of requests to the GitHub API in a very short period. With unfettered access to GitHub application of the time, we were causing them problems.

Eventually, GitHub contacted us and requested that we scale back how much we were using their API. We would still have unlimited access, just needed to give them breathing room. We complied, checking data once per day instead of by the hour, and at a more reasonable rate. We continue to do so to this day.

While modern GitHub can certainly handle much, much larger volumes of API access then it could in late 2010, we like to think we learned a shared lesson about unfettered access to an API: Grant such access cautiously.

16.7.2 REST Frameworks Must Come with Rate Limiting

One of the features usually delegated to a feature bullet when describing a REST API framework is if it allows for rate limiting of API users. Yet when evaluating which one to use, this is a must-have. Being able to control this can mean the difference between joyful triumph or utter disaster.

> **TIP: HTTP Server Rate Limiting**
>
> It's possible to use nginx or apache for rate limiting. The upside is faster performance. The downside is that it removes this functionality from the Python code.

16.7.3 Rate Limit Can Be A Business Plan

Imagine we launch an API-based startup that lets users add images of toppings to images of ice cream. We know that everyone will want to use this API, and come up with several tiers of access that we tie into pricing:

Developer tier is free, but only allows 10 API requests per hour.
One Scoop is $24/month, allows 25 requests per minute.
Two Scoops is $79/month, allows 50 requests per minute.
Corporate is $5000/month, allows for 200 requests per minute.

Now all we have to do is get people to use our API.

16.8 Advertising Your REST API

Let's assume we've built our REST API and want outside coders and companies to use it. How do we go about doing that?

16.8.1 Documentation

The most important thing to do is to provide comprehensive documentation. The easier to read and understand the better. Providing easy-to-use code examples is a must. You can write it from scratch, use the auto-documentation provided by tools like django-rest-framework, Sphinx, and Markdown or even embrace a commercial documentation generation service like `swagger.io`.

Some of the material in chapter 23, '*Documentation: Be Obsessed*' might prove useful for forward-facing REST API documentation.

16.8.2 Provide Client SDKs

Something that may help spread use of your API is to provide a **software development kits (SDK)** for various programming languages. The more programming languages covered the better. For us, we've found the must-have languages include Python, JavaScript, Ruby, PHP, Go, and Java.

In our experience, it's a good idea to write at least one of these libraries ourselves and create a demo project. The reason is that it not only advertises our API, it forces us to experience our API from the same vantage point as our consumers.

For building client SDKs, reading section 21.9, 'Releasing Your Own Django Packages' might prove useful.

16.9 Additional Reading

We highly recommend reading the following:

- `http://en.wikipedia.org/wiki/REST`

- http://en.wikipedia.org/wiki/List_of_HTTP_status_codes
- http://jacobian.org/writing/rest-worst-practices/

16.10 Summary

In this chapter we covered:

- API creation libraries.
- Grouping strategies.
- Fundamentals of basic REST API design.
- Implementing a simple JSON API.

Coming up next, we'll go over the other side of REST APIs in chapter 17, *Consuming REST APIs.*

17 | Consuming REST APIs

Now that we've covered both creating REST APIs and template best practices, let's combine them. In other words, these are best practices for using Django-powered tools to display content to the end user in the browser using content managed by REST APIs and presented by modern JavaScript frameworks.

> **WARNING: This Chapter Will Be Brief**
>
> Our challenge in writing this chapter is twofold:
>
> - Django is a backend framework.
> - The modern JavaScript/HTML5 landscape is evolving too fast to document.
>
> Therefore, we're going to cover best practices at a very high level.

With the advent of faster JavaScript engines and a maturation of the associated community, there has been a rise in new JavaScript frameworks that make integration of RESTful APIs easy. Here are some of them:

React.js `https://facebook.github.io/react/`
: A JavaScript framework and ecosystem created and maintained by Facebook. Designed for creation of HTML, iOS, and android applications.

Angular.js `http://angularjs.org`
: A JavaScript framework, maintained by Google, that assists with running single-page applications. Popular in the Django community. As of the release of this book, Angular.js is in the midst of controversy due to the incompatible break between the 1.x and 2.x.

Backbone.js http://backbonejs.org
: The first of the modern JavaScript libraries to really hit critical mass in popularity. It's built on top of the really useful underscore.js library.

jQuery http://jquery.com/
: While it's no longer the cool kid on the block, 75 percent of the web can't be wrong.

These libraries can really improve what we like to call the 'immediate user experience'. However, with every good thing there are always things to consider and things to do.

17.1 Learn How to Debug the Client

Debugging client-side JavaScript is a lot more than simply writing `console.log()` and `console.dir()` statements. There are a number of tools for debugging and finding errors, and some of them are specifically written for particular JavaScript frameworks. Once a tool of choice is chosen, it's an excellent idea to take a day to learn how to write client-side tests.

Reference material:

- http://2scoops.co/chrome-developer-tools
- https://developer.mozilla.org/en-US/docs/Debugging_JavaScript

Figure 17.1: Server-side vs. client-side ice cream.

17.2 Consider Using JavaScript-Powered Static Asset Preprocessors

In the past, we used Python everywhere, including JavaScript and CSS minification. However, as of the publication of the 1.6 edition of this book, it was clear that the JavaScript community was maintaining their version of these tools better than the Python community. That's perfectly okay, because since they've done the work on this part of the toolchain, we can focus on other things.

As we write this, the most commonly used tool for this kind of work is **Gulp**, found at `http://gulpjs.com/`. Think of it as an automation tool like python's Fabric or Invoke, but for JavaScript. Gulp.js requires **node.js** to be installed, but since that works everywhere Python does (including Windows), it won't be a problem.

17.3 Making Content Indexable by Search Engines

Single-page applications or content served by REST APIs are increasingly popular. However, without care this content won't be indexed by search engines such as Google or Baidu. If all the content is only available to authenticated users this isn't a big deal, but if reaching search engines is important, then here are some steps that can be used to address the problem.

17.3.1 Read the Search Engine Documentation

The teams behind Google Search and other search engines are very well aware of the growing use of single page apps. Which is why they provide instructions on how to make your AJAX powered content searchable.

- `https://developers.google.com/webmasters/ajax-crawling/`
- `http://www.2scoops.co/bing-search-engine-best-practices/`

In theory some of them are already searching through content rendered by client-side JavaScript. Over time, their ability to weed the chaff from real content is only going to grow. If SEO isn't important to you right now but will be in the future, consider waiting until they figure it out.

17.3.2 Hand-Craft the sitemap.xml

Some search engines, such as Baidu, don't have instructions for site developers wanting their content index. The answer to this is to use the old ***sitemap.xml*** method to instruct the search engine. Since the AJAX views are not concrete HTML, we'll need to create a custom view instead of Django's built-in sitemap app:

Example 17.1

```python
# core/views.py
from __future__ import absolute_import

from django.views.generic import TemplateView

from .flavors.models import Flavor

class SiteMapView(TemplateView):
    template_name = "sitemap.xml"

    def flavors(self):
        return Flavor.objects.all()
```

Then hand-craft the sitemap.xml (note: this is a *simple* example):

Example 17.2

```xml
<?xml version="1.0" encoding="UTF-8"?>
<urlset xmlns="http://www.sitemaps.org/schemas/sitemap/0.9">
    {# Snip the home page, contact, etc #}
    {% for flavor in view.flavors %}
        <url>
            <loc>{{ site.domain }}/app/#{{ flavor.slug }}</loc>
            <lastmod>{{ flavor.modified }}</lastmod>
            <changefreq>monthly</changefreq>
            <priority>0.8</priority>
        </url>
    {% endfor %}
</urlset>
```

There are a lot of other things you can do, making Google's web crawling specification an important resource for anyone creating single page apps:
`https://developers.google.com/webmasters/ajax-crawling/`.

17.3.3 Use a Service to Make Your Site Crawlable

Rather than do the work of generating a sitemap yourself, consider using a service to do the work for you. For example, for a fee, `brombone.com` crawls your Angular.js, Ember.js, or Backbone.js site and shows Google pre-rendered HTML representing the data that you want to display.

17.4 Real-Time Woes a.k.a. Latency

Let's say we've put together a well-designed, well-indexed, well-cached real-time project with the widest bandwidth piping content to the world. We can handle any load, and our test users applaud the speed and functionality of the project. Things look great, and we look forward to bonuses and raises.

Then the complaints from the other side of the planet start coming in about the slow speed of the application. Our effort isn't 'real-time' to any of a potentially large block of users and our client/boss is really unhappy.

Congratulations, we've just hit the speed of light!

This isn't a joke, it's a very real problem. Here, Django isn't the problem. Instead, it's physics. The time it takes for HTTP requests to transmit back and forth across half the circumference of the planet is noticeable to human beings. Add in server-side and client-side processing, and we risk alienating potential or existing users.

Also, keep in mind that even the fastest local connections have hiccups and slow-downs. So it's not uncommon for 'real-time' applications to have ways to handle this sort of behavior.

17.4.1 Solution: Mask the Latency With Animations

One of the more common fixes is to have JavaScript-powered animation distract the user from latency issues. We encounter this every time we use a single page app with an attractive interface, including all modern web-based email clients.

17.4.2 Solution: Fake Successful Transactions

Another solution involves processing the request on the client-side as if the request successfully made it to the server. We'll need to include client-side logic to handle failures, but JavaScript frameworks handling HTTP requests are asynchronous, making this feasible, albeit possibly complicated.

If you've ever suddenly discovered that your cloud-based spreadsheet hadn't save the data entered for the past 30 seconds, you've uncovered this kind of JavaScript powered trickery in action.

17.4.3 Solution: Geographically Based Servers

Geographically-based servers across all seven continents is an option. However, for Django this is not trivial to implement, not at the programming or database level. It requires a significant volume of skills and expertise that's outside the scope of this book.

If you have the time and budget, this can be an exciting avenue to explore and we encourage it. However, unless you've done this before there is a good chance you are going to underestimate the effort involved.

17.4.4 Solution: Restrict Users Geographically

Sometimes we just don't have a choice. Perhaps our application is too reliant on 'real-time' performance and geolocating servers might be outside the budget. We might make some people unhappy, but that can be mitigated to some degree by saying things like, 'Support in your country is coming soon!'

17.5 Avoid the Anti-Patterns

Here are a number of anti-patterns that we've discovered when it comes to projects consuming REST APIs for content.

17.5.1 Building Single Page Apps When Multi-Page Apps Suffice

Single-page apps are challenging and fun to build, but does a traditional CMS-site need to be one? Certainly the content pages can include API-powered editing controls, but when building this kind of site, there is something to be said for traditional HTML pages.

However, when working with legacy projects, it's often easier to add new features as single-page apps. This allows for the maintainers of the project to deliver improved experiences with new features, while preserving the stability of the existing code base. A good example of this might be adding a calendar application to an existing project.

17.5.2 Not Writing Tests

When you first begin working in a new language or framework, including client-side JavaScript, it's tempting to skip the tests. In a word, don't. Working in the client is getting more complicated and sophisticated every year. Between evolving client-side standards, things are simply not as readable there as on the server side.

We cover Django/Python testing in chapter 22. A good reference for JavaScript testing is `http://2scoops.co/stack-overflow-javascript-unit-test-tools-for-tdd`

17.5.3 Not Understanding JavaScript Memory Management

Single-page apps are great, but the complex implementations where users keep them open constantly will hold objects in the browser for a very long time. Eventually, if not managed, this can cause browser slowdowns and crashes. Each JavaScript framework comes with tools or advice on how to handle this potential problem, and it's a good idea to know the recommended approach.

17.5.4 Storing Data in the DOM When It's Not jQuery

After years of using jQuery, some of us have grown used to using DOM elements to store data (especially Daniel). However, when using other JavaScript frameworks this isn't ideal.

They have their own mechanisms for handling client data, and by not following them we risk losing out on some of the features promised by these frameworks.

We recommend looking up the data management methods for your chosen JavaScript framework and embracing them as deeply as possible.

17.6 AJAX and the CSRF Token

If you use AJAX with Django, you may discover that triggering the CSRF token validation blocks your ability to use your API. In each subsection below we'll provide a base example, as well as link to at least one useful reference.

17.6.1 JQuery and the CSRF Token

Django's CSRF protection seems like an inconvenience when writing AJAX. However, if you're using **jQuery** then you can just create a *csrf.js* and use the following on any page with AJAX that is updating data.

Example 17.3

```
// Place at /static/js/csrf.js
// CSRF helper functions taken directly from Django docs
function getCookie(name) {
  var cookieValue = null;
  if (document.cookie && document.cookie != '') {
    var cookies = document.cookie.split(';');
    for (var i = 0; i < cookies.length; i++) {
      var cookie = jQuery.trim(cookies[i]);
      // Does this cookie string begin with the name we want?
      if (cookie.substring(0, name.length + 1) == (name + '=')) {
        cookieValue = decodeURIComponent(cookie.substring(name.length + 1));
        break;
      }
    }
  }
  return cookieValue;
}
```

```
var csrftoken = getCookie('csrftoken');
function csrfSafeMethod(method) {
  // these HTTP methods do not require CSRF protection
  return (/^(GET|HEAD|OPTIONS|TRACE)$/.test(method));
}
$.ajaxSetup({
  beforeSend: function(xhr, settings) {
    if (!csrfSafeMethod(settings.type) && !this.crossDomain) {
        xhr.setRequestHeader("X-CSRFToken", csrftoken);
    }
  }
});
```

Now let's include the JavaScript on a page which has a shopping cart form for ordering ice cream:

Example 17.4

```
{% extends "base.html" %}
{% load static %}

{% block title %}Ice Cream Shopping Cart{% endblock %}

{% block content %}
    <h1>Ice Cream Shopping Cart</h1>
    <div class="shopping-cart"></div>
{% endblock %}

{% block javascript %}
    {{ block.super }}
    <script type="text/javascript"
        src="{% static "js/csrf.js" %}"></script>
    <script type="text/javascript"
        src="{% static "js/shopping_cart.js" %}"></script>
{% endblock %}
```

Reference:

- https://docs.djangoproject.com/en/1.8/ref/csrf/

17.6.2 Backbone.js and the CSRF Token

Working with the CSRF token and **Backbone.js** project is pretty straight-forward:

Example 17.5

```
// Place at /static/models.js
var newSync = Backbone.sync;
Backbone.sync = function(method, model, options){
    options.beforeSend = function(xhr){
        xhr.setRequestHeader('X-CSRFToken', CSRF_TOKEN);
    };
    return newSync(method, model, options);
};
```

17.6.3 AngularJS and the CSRF Token

The pattern we like to follow with AngularJS is to place the CSRF token in the HTTP header. It is not uncommon to see the CSRF token added to the header thus:

Example 17.6

```
<script>
var app = angular.module('icecreamlandia.app');
app.config(['$httpProvider', function($httpProvider) {
  // The next two lines should just be one, but we had to break it
  //     up in order to preserve book formatting.
  var common = $httpProvider.defaults.headers.common;
  common['X-CSRFToken'] = '{{ csrf_token|escapejs }}';
}]);
</script>
```

AngularJS Resources:

- http://2scoops.co/kevin-stone-django-angular-tutorial

17.7 Improving JavaScript Skills

One of the best things we can do when implementing the consumption of REST APIs in templates is to ensure our JavaScript skills are up to par. While Python developers sometimes like to grumble about JavaScript, it is a very capable language in its own right. Any responsible web developer will take the time to ramp up their skills so they can reap the benefits of modern JavaScript frameworks.

17.7.1 Assessing Skill Levels

Noted JavaScript developer Rebecca Murphey created a JavaScript assessment tool. We found it a wonderful way to determine how much JavaScript we actually knew, and what we needed to improve.

See `https://github.com/rmurphey/js-assessment`

17.7.2 Learn More JavaScript!

There are a plethora of JavaScript resources for taking basic skills and making them better. We list our favorites at the end of Appendix C: 'Additional Resources.'

17.8 Follow JavaScript Coding Standards

In the case of JavaScript, we advocate the following guides for both front- and back-end work:

- *Felix's Node.js Style Guide*
  `http://nodeguide.com/style.html`
- *idiomatic.js*
  `https://github.com/rwaldron/idiomatic.js/`

17.9 Useful Resources

Tutorials:

- http://2scoops.co/lightweight-django A good, mostly front-end focused Django book by Julia Elman and Mark Lavin
- http://2scoops.co/kevin-stone-django-angular-tutorial Kevin Stone's extensive tutorial on Django and Angular.
- http://www.2scoops.co/joseph-misiti-django-backbone-tutorial/

17.10 Summary

Material covered in this chapter included:

- Debugging the client.
- JavaScript static asset preprocessors.
- Making content indexable by search engines.
- Real-time woes.
- Client-side anti-patterns.
- AJAX and CSRF tokens.
- Improving JavaScript skills.
- Useful resources

18 Tradeoffs of Replacing Core Components

There's a lot of hype around swapping out core parts of Django's stack for other pieces. Should you do it?

Short Answer: Don't do it. These days, even Instagram says on Forbes.com that it's completely unnecessary: `http://2scoops.co/instagram-insights`.

Long Answer: It's certainly possible, since Django modules are simply just Python modules. Is it worth it? Well, it's worth it only if:

- You are okay with sacrificing some or all of your ability to use third-party Django packages.
- You have no problem giving up the powerful Django admin.
- You have already made a determined effort to build your project with core Django components, but you are running into walls that are major blockers.
- You have already analyzed your own code to find and fix the root causes of your problems. For example, you've done all the work you can to reduce the numbers of queries made in your templates.
- You've explored all other options including caching, denormalization, etc.
- Your project is a real, live production site with tons of users. In other words, you're certain that you're not just optimizing prematurely.
- You've looked at and rejected adopting a Service Oriented Approach (SOA) for those cases Django has problems dealing with.
- You're willing to accept the fact that upgrading Django will be extremely painful or impossible going forward.

That doesn't sound so great anymore, does it?

18.1 The Temptation to Build FrankenDjango

Every year, a new fad leads waves of developers to replace some particular core Django component. Here's a summary of some of the fads we've seen come and go.

Fad	Reasons
For performance reasons, replacing the database/ORM with a NoSQL database and corresponding ORM replacement.	Not okay: ``I have an idea for a social network for ice cream haters. I just started building it last month. I need it to be web-scale!!!1!''  Okay: ``Our site has 50M users and I'm hitting the limits of what I can do with indexes, query optimization, caching, etc. We're also pushing the limits of our Postgres cluster. I've done a lot of research on this and am going to try storing a simple denormalized view of data in Cassandra to see if it helps. I'm aware of the CAP theorem (`http://www.2scoops.co/CAP-theorem/`), and for this view, eventual consistency is fine.''
For data processing reasons, replacing the database/ORM with a NoSQL database and corresponding ORM replacement.	Not okay: ``SQL Sucks! We're going with a document-oriented database like MongoDB!''  Okay: ``While PostgreSQL's HSTORE datatype replicates nearly every aspect of MongoDB's data storage system, we want to use MongoDB's built-in MapReduce functionality.''
Replacing Django's template engine with Jinja2, Mako, or something else.	Not okay: ``I read on Hacker News that Jinja2 is faster. I don't know anything about caching or optimization, but I need Jinja2!''  Not okay: ``I hate having logic in Python modules. I want logic in my templates!'' Okay: ``I have a small number of views which generate 1MB+ HTML pages designed for Google to index. I'll use Django's native support for multiple template languages to render the 1MB+ sized pages with Jinja2, and serve the rest with Django Template Language.''

Table 18.1: Fad-based Reasons to Replace Components of Django

Figure 18.1: Replacing more core components of cake with ice cream seems like a good idea. Which cake would win? The one on the right, of course.

18.2 Non-Relational Databases vs. Relational Databases

Even Django projects that use relational databases for persistent data storage rely on non-relational databases. If a project relies on tools like Memcached for caching and Redis for queuing, then it's using non-relational databases.

The problem occurs when NoSQL solutions are used to completely replace Django's relational database functionality without considering in-depth the long-term implications.

18.2.1 Not All Non-Relational Databases Are ACID Compliant

ACID is an acronym for:

Atomicity means that all parts of a transaction work or it all fails. Without this, you risk data corruption.

Consistency means that any transaction will keep data in a valid state. Strings remain strings and integers remain integers. Without this, you risk data corruption.

Isolation means that concurrent execution of data within a transaction will not collide or leak into another transaction. Without this, you risk data corruption.

Durability means that once a transaction is committed, it will remain so even if the database server is shut down. Without this, you risk data corruption.

Did you notice how each of those descriptions ended with *'Without this, you risk data corruption.'*? This is because in the case of most NoSQL engines, there is little-to-no mechanism for *ACID* compliance. It's much easier to corrupt the data, which is mostly a non-issue for things like caching but another thing altogether for projects handling processing of persistent medical or e-commerce data.

18.2.2 Don't Use Non-Relational Databases for Relational Tasks

Imagine if we were to use a non-relational database to track the sale of properties, property owners, and how property laws worked for them in 50 US states. There a lot of unpredictable details, so wouldn't a schemaless datastore be perfect for this task?

Perhaps...

We would need to track the *relationship* between properties, property owners, and laws of 50 states. Our Python code would have to maintain the referential integrity between all the components. We would also need to ensure that the right data goes into the right place.

For a task like this, stick with a relational database.

18.2.3 Ignore the Hype and Do Your Own Research

It's often said that non-relational databases are faster and scale better than relational databases. Whether or not this is true, don't blindly swallow the marketing hype of the companies behind any particular alternative database solution.

Instead, do as we do: search for benchmarks, read case studies describing when things went right or wrong, and form opinions as independently as possible.

Also, experiment with unfamiliar NoSQL databases on small hobby side projects before you make major changes to your main project infrastructure. Your main codebase is not a playground.

Lessons learned by companies and individuals:

- Pinterest: `2scoops.co/learn-to-stop-using-shiny-new-things/`
- Etsy engineer: `mcfunley.com/why-mongodb-never-worked-out-at-etsy`

18.2.4 How We Use Non-Relational Databases With Django

This is how we prefer to do things:

- If we use a *non-relational data store*, limit usage to short-term things like caches, queues, and sometimes denormalized data. But avoid it if possible, to reduce the number of moving parts.
- Use *relational data stores* for long-term, relational data and sometimes denormalized data (PostgreSQL's array and HStore fields work great for this task).

For us, this is the sweet spot that makes our Django projects shine.

18.3 What About Replacing the Django Template Language?

We advocate the practice of sticking entirely to the Django Template Language (DTL) with the exception of rendered content of huge size. However, as this use case is now covered by Django's native support of alternate template systems, we've moved discussion of this topic to chapter 15, *Using Alternate Template Systems*.

18.4 Summary

Always use the right tool for the right job. We prefer to go with stock Django components, just like we prefer using a scoop when serving ice cream. However, there are times when other tools make sense.

Just don't follow the fad of mixing vegetables into your ice cream. You simply can't replace the classic strawberry, chocolate, and vanilla with supposedly "high-performance" flavors such as broccoli, corn, and spinach. That's taking it too far.

19 | Working With the Django Admin

When people ask, "*What are the benefits of Django over other web frameworks?*" the admin is what usually comes to mind.

Imagine if every gallon of ice cream came with an admin interface. You'd be able to not just see the list of ingredients, but also add/edit/delete ingredients. If someone was messing around with your ice cream in a way that you didn't like, you could limit or revoke their access.

Figure 19.1: Chocolate chip ice cream with an admin interface.

Pretty surreal, isn't it? Well, that's what web developers coming from another background feel like when they first use the Django admin interface. It gives you so much power over your web application automatically, with little work required.

19.1 It's Not for End Users

The Django admin interface is designed for site administrators, not end users. It's a place for your site administrators to add/edit/delete data and perform site management tasks.

Although it's possible to stretch it into something that your end users could use, you really shouldn't. It's just not designed for use by every site visitor.

19.2 Admin Customization vs. New Views

It's usually not worth it to heavily customize the Django admin. Sometimes, creating a simple view or form from scratch results in the same desired functionality with a lot less work.

We've always had better results with creating custom management dashboards for client projects than we have with modifying the admin to fit the need of the client.

19.3 Viewing String Representations of Objects

The default admin page for a Django app looks something like this:

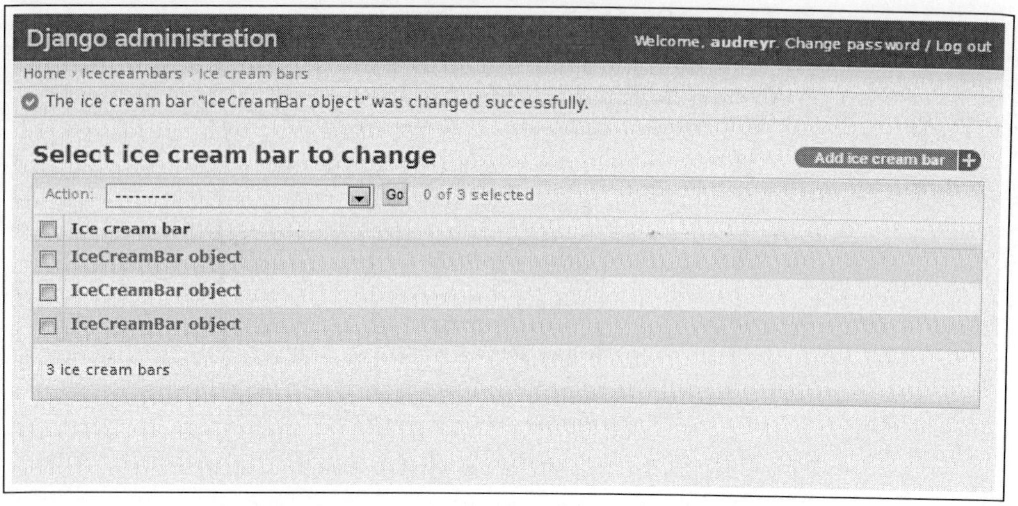

Figure 19.2: Admin list page for an ice cream bar app.

That's because the default string representation of an `IceCreamBar` object is "IceCreamBar object".

It would be helpful to display something better here. We recommend that you do the following as standard practice:

1. Always implement the `__str__()` method for each of your Django models. If you are using Python 2.7, decorate the model's class with `django.utils.encoding.python_2_unicode_compatible`. This will give you a better default string representation in the admin and everywhere else.
2. If you want to change the admin list display in a way that isn't quite a string representation of the object, then use `list_display`.

Implementing `__str__()` is simple:

Example 19.1

```
from django.db import models
from django.utils.encoding import python_2_unicode_compatible

@python_2_unicode_compatible  # For Python 3.4 and 2.7
class IceCreamBar(models.Model):
    name = models.CharField(max_length=100)
    shell = models.CharField(max_length=100)
    filling = models.CharField(max_length=100)
    has_stick = models.BooleanField(default=True)

    def __str__(self):
        return self.name
```

The result is on the next page:

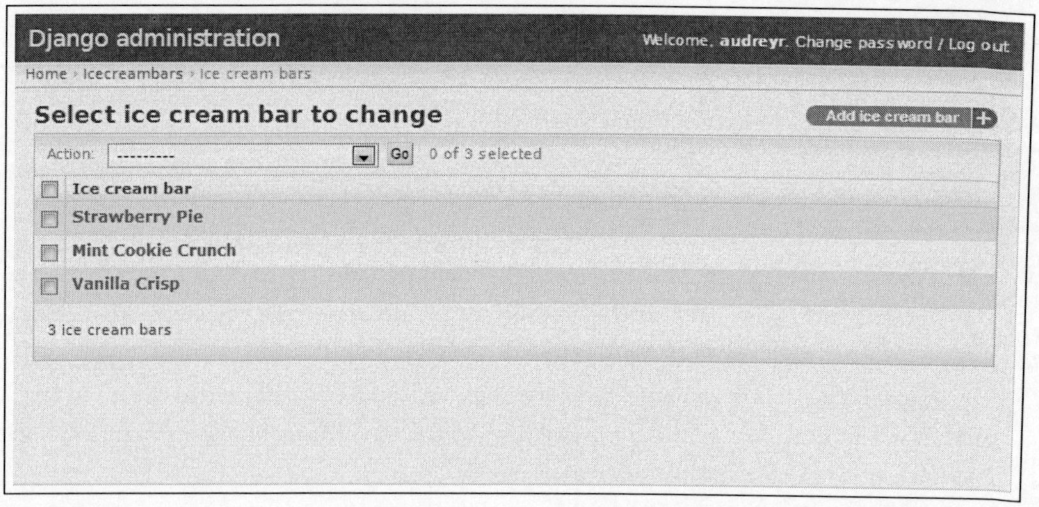

Figure 19.3: Improved admin list page with better string representation of our objects.

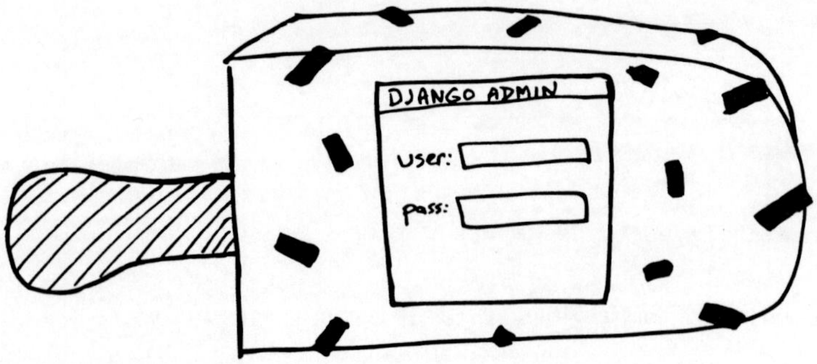

Figure 19.4: What? An admin interface for ice cream bars?

It's more than that. When you're in the shell, you see the better string representation:

Example 19.2

```
>>> IceCreamBar.objects.all()
[<IceCreamBar: Vanilla Crisp>, <IceCreamBar: Mint Cookie Crunch>,
<IceCreamBar: Strawberry Pie>]
```

The `__str__()` method is called whenever you call `unicode()` on an object. This occurs in the Django shell, templates, and by extension the Django admin. Therefore, try to make the results of `__str__()` nice, readable representation of Django model instances.

For working in Python 2.7, Django also provides the `__unicode__()` method as a default if we don't add a `__str__()` method.

If you still want to show data for additional fields on the app's admin list page, you can then use `list_display`:

Example 19.3

```
from django.contrib import admin

from .models import IceCreamBar

class IceCreamBarAdmin(admin.ModelAdmin):
    list_display = ("name", "shell", "filling",)

admin.site.register(IceCreamBar, IceCreamBarAdmin)
```

The result with the specified fields:

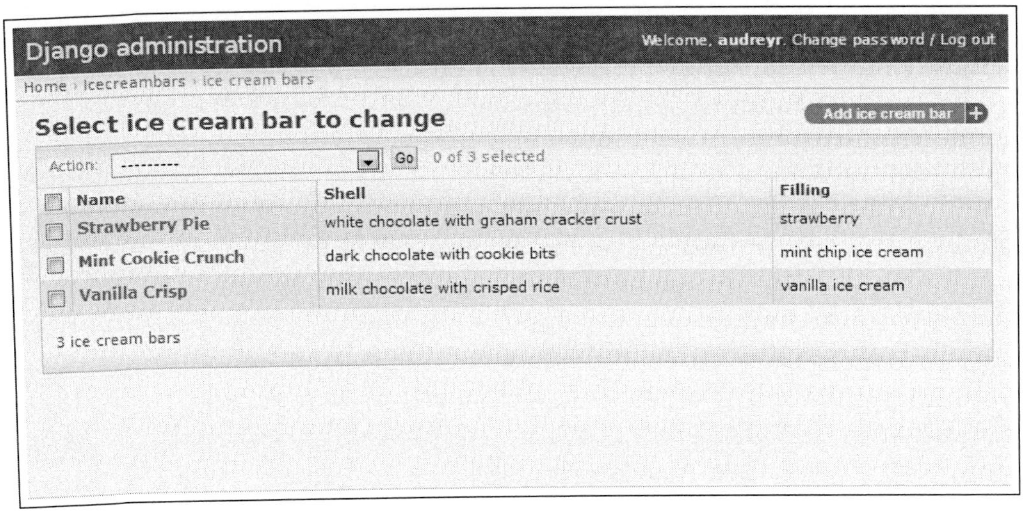

Figure 19.5: Further improvements to the admin list page.

19.4 Adding Callables to ModelAdmin Classes

You can use callables such as methods and functions to add functionality to the Django `django.contrib.admin.ModelAdmin` class. This allows you to really modify the list and display screens to suit your ice cream project needs.

For example, it's not uncommon to want to see the exact URL of a model instance in the Django admin. If you define a `get_absolute_url()` method for your model, what Django provides in the admin is a link to a redirect view whose URL is very different from the actual object URL. Also, there are cases where the `get_absolute_url()` method is meaningless (REST APIs come to mind). In the example below, we demonstrate how to use a simple callable to provide a link to our target URL:

Example 19.4

```
from django.contrib import admin
from django.core.urlresolvers import reverse
from django.utils.html import format_html

from icecreambars.models import IceCreamBar

class IceCreamBarAdmin(admin.ModelAdmin):

    list_display = ("name", "shell", "filling",)
    readonly_fields = ("show_url",)

    def show_url(self, instance):
        url = reverse("ice_cream_bar_detail",
                      kwargs={"pk": instance.pk})
        response = format_html("""<a href="{0}">{1}</a>""", url, url)
        return response

    show_url.short_description = "Ice Cream Bar URL"
    # Displays HTML tags
    # Never set allow_tags to True against user submitted data!!!
    show_url.allow_tags = True

admin.site.register(IceCreamBar, IceCreamBarAdmin)
```

Since a picture is worth a thousand words, here is what our callable does for us:

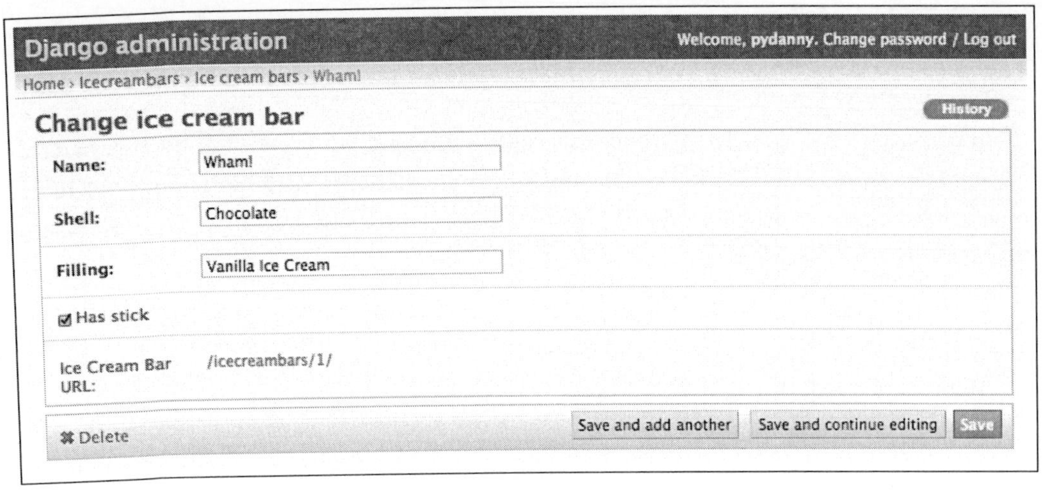

Figure 19.6: Displaying URL in the Django Admin.

> **WARNING: Use the allow_tags Attribute With Caution**
>
> The `allow_tags` attribute, which is set to `False` by default, can be a security issue. When `allow_tags` is set to `True`, HTML tags are allowed to be displayed in the admin.
>
> Our hard rule is `allow_tags` can only be used on system generated data like primary keys, dates, and calculated values. Data such as character and text fields are completely out, as is any other user entered data.

19.5 Don't Use list_editable in Multiuser Environments

This is a feature of `django.contrib.admin` that replaces the normal admin list view with a form, allowing for a user to edit multiple records at the same time. Unfortunately, records are identified not by primary keys, but by their ordered position. While this is fine for a project with a single person with admin-level access, on a multi-user project it's a very serious problem. Here is what happens:

1. Ice cream bars are in descending `created` order.
2. Daniel brings up the list field for ice cream bars and begins making changes.
3. Audrey decides to add a "Peppermint Sundae" ice cream bar. Since it's the last item added, it's now the first IceCreamBar object returned.

4. Daniel finally saves his changes, but the records he saw all receive the data from the next record, corrupting at least 50 records (Django's default admin display number).

Pointed out to us originally by Tomasz Paczkowski, our good friend and co-organizer of Django Circus 2013, this is a known bug in Django. It will hopefully be correcting in a future release of the project. In the meantime, if there is a need for this kind of display, it's best to generate your own list update view.

Related Django tickets:

- `https://code.djangoproject.com/ticket/11313`
- `https://code.djangoproject.com/ticket/17118`

19.6 Django's Admin Documentation Generator

One of the more interesting developer tools that Django provides is the `django.contrib.admindocs` package. Created in an era before the advent of the documentation tools that we cover in chapter 23, *Documentation: Be Obsessed*, it remains a useful tool.

It's useful because it introspects the Django framework to display docstrings for project components like models, views, custom template tags, and custom filters. Even if a project's components don't contain any docstrings, simply seeing a list of harder-to-introspect items like oddly named custom template tags and custom filters can be really useful in exploring the architecture of a complicated, existing application.

Using `django.contrib.admindocs` is easy, but we like to to reorder the steps described in the formal documentation:

1. `pip install docutils` into your project's **virtualenv**.
2. Add `django.contrib.admindocs` to your `INSTALLED_APPS`.
3. Add `(r'^admin/doc/', include('django.contrib.admindocs.urls'))` to your root URLConf. Make sure it's included before the `r'^admin/'` entry, so that requests to `/admin/doc/` don't get handled by the latter entry.
4. *Optional*: Linking to templates requires the `ADMIN_FOR` setting to be configured.
5. *Optional*: Using the admindocs bookmarklets requires the `XViewMiddleware` to be installed.

Once you have this in place, go to `/admin/doc/` and explore. You may notice a lot of your project's code lacks any sort of documentation. This is addressed in the formal documentation on `django.contrib.admindocs`: http://2scoops.co/1.8-admindocs and our own chapter on chapter 23, *Documentation: Be Obsessed.*

19.7 Securing the Django Admin and Django Admin Docs

It's worth the effort to take the few extra steps to prevent hackers from accessing the admin, since the admin gives you so much power over your site. See chapter 26, *Security Best Practices* for details, specifically section 26.17, 'Securing the Django Admin,' and section 26.18, 'Securing Admin Docs.'

19.8 Using Custom Skins With the Django Admin

Over the years there have been a number of efforts to reskin or theme the Django Admin. These range from the venerable, stable, and very popular django-grappelli to more recent up-and-comers. They turn Django's 2005-era admin design into lovely styles more friendly to the modern eye.

PACKAGE TIP: Custom django.contrib.admin Skins

Here are some of the more popular custom skins that are generally Python 2 and 3 compatible:

- **django-grappelli** is the grand-daddy of all custom Django skins. Stable, robust, and with a unique but friendly style.
- **django-suit** is a relatively recent project and like many modern custom Django skins, is built using the familiar Twitter Bootstrap front-end framework.
- **django-admin-bootstrapped** is another port of the Django admin to Twitter Bootstrap.

A more complete list can be found at https://www.djangopackages.com/grids/g/admin-styling/.

Django has a gigantic community, so why aren't there more skins?

It turns out that besides the most basic CSS-based modifications, creating custom Django themes is very challenging. For anyone who has delved into the source code for these projects, it's clear that custom admin skins require arcane code to account for some of the idiosyncrasies of `django.contrib.admin`.

Patrick Kranzlmueller, maintainer of django-grappelli, goes into great detail in his article on the subject, 'A Frontend Framework for the Django Admin Interface', which you can read at the link below:

- http://sehmaschine.net/blog/django-admin-frontend-framework.

Here are some tips when working with custom `django.contrib.admin` skins:

19.8.1 Evaluation Point: Documentation is Everything

As mentioned earlier, writing a custom skin for `django.contrib.admin` is hard. While the successful skins are relatively easy to add to a project, it's the edge cases (invariably involved in extending the `ModelAdmin` object) that can hurt.

Therefore, when evaluating one of these projects for use on a project, check to see how far the documentation goes beyond installation instructions.

19.8.2 Write Tests for Any Admin Extensions You Create

For our purposes, we've found that while clients enjoy the more modern themes, you have to be careful of how far you extend these admin skins. What works great in vanilla `django.contrib.admin` can break in a custom skin. Since the custom skins have to wrap portions of `django.contrib.admin` abstractions in curious ways, debugging these problems can prove to be a mind-numbing nightmare.

Therefore, if you use a custom skin, the best practice is to write tests of the admin, especially for any customization. Yes, it is a bit of work up front, but it means catching these bugs much, much earlier.

For more on testing, see chapter 22.

19.9 Summary

In this chapter we covered the following:

- Who should be using the Django admin.
- When to use the Django admin and when to roll a new dashboard.
- String representation of objects.
- Adding callables to Django admin classes.
- Warned about using `django.contrib.admin.ModelAdmin.list_editable`.
- Using Django's admin docs.
- Encouraging you to secure the Django admin.
- Advised on working with custom Django skins.

20 Dealing With the User Model

The best practices for this changed significantly in Django 1.5. The "right way" before Django 1.5 was a bit confusing, and there's still confusion around pre-1.5, so it's especially important that what we describe here is only applied to Django 1.5 or higher.

So let's go over best practices for Django 1.8.

20.1 Use Django's Tools for Finding the User Model

The advised way to get to the user class is as follows:

Example 20.1

```
# Stock user model definition
>>> from django.contrib.auth import get_user_model
>>> get_user_model()
<class 'django.contrib.auth.models.User'>

# When the project has a custom user model definition
>>> from django.contrib.auth import get_user_model
>>> get_user_model()
<class 'profiles.models.UserProfile'>
```

It is now possible to get two different `User` model definitions depending on the project configuration. This doesn't mean that a project can have two different `User` models; it means that every project can customize its own `User` model. This was introduced in Django 1.5 and a radical departure from earlier versions of Django.

20.1.1 Use settings.AUTH_USER_MODEL for Foreign Keys to User

In Django 1.8, the official preferred way to attach `ForeignKey`, `OneToOneField`, or `ManyToManyField` to `User` is as follows:

Example 20.2

```
from django.conf import settings
from django.db import models

class IceCreamStore(models.Model):

    owner = models.OneToOneField(settings.AUTH_USER_MODEL)
    title = models.CharField(max_length=255)
```

Yes, it looks a bit strange, but that's what the official Django docs advise.

Figure 20.1: This looks strange too.

WARNING: Don't Change settings.AUTH_USER_MODEL!

Once set in a project, changing `settings.AUTH_USER_MODEL` requires changing your database schema accordingly. It's one thing to add or modify User model fields, it's another thing to create a whole new User object.

20.1.2 Don't Use get_user_model() for Foreign Keys to User

This is bad, as it tends to create import loops.

Bad Example 20.1

```
# DON'T DO THIS!
from django.db import models
from django.contrib.auth import get_user_model

class IceCreamStore(models.Model):

    # This following line tends to create import loops.
    owner = models.OneToOneField(get_user_model())
    title = models.CharField(max_length=255)
```

20.2 Migrating Pre-1.5 User Models to 1.5+'s Custom User Models

This isn't for the timid. As always, before starting a large intrusive effort, there should be significant test coverage as well as continuous integration in place. Also, if there was ever a reason to test the backup system, this is it.

As documenting this is outside the scope of this book, we recommend reading the following:

Tobias McNulty's Tutorial
: http://www.2scoops.co/caktusgroup-migrating-custom-user-model

django-authtool's Tutorial
: http://www.2scoops.co/authtools-migrate-to-custom-user-model

20.3 Custom User Fields for Django 1.8 Projects

In Django 1.8, as long as we incorporate the required methods and attributes, we can create our own user model with its own fields. We can still do things the old pre-Django 1.5 way, but we're not stuck with having a `User` model with just `email`, `first_name`, `last_name`, and `username` fields for identity.

PACKAGE TIP: Libraries for Defining Custom User Models

django-authtools is a library that makes defining custom user models easier. Of particular use are the `AbstractEmailUser` and `AbstractNamedUser` models. Even if you don't end up using django-authtools, the source code is well worth examining.

WARNING: Third-Party Libraries Should Not Be Defining the User Model

Unless the express purpose of the library is to define custom user models for a project (à la django-authtools), third-party libraries shouldn't be using options #1 or #2 to add fields to user models. Instead, they should rely on option #3.

20.3.1 Option 1: Subclass AbstractUser

Choose this option if you like Django's `User` model fields the way they are, but need extra fields. For what it's worth, this is the first approach that we look at anytime we start a new project. When using django-authtools' base models, forms, and admin objects, we find that it's the quickest and easiest way to implement custom user models.

Here's an example of how to subclass `AbstractUser`:

Example 20.3

```
# profiles/models.py
from django.contrib.auth.models import AbstractUser
from django.db import models
from django.utils.translation import ugettext_lazy as _

class KarmaUser(AbstractUser):
    karma = models.PositiveIntegerField(verbose_name=_("karma"),
                                        default=0,
                                        blank=True)
```

It's much more elegant than the pre-1.5 way, isn't it?

The other thing you have to do is set this in your settings:

Example 20.4
```
AUTH_USER_MODEL = "profiles.KarmaUser"
```

20.3.2 Option 2: Subclass AbstractBaseUser

`AbstractBaseUser` is the bare-bones option with only 3 fields: `password`, `last_login`, and `is_active`.

Choose this option if:

- You're unhappy with the fields that the `User` model provides by default, such as `first_name` and `last_name`.
- You prefer to subclass from an extremely bare-bones clean slate but want to take advantage of the `AbstractBaseUser` sane default approach to storing passwords.

If you want to go down this path, we recommend the following reading:

Official Django Documentation Example
 http://2scoops.co/1.8-custom-user-model-example
Source code of django-authtools (Especially `admin.py`, `forms.py`, and `models.py`)
 https://github.com/fusionbox/django-authtools

20.3.3 Option 3: Linking Back From a Related Model

This code is very similar to the pre-Django 1.5 project technique of creating 'Profile' models. Before discarding this approach as legacy, consider the following use cases:

Use Case: Creating a Third Party Package

- We are creating a third-party package for publication on PyPI.
- The package needs to store additional information per user, perhaps a Stripe ID or another payment gateway identifier.
- We want to be as unobtrusive to the existing project code as possible. Loose coupling!

Use Case: Internal Project Needs

- We are working on our own Django project.
- We want different types of users to have different fields.
- We might have some users with a combination of different user types.
- We want to handle this at the model level, instead of at other levels.
- We want this to be used in conjunction with a custom user model from options #1 or #2.

Either of these use cases provide motive for the continued use of this technique.

To make this technique work, we continue to use `django.contrib.models.User` (called preferably via `django.contrib.auth.get_user_model()`) and keep your related fields in separate models (e.g. `Profiles`). Here's an example:

Example 20.5

```
# profiles/models.py

from django.conf import settings
from django.db import models

from flavors.models import Flavor

class EaterProfile(models.Model):

    # Default user profile
    # If you do this you need to either have a post_save signal or
    #     redirect to a profile_edit view on initial login.
    user = models.OneToOneField(settings.AUTH_USER_MODEL)
    favorite_ice_cream = models.ForeignKey(Flavor, null=True, blank=True)

class ScooperProfile(models.Model):

    user = models.OneToOneField(settings.AUTH_USER_MODEL)
    scoops_scooped = models.IntegerField(default=0)

class InventorProfile(models.Model):

    user = models.OneToOneField(settings.AUTH_USER_MODEL)
```

```
flavors_invented = models.ManyToManyField(Flavor, null=True, blank=True)
```

Using this approach, we can query for any user's favorite ice cream trivially with the ORM: `user.eaterprofile.favorite_ice_cream`. In addition, `Scooper` and `Inventor` profiles provide individual data that only applies to those users. Since that data is isolated into dedicated models, it's much harder for accidents between user types to occur.

The only downside to this approach is that it's possible to take it too far in complexity of profiles or in the supporting code. As always, keep your code as simple and clean as possible.

> **TIP: The user.get_profile() Method is Gone**
>
> If you are migrating forward from Django 1.6 or lower, please note that the `user.get_profile()` method was removed in Django 1.7.

20.4 Summary

The new `User` model makes this an exciting time to be involved in Django. We are getting to participate in a major infrastructure change with wide-ranging implications. We are the ones who get to pioneer the best practices.

In this chapter we covered the new method to find the `User` model and define our own custom ones. Depending on the needs of a project, they can either continue with the current way of doing things or customize the actual user model.

The next chapter is a dive into the world of third-party packages.

21 | Django's Secret Sauce: Third-Party Packages

The real power of Django is more than just the framework and documentation available at `https://djangoproject.com`. It's the vast, growing selection of third-party Django and Python packages provided by the open source community. There are many, many third-party packages available for your Django projects which can do an incredible amount of work for you. These packages have been written by people from all walks of life, and they power much of the world today.

Figure 21.1: A jar of Django's mysterious secret sauce. Most don't have a clue what this is.

Much of professional Django and Python development is about the incorporation of third-party packages into Django projects. If you try to write every single tool that you need from scratch, you'll have a hard time getting things done.

This is especially true for us in the consulting world, where client projects consist of many of the same or similar building blocks.

Figure 21.2: The secret is out. It's just hot fudge.

21.1 Examples of Third-Party Packages

Appendix A: *Packages Mentioned In This Book* covers all of the packages mentioned throughout Two Scoops of Django. This list is a great starting point if you're looking for highly-useful packages to consider adding to your projects.

Note that not all of those packages are Django-specific, which means that you can use some of them in other Python projects. (Generally, Django-specific packages generally have names prefixed with "django-", but there are many exceptions.)

21.2 Know About the Python Package Index

The **Python Package Index** (**PyPI**), located at https://pypi.python.org/pypi, is a repository of software for the Python programming language. As of the time this sentence was written, it lists over 55,000 packages, including Django itself.

For the vast majority of Python community, no open source project release is considered official until it occurs on the Python Package Index.

The Python Package Index is much more than just a directory. Think of it as the world's largest center for Python package information and files. Whenever you use **pip** to install a particular release of Django, pip downloads the files from the Python Package Index. Most Python and Django packages are downloadable from the Python Package Index in addition to pip.

21.3 Know About DjangoPackages.com

Django Packages (https://www.djangopackages.com/) is a directory of reusable apps, sites, tools and more for your Django projects. Unlike PyPI, it doesn't store the packages themselves, instead providing a mix of hard metrics gathered from the Python Package Index, GitHub, Bitbucket, ReadTheDocs, and "soft" data entered by users.

Django Packages is best known as a comparison site for evaluating package features. On Django Packages, packages are organized into handy grids so they can be compared against each other.

Django Packages also happens to have been created by the authors of this book, with contributions from many, many people in the Python community. We continue to maintain and improve it as a helpful resource for Django users.

21.4 Know Your Resources

Django developers unaware of the critical resources of Django Packages and the Python Package Index are denying themselves one of the most important advantages of using Django and Python. If you are not aware of these tools, it's well worth the time you spend educating yourself.

As a Django (and Python) developer, make it your mission to use third-party libraries instead of reinventing the wheel whenever possible. The best libraries have been written, documented, and tested by amazingly competent developers working around the world. Standing on the shoulders of these giants is the difference between amazing success and tragic downfall.

As you use various packages, study and learn from their code. You'll learn patterns and tricks that will make you a better developer.

On the other hand, it's very important to be able to identify the good packages from the bad. It's well worth taking the time to evaluate packages written by others the same way we evaluate our own work. We cover this later in this chapter in section 21.10, 'What Makes a Good Package.'

21.5 Tools for Installing and Managing Packages

To take full advantage of all the packages available for your projects, having **virtualenv** and **pip** installed isn't something you can skip over. It's mandatory.

Refer to chapter 2, *The Optimal Django Environment Setup*, for more details.

21.6 Package Requirements

As we mentioned earlier in chapter 5, *Settings and Requirements Files*, we manage our Django/Python dependencies with requirements files. These files go into the ***requirements/*** directory that exists in the root of our projects.

> **TIP: Researching Third-Party Packages to Use**
>
> If you want to learn more about the dependencies we list in this and other chapters, please refer to Appendix A: *Packages Mentioned In This Book*.

21.7 Wiring Up Django Packages: The Basics

When you find a third-party package that you want to use, follow these steps:

21.7.1 Step 1: Read the Documentation for the Package

Are you sure you want to use it? Make sure you know what you're getting into before you install any package.

21.7.2 Step 2: Add Package and Version Number to Your Requirements

If you recall from chapter 5, *Settings and Requirements Files*, a ***requirements/base.txt*** file looks something like this (but probably longer):

Example 21.1

```
Django==1.8
coverage==3.7.1
django-extensions==1.5.2
django-braces==1.4
```

Note that each package is pinned to a specific version number. *Always* pin your package dependencies to version numbers.

What happens if you don't pin your dependencies? You are almost guaranteed to run into problems at some point when you try to reinstall or change your Django project. When new versions of packages are released, you can't expect them to be backwards-compatible.

Our sad example: Once we followed a software-as-a-service platform's instructions for using their library. As they didn't have their own Python client, but an early adopter had a working implementation on GitHub, those instructions told us to put the following into our ***requirements/base.txt***:

Bad Example 21.1

```
-e git+https://github.com/erly-adptr/py-junk.git#egg=py-jnk
```

Our mistake. We should have known better and pinned it to a particular git revision number.

Not the early adopter's fault at all, but they pushed up a broken commit to their repo. Once we had to fix a problem on a site very quickly, so we wrote a bug fix and tested it locally in development. It passed the tests. Then we deployed it to production in a process that grabs all dependency changes; of course the broken commit was interpreted as a valid change. Which meant, while fixing one bug, we crashed the site.

Not a fun day.

The purpose of using pinned releases is to add a little formality and process to our published work. Especially in Python, GitHub and other repos are a place for developers to publish their work-in-progress, not the final, stable work upon which our production-quality projects depend.

One more thing, when pinning dependencies, try to pin the dependencies of dependencies. It just makes deployment and testing that much more predictable.

21.7.3 Step 3: Install the Requirements Into Your Virtualenv

Assuming you are already in a working virtualenv and are at the **<repo_root>** of your project, you `pip install` the appropriate requirements file for your setup, e.g. *requirements/dev.txt*.

If this is the first time you've done this for a particular virtualenv, it's going to take a while for it to grab all the dependencies and install them.

21.7.4 Step 4: Follow the Package's Installation Instructions Exactly

Resist the temptation to skip steps unless you're very familiar with the package. Since open source Django package developers tend to take pride in their documentation and love to get people to use their packages, most of the time the installation instructions they've authored make it easy to get things running.

21.8 Troubleshooting Third-Party Packages

Sometimes you run into problems setting up a package. What should you do?

First, make a serious effort to determine and solve the problem yourself. Pore over the documentation and make sure you didn't miss a step. Search online to see if others have run into the same issue. Be willing to roll up your sleeves and look at the package source code, as you may have found a bug.

If it appears to be a bug, see if someone has already reported it in the package repository's issue tracker. Sometimes you'll find workarounds and fixes there. If it's a bug that no one has reported, go ahead and file it.

If you still get stuck, try asking for help in all the usual places: StackOverflow, IRC #django, the project's IRC channel if it has its own one, and your local Python user group. Be as descriptive and provide as much context as possible about your issue.

21.9 Releasing Your Own Django Packages

Whenever you write a particularly useful Django app, consider packaging it up for reuse in other projects.

The best way to get started is to follow Django's *Advanced Tutorial: How to Write Reusable Apps,* for the basics: `https://docs.djangoproject.com/en/1.8/intro/reusable-apps/`

In addition to what is described in that tutorial, we recommend that you also:

- Create a public repo containing the code. Most Django packages are hosted on GitHub these days, so it's easiest to attract contributors there, but various alternatives exist (Gitlab, Sourceforge, Bitbucket, Launchpad, Assembla, etc.).
- Release the package on the Python Package Index (`http://pypi.python.org`). Follow the submission instructions at `http://2scoops.co/submit-to-pypi`.
- Add the package to Django Packages (`https://www.djangopackages.com`).
- Use Read the Docs (`https://readthedocs.org/`) to host your **Sphinx** documentation.

> **TIP: Where Should I Create a Public Repo?**
>
> There are websites that offer free source code hosting and version control for open source projects. As mentioned in chapter 2, "The Optimal Django Environment Setup", GitHub or Bitbucket are two popular options.
>
> When choosing a hosted version control service, keep in mind that pip only supports Git, Mercurial, Bazaar, and Subversion.

21.10 What Makes a Good Django Package?

Here's a checklist for you to use when creating a new open source Django package. Much of this applies to Python packages that are not Django-specific. This checklist is also helpful for when you're evaluating a Django package to use in any of your projects.

21.10.1 Purpose

Your package should do something useful and do it well. The name should be descriptive. The package repo's root folder should be prefixed with 'django-' to help make it easier to find.

If part of the package's purpose can be accomplished with a related Python package that doesn't depend on Django, then create a separate Python package and use it as a dependency.

21.10.2 Scope

Your package's scope should be tightly focused on one small task. This means that your application logic will be tighter, and users will have an easier time patching or replacing the package.

21.10.3 Documentation

A package without documentation is a pre-alpha package. Docstrings don't suffice as documentation.

As described in chapter 23, *Documentation: Be Obsessed*, your docs should be written in **ReStructuredText**. A nicely-formatted version of your docs should be generated with Sphinx and hosted publicly. We encourage you to use `https://readthedocs.org/` with webhooks so that your formatted documentation automatically updates whenever you make a change.

If your package has dependencies, they should be documented. Your package's installation instructions should also be documented. The installation steps should be bulletproof.

21.10.4 Tests

Your package should have tests. Tests improve reliability, make it easier to advance Python/Django versions, and make it easier for others to contribute effectively. Write up instructions on how to run your package's test suite. If you or any contributor can run your tests easily before submitting a pull request, then you're more likely to get better quality contributions.

21.10.5 Templates

In the past, some Django packages provided instructions for creating templates in their docs in lieu of actual template files. However, nowadays it's pretty standard for Django packages to come with a set of barebones templates that demonstrate basic functionality. Typically these templates contain only minimalist HTML, any needed JavaScript, and no CSS. The exception is for packages containing widgets that require CSS styling.

21.10.6 Activity

Your package should receive regular updates from you or contributors if/when needed. When you update the code in your repo, you should consider uploading a minor or major release to the Python Package Index.

21.10.7 Community

Great open source packages, including those for Django, often end up receiving contributions from other developers in the open source community. All contributors should receive attribution in a *CONTRIBUTORS.rst* or *AUTHORS.rst* file.

Be an active community leader if you have contributors or forks of your package. If your package is forked by other developers, pay attention to their work. Consider if there are ways that parts or all of their work can be merged into your fork. If the package's functionality diverges a lot from your package's purpose, be humble and consider asking the other developer to give their fork a new name.

21.10.8 Modularity

Your package should be as easily pluggable into any Django project that doesn't replace core components (templates, ORM, etc) with alternatives. Installation should be minimally invasive. Be careful not to confuse modularity with over-engineering, though.

21.10.9 Availability on PyPI

All major and minor releases of your package should be available for download from the Python Package Index. Developers who wish to use your package should not have to go to your repo to get a working version of it. Use proper version numbers per the next section.

21.10.10 Uses the Broadest Requirements Specifiers Possible

Your third-party package should specify in ***setup.py*** the `install_requires` argument what other libraries your package requires in the broadest terms possible. However, this is a terrible way to define a package's requirements:

Bad Example 21.2

```
# DON'T DO THIS!
# requirements for django-blarg

Django==1.7.2
requests==1.2.3
```

The reason is dependency graphs. Every so often something that you absolutely pin to a specific version of Django or another library will break on someone else's site project. For example, what if *icecreamratings.com* was our site and this was its deployed project's requirements.txt file, and we installed django-blarg?

Example 21.2

```
# requirements.txt for the mythical web site 'icecreamratings.com'
Django==1.8
requests==2.6.0-
djangoblarg==1.0

# Note that unlike the -djangoblarg library , we explicitly pin
# the requirements so we have total control over the environment
```

What would happen if Bad Example 21.2 were installed to a project with Example 21.3 requirements is that the Django 1.7.2 requirement would overwrite the Django 1.8 specification during installation of ***icecreamratings.com*** requirements. As there are several backwards incompatibilities between Django 1.7.2 and 1.8, django-blarg could make ***icecreamratings.com*** site simply throw HTTP 500 errors.

Your third-party package should specify what other libraries your package requires in the broadest terms possible:

EXAMPLE 21.3

```
# requirements for django-blarg

Django>=1.5,<1.9
requests>=1.2.3,<=2.6.0
```

Additional Reading:

- http://www.pip-installer.org/en/latest/logic.html#requirement-specifiers
- http://nvie.com/posts/pin-your-packages/

21.10.11 Proper Version Numbers

Like Django and Python, we prefer to adhere to the strict version of **PEP 386** naming schema. In fact we follow the '**A.B.C**' pattern. Let's go through each element:

'A' represents the major version number. Increments should only happen with large changes that break backwards compatibility from the previous major version. It's not uncommon to see large API changes between versions.

'B' is the minor version number. Increments include less breaking changes, or deprecation notices about forthcoming changes.

'C' represents bug fix releases, and purists call this the 'micro' release. It's not uncommon for developers to wait until a project has its first release at this level before trying the latest major or minor release of an existing project.

For alpha, beta, or release-candidates for a project, the convention is to place this information as a suffix to the upcoming version number. So you might have:

- Django 1.8-alpha

- django-crispy-forms 1.4.0-beta

WARNING: Don't Upload Unfinished Code to PyPI

PyPI, the Python Package Index, is meant to be the place where dependable, stable packages can be harnessed to build Python projects. *PyPI is not the place for Alpha, Beta, or Release Candidate code*, especially as pip and other tools will fetch the latest release by default.

Be nice to other developers and follow the convention of only placing proper releases on PyPI.

Note: While recent versions of pip no longer install pre-releases by default, it's dangerous to expect users of code to have the latest pip version installed.

Additional Reading:

- `http://www.python.org/dev/peps/pep-0386`
- `http://semver.org/`

21.10.12 Name

The name of the project is absolutely critical. A well-named project makes it easy to discover and remember, a poor name hides it from potential users, can scare off its use from some developer shops, and even block it from being listed on PyPI, Django Packages, and other resources.

We did cover the basics in section 4.2, 'What to Name Your Django Apps,' but here are tips that apply to open source Django packages:

- *Check to see that the name isn't already registered on PyPI.* Otherwise, it won't be trivial to install with **pip**.
- *Check to see that the name isn't on Django Packages.* This applies only to packages designed for use with Django.
- *Don't use names that include obscenity.* While you might find them funny, it's unfortunate for others. For example a noted developer once created a library that couldn't be used at NASA until he agreed to change the name.

21.10.13 License

Your package needs a license. Preferably, for individuals it should be licensed under the **MIT** licenses, which are generally accepted for being permissive enough for most commercial or noncommercial uses. If you are worried about patents, then go with the **Apache** license.

Create a ***LICENSE.rst*** file in your repo root, mention the license name at the top, and paste in the appropriate text from the (OSI) approved list at `http://choosealicense.com/`.

> **TIP: Licenses Protect You and the World**
>
> In this era of casual litigation and patent trolls adding a software license isn't just a matter of protecting your ownership of the code. It's much, much more. If you don't license your code, or use an unapproved license not vetted by real lawyers, you run the risk of your work being used as a weapon by a patent troll, or in the case of financial or medical disaster, you could be held liable.
> OSI-approved licenses all include a couple critical statements on **copyright**, **redistribution**, **disclaimer of warranty**, and **limitation of liability**.

21.10.14 Clarity of Code

The code in your Django package should be as clear and simple as possible, of course. Don't use weird, unusual Python/Django hacks without explaining what you are doing.

21.10.15 Use URL Namespaces

Described in section 8.4, URL namespaces allow for greater Interoperability. Using means it's easier to manage collisions between projects, or even prepare for it ahead of time.

If there is concern about future collisions, settings-based URL namespace systems can be implemented. This is where the project defines its URL namespace as a setting, then provides a Django context processor and detailed instructions on use. While it's not hard to implement, it does create a level of abstraction that can make a project a little bit harder to maintain.

21.11 Creating Your Own Packages the Easy Way

Releasing your own bit of code can be a wonderfully rewarding experience. Everyone should do it!

That said, putting all the pieces together in order to make a reusable Django package is a lot of work, and it's common to get things wrong. Fortunately, **Cookiecutter** makes this easy.

> **PACKAGE TIP: Cookiecutter: Project Templates Made Easy**
>
> Audrey has created a popular utility for generating project templates. It's easy to use and very powerful. Numerous templates exist for Python and Django packages.
> - https://github.com/audreyr/cookiecutter
> - http://cookiecutter.readthedocs.org/

In the Cookiecutter templates referenced below, we have vetted them by aggressively asking for them to be reviewed by leaders in both the Django and Python communities. Just use the following bash example at the command-line:

Example 21.4

```
# Only if you installed cookiecutter yet
$ pip install cookiecutter

# Creating a Django Package from scratch
$ cookiecutter https://github.com/pydanny/cookiecutter-djangopackage.git

# Creating a Python Package from scratch
$ cookiecutter https://github.com/audreyr/cookiecutter-pypackage.git
```

You'll be prompted to provide information. The generated result will be an implementation of a base Django/Python/etc package template that includes code, documentation, tests, license, and much more.

21.12 Maintaining Your Open Source Package

WARNING: Open Source Burnout and Giving Too Much

Unless you are getting paid professionally to do open source work, remember that this is volunteer work done for pleasure. Do what you can at your own pace, and just try your best.

The open source packages that you create have a life of their own. They mature over time, changing as their needs and the development standards grow over time. Here are some things we should do when maintaining open source projects:

21.12.1 Give Credit for Pull Requests

When someone submits a pull request that's accepted, treat them right. Make sure to add the contributor to a project's author document called something like *CONTRIBUTORS.txt* or *AUTHORS.txt*.

21.12.2 Handling Bad Pull Requests

Sometimes you get pull requests that you just have to reject. Be nice and positive about it, since a well-handled rejected pull request can make a friend for life.

Here are problematic pull requests that should be considered for rejection:

- *Any pull request that fails the tests.* Ask for fixes. See chapter 22.
- *Any added code that reduces test coverage.* Again, see chapter 22.
- *Pull requests should change/fix as little as possible.* Large, wide-sweeping changes in a pull request should be rejected, with comments to isolate changes in smaller, atomic pull requests.
- *Overly complex code submissions should be carefully considered.* There is nothing wrong with asking for simplification, better comments, or even rejecting an overly complex pull request.

- *Code that breaks PEP-8 needs to be resubmitted.* The Django world follows PEP-8 very closely, and so should your project. Submissions that violate PEP 8 can be requested to be improved.
- *Code changes combined with major whitespace cleanup.* If someone submits a change of two lines of code and corrects 200 lines of whitespace issues, the diff on that pull request is functionally unreadable and should be rejected. Whitespace cleanups need to be in their own pull request.

WARNING: Code Changes Combined With Major Whitespace Cleanup

We're adding a warning because this is arguably a form of code obfuscation by a third party. One could argue it's potentially a security risk. What better way to inject malignant code than through a pull request?

21.12.3 Do Formal PyPI Releases

In the Python community, it's considered irresponsible to force developers to rely on a 'stable' master or trunk branch of critical open source projects because the PyPI version is out of date. This can cause problems as open source code repositories are not considered to be good sources of production quality code. For example, which particular commit or tag should be used? On the other hand, PyPI, is a known resource designed to securely provide valid installable packages.

In the Python world, the accepted best practice is to release when significant (or even minor) changes or bug fixes happen on trunk or master. In fact, minor bug fix releases are a part of every ongoing software project and no one faults anyone for these kinds of things (except in US government IT contracts, but that's outside the scope of this book).

If you aren't sure how this works, please look at python-request's change history, it being one of Python's most popular projects: `http://2scoops.co/requests-history`

To create and upload your distribution, use the following steps:

Example 21.5

```
$ pip install twine
$ python setup.py sdist
$ twine upload dist/*
```

PACKAGE TIP: What is Twine?

Twine is the preferred library for uploading packages to PyPI. The problem with `python setup.py` is that it sends files over a non-SSH connection, exposing your library to a man-in-the-middle attack. In contrast, twine uses only verified TLS to upload your package.

That's not all! Twine works better at uploading Wheels (see the next subsection), doesn't require executing the setup.py, and even pre-signs your releases. If you are seriously security minded, it's the tool of choice.

21.12.4 Create and Deploy Wheels to PyPI

According to PEP 427, Wheels are the new standard of python distribution. They are intended to replace eggs and provide a number of advantages including faster installation and allow secure digital signing. Support is offered in pip >= 1.4 and setuptools >= 0.8.

Example 21.6

```
$ pip install wheel
$ pip install twine
```

Then, after you've deployed your package to PyPI, run the following commands:

Example 21.7

```
$ python setup.py bdist_wheel
$ twine upload dist/*
```

For supporting Python 2.7 and 3.3+, Twine makes universal wheels when the optional ***setup.cfg*** file is at the same level as ***setup.py*** and includes this snippet:

Example 21.8

```
# setup.cfg
[wheel]
universal = 1
```

Wheel Resources:

Specification: PEP 427 http://www.python.org/dev/peps/pep-0427/
Wheel Package on PyPI https://pypi.python.org/pypi/wheel
Documentation http://wheel.readthedocs.org/
Advocacy http://pythonwheels.com/

21.12.5 Upgrade the Package to New Versions of Django

Every once in awhile, Django is updated with a minor release. Approximately once a year there is a major Django release. When this happens, it's very important to run our package's test suite in a **virtualenv** that contain Django's latest release.

If for no other reason, this is an excellent reason to include tests in your project.

21.12.6 Follow Good Security Practices

We discuss security in-depth in chapter 26, *Security Best Practices*. However, core Django, Python, and PyPy developer Alex Gaynor has an incredibly useful article for maintainers of any open source project:
https://alexgaynor.net/2013/oct/19/security-process-open-source-projects/

> **TIP: Alex Gaynor on Security for Open Source Projects**
>
> "Security vulnerabilities put your users, and often, in turn, their users at risk. As an author and distributor of software, you have a responsibility to your users to handle security releases in a way most likely to help them avoid being exploited."

21.12.7 Provide Sample Base Templates

Always include some basic templates for views using your project. We prefer to write either incredibly simple HTML or use a common front-end frameworks such as Twitter Bootstrap. This makes 'test-driving' the project much easier for developers who are considering using it to solve their problems. Invariably they'll modify the templates inside their own ***templates/*** directory, but this just makes everything so much easier.

In addition, include a ***templates/myapp/base.html*** to increase interoperability. You can see a description and example of this in cookiecutter-djangopackage:

`http://2scoops.co/cookiecutter-djangopackage-base.html`

21.12.8 Give the Package Away

Sometimes, life takes you away from maintaining a package. It might be family or a new job, but sometimes you just have no need for a particular open source project. Time considerations might mean that you don't have the ability to review pull requests or explore ideas for new features. If you're the creator of a project it can be extremely challenging to let it go.

However, by giving a project away to an active maintainer, it can be reborn and prove more useful. It also earns the respect of the developer community at large.

Some notable giveaways in the Django and Python communities include:

- Ian Bicking and pip/virtualenv.
- Jesper Nøhr and django-piston.

- Daniel Roy Greenfeld and django-uni-form.
- Rob Hudson and django-debug-toolbar.

21.13 Additional Reading

The following are links to useful articles for anyone contributing to, creating, or maintaining open source libraries:

- `http://alexgaynor.net/2013/sep/26/effective-code-review/`
- `http://2scoops.co/sharing-your-labor-of-love-pypi-quick-and-dirty`
- `http://2scoops.co/jeff-knupp-open-sourcing-a-python-project`

21.14 Summary

Django's real power is in the vast selection of third-party packages available to you for use in your Django projects.

Make sure that you have pip and virtualenv installed and know how to use them, since they're your best tools for installing packages on your system in a manageable way.

Get to know the packages that exist. The Python Package Index and Django Packages are a great starting point for finding information about packages.

Package maturity, documentation, tests, and code quality are good starting criteria when evaluating a Django package.

Installation of stable packages is the foundation of Django projects big and small. Being able to use packages means sticking to specific releases, not just the trunk or master of a project. Barring a specific release, you can rely on a particular commit. Fixing problems that a package has with your project takes diligence and time, but remember to ask for help if you get stuck.

We also covered how to create your own third-party package, and provided basic instruction on how to use cookiecutter to jump-start you on your way to releasing something on the Python Package Index. We also included instructions on using the new Wheel format.

Finally, we provided guidance on how to maintain a package.

22 Testing Stinks and Is a Waste of Money!

There, got you to this chapter.

Now you have to read it.

We'll try and make this chapter interesting.

22.1 Testing Saves Money, Jobs, and Lives

Daniel's Story: Ever hear the term "smoke test"?

Gretchen Davidian, a Management and Program Analyst at **NASA**, told me that when she was still an engineer, her job as a tester was to put equipment intended to get into space through such rigorous conditions that they would begin emitting smoke and eventually catch on fire.

That sounds exciting! Employment, money, and lives were on the line, and knowing Gretchen's attention to detail, I'm sure she set a lot of hardware on fire.

Keep in mind that for a lot of us, as software engineers, the same risks are on the line as NASA. I recall in 2004 while working for a private company how a single miles-vs-kilometers mistake cost a company hundreds of thousands of dollars in a matter of hours. Quality Assurance (QA) staff lost their jobs, which meant that money and health benefits were gone. In other words, employment, money, and possibly lives can be lost without adequate tests. While the QA staff were very dedicated, everything was done via manually clicking through projects, and human error simply crept into the testing process.

Today, as Django moves into a wider and wider set of applications, the need for automated testing is just as important as it was for Gretchen at NASA and for the poor QA staff in 2004. Here are some cases where Django is used today that have similar quality requirements:

- Your application handles medical information.
- Your application provides life-critical resources to people in need.
- Your application works with other people's money now or will at some point in the future.

> **PACKAGE TIP: Useful Library for Testing Django Projects**
>
> We like to use **coverage.py**.
>
> This tool provides clear insight into what parts of your code base are covered by tests, and what lines haven't been touched by tests. You also get a handy percentage of how much of your code is covered by tests. Even 100% test coverage doesn't guarantee a bug-free application, but it helps.
>
> We want to thank Ned Batchelder for his incredible work in maintaining coverage.py. It's a superb project and is useful for any Python related project.

22.2 How to Structure Tests

Let's say we've just created a new Django app. The first thing we do is delete the default but useless ***tests.py*** module that `django-admin.py startapp` creates.

In its place, because most apps need them, we create ***test_forms.py***, ***test_models.py***, ***test_views.py*** modules. Tests that apply to forms go into ***test_forms.py***, model tests go into ***test_models.py***, and so on.

Here's what it looks like:

Example 22.1

```
popsicles/
    __init__.py
    admin.py
    forms.py
    models.py
    test_forms.py
    test_models.py
    test_views.py
    views.py
```

Also, if we have other files besides *forms.py*, *models.py* and *views.py* that need testing, we create corresponding test files.

We like this approach because per the *Zen of Python*'s statement that "*Flat is better than nested,*" this makes it easier to navigate a Django app.

> **TIP: Prefix Test Modules With test_**
>
> It's critically important that we always prefix test modules with ***test_***, otherwise Django's test runner can't discover our test files.

22.3 How to Write Unit Tests

It's not uncommon for programmers to feel at the top of their game at the moment they are writing code. When they revisit that same code in months, weeks, days, or even hours and it's not uncommon for programmers to feel as if that same code is of poor quality.

The same applies to writing unit tests.

Over the years, we've evolved a number of practices we like to follow when writing tests, including **unit tests**. Our goal is always to write the most meaningful tests in the shortest amount of time. Hence the following:

22.3.1 Each Test Method Tests One Thing

A test method must be extremely narrow in what it tests. A single unit test *should never* assert the behavior of multiple views, models, forms, or even multiple methods within a class. Instead, a single test should assert the behavior of a single view, model, form, method or function.

Of course, therein lies a conundrum. How does one run a test for a view, when views often require the use of models, forms, methods, and functions?

The trick is to be absolutely minimalistic when constructing the environment for a particular test, as shown in the example below:

EXAMPLE 22.2

```
# flavors/test_api.py
import json

from django.core.urlresolvers import reverse
from django.test import TestCase

from flavors.models import Flavor

class FlavorAPITests(TestCase):

    def setUp(self):
        Flavor.objects.get_or_create(title="A Title", slug="a-slug")

    def test_list(self):
        url = reverse("flavor_object_api")
        response = self.client.get(url)
        self.assertEquals(response.status_code, 200)
        data = json.loads(response.content)
        self.assertEquals(len(data), 1)
```

In this test, taken from code testing the API we presented in section 16.2, 'Implementing a Simple JSON API,' chapter 16, *Building REST APIs,* we use the `setUp()` method to create the minimum possible number of records needed to run the test.

Here's a much larger example, one based on the REST API example that we provided in chapter 16.

Example 22.3

```
# flavors/test_api.py
import json

from django.core.urlresolvers import reverse
from django.test import TestCase

from flavors.models import Flavor

class DjangoRestFrameworkTests(TestCase):

    def setUp(self):
        Flavor.objects.get_or_create(title="title1", slug="slug1")
        Flavor.objects.get_or_create(title="title2", slug="slug2")

        self.create_read_url = reverse("flavor_rest_api")
        self.read_update_delete_url = \
            reverse("flavor_rest_api", kwargs={"slug": "slug1"})

    def test_list(self):
        response = self.client.get(self.create_read_url)

        # Are both titles in the content?
        self.assertContains(response, "title1")
        self.assertContains(response, "title2")

    def test_detail(self):
        response = self.client.get(self.read_update_delete_url)
        data = json.loads(response.content)
        content = {"id": 1, "title": "title1", "slug": "slug1",
                                            "scoops_remaining": 0}
        self.assertEquals(data, content)

    def test_create(self):
        post = {"title": "title3", "slug": "slug3"}
        response = self.client.post(self.create_read_url, post)
```

```
        data = json.loads(response.content)
        self.assertEquals(response.status_code, 201)
        content = {"id": 3, "title": "title3", "slug": "slug3",
                                            "scoops_remaining": 0}
        self.assertEquals(data, content)
        self.assertEquals(Flavor.objects.count(), 3)

    def test_delete(self):
        response = self.client.delete(self.read_update_delete_url)
        self.assertEquals(response.status_code, 204)
        self.assertEquals(Flavor.objects.count(), 1)
```

22.3.2 For Views, When Possible Use the Request Factory

The `django.test.client.RequestFactory` provides a way to generate a request instance that can be used as the first argument to any view. This provides a greater amount of isolation than the standard Django test client, but it does require a little bit of extra work on the part of the test writer. This is because the request factory doesn't support middleware, including session and authentication.

See http://2scoops.co/1.8-request-factory

Unfortunately the documentation doesn't cover when you want to test a view wrapped with a single `middleware` class. For example, if your view required sessions, this is how you would do it:

Example 22.4

```
from django.contrib.auth.models import AnonymousUser
from django.contrib.sessions.middleware import SessionMiddleware
from django.test import TestCase, RequestFactory

from .views import cheese_flavors

def add_middleware_to_request(request, middleware_class):
    middleware = middleware_class()
```

```python
    middleware.process_request(request)
    return request

def add_middleware_to_response(request, middleware_class):
    middleware = middleware_class()
    middleware.process_request(request)
    return request

class SavoryIceCreamTest(TestCase):
    def setUp(self):
        # Every test needs access to the request factory.
        self.factory = RequestFactory()

    def test_cheese_flavors(self):
        request = self.factory.get('/cheesy/broccoli/')
        request.user = AnonymousUser()

        # Annotate the request object with a session
        request = add_middleware_to_request(request, SessionMiddleware)
        request.session.save()

        # process and test the request
        response = cheese_flavors(request)
        self.assertContains(response, "bleah!")
```

22.3.3 Don't Write Tests That Have to Be Tested

Tests should be written as simply as possible. If the code in a test (or the code called to help run a test) feels complicated or abstracted, then you have a problem. In fact, we ourselves are guilty of writing overly complicated utility test functions that required their own tests in the past. As you can imagine, this made debugging the actual tests a nightmare.

22.3.4 Don't Repeat Yourself Doesn't Apply to Writing Tests

The `setUp()` method is really useful for generating reusable data across all test methods in a test class. However, sometimes we need similar but different data between test methods, which is where we often fall into the trap of writing fancy test utilities. Or worse, we decide that rather than write 20 similar tests, we can write a single method that when passed certain arguments will handle all the work for us.

Our favorite method of handling these actions is to just dig in and write the same or similar code multiple times. In fact, we'll quietly admit to copy/pasting code between tests to expedite our work.

22.3.5 Don't Rely on Fixtures

We've learned over time that using fixtures is problematic. The problem is that fixtures are hard to maintain as a project's data changes over time. Modifying JSON-formatted files to match your last migration is hard, especially as it can be difficult to identify during the JSON load process where your JSON file(s) is either broken or a subtly inaccurate representation of the database.

Rather than wrestle with fixtures, we've found it's easier to write code that relies on the ORM. Other people like to use third-party packages.

PACKAGE TIP: Tools to Generate Test Data

The following are popular tools for test data generation:

- **factory boy** A package that generates model test data.
- **model mommy** Another package that generates model test data.
- **mock** Not explicitly for Django, this allows you to replace parts of your system with mock objects. This project made its way into the standard library as of Python 3.3.

22.3.6 Things That Should Be Tested

Everything! Seriously, you should test whatever you can, including:

Views: Viewing of data, changing of data, and custom class-based view methods.

Models: Creating/updating/deleting of models, model methods, model manager methods.

Forms: Form methods, clean() methods, and custom fields.

Validators: Really dig in and write multiple test methods against each custom validator you write. Pretend you are a malignant intruder attempting to damage the data in the site.

Signals: Since they act at a distance, signals can cause grief especially if you lack tests on them.

Filters: Since filters are essentially just functions accepting one or two arguments, writing tests for them should be easy.

Template Tags: Since template tags can do anything and can even accept template context, writing tests often becomes much more challenging. This means you really need to test them, since otherwise you may run into edge cases.

Miscellany: Context processors, middleware, email, and anything else not covered in this list.

Failure What happens when any of the above fail? See

The only things that shouldn't be tested are parts of your project that are already covered by tests in core Django and third-party packages. For example, a model's fields don't have to be tested if you're using Django's standard fields as-is. However, if you're creating a new type of field (e.g. by subclassing `FileField`), then you should write detailed tests for anything that could go wrong with your new field type.

Figure 22.1: Test as much of your project as you can, as if it were free ice cream.

22.3.7 Test for Failure

Let's say we have a view that allows users to edit their own ice cream shop reviews. The obvious tests involve logging in, attempting to change the review, and then checking whether they've actually changed. Test success, coverage 100%. Right?

However, this only tests part of the scenario. What if the user isn't logged in? What if the user is trying to edit someone else's review? Does the view produce an error and most importantly: is the object left unchanged? It has been argued that this test is even more important than the success scenario: a failure in the success scenario will cause inconvenience for users, but will be reported. A failure in the fail scenario will cause a silent security hole that could go undetected until it's too late.

This is only a sampling of the things that can go wrong when we don't test for what happens when our systems break down. It is up to us to learn how to test for the exceptions our code my throw:

- `2scoops.co/unittest-assert-raises-docs/`
- `2scoops.co/pytest-assertions-about-expected-exceptions/`

22.3.8 Use Mock to Keep Unit Tests From Touching the World

Unit tests are not supposed to test things external to the function or method they are calling. Which means that during tests we should not access external APIs, receive emails or webhooks, or anything that is not part of of the tested action. Alas, this causes a conundrum when you are trying to write a unit test for a function that interacts with an external API.

At this point you have two choices:

- Choice #1: Change the unit test to be an Integration Test.
- Choice #2: Use the **Mock** library to fake the response from the external API.

The Mock library, created by Michael Foord, has as one of its features the capability to briefly monkey-patch libraries in order to make them return the exact value that we want. This way we are testing not the availability of the external API, but instead just the logic of our code.

In the example displayed below, we are monkey-patching a function in a mythical Ice Cream API library so our test code doesn't access anything external to our application.

Example 22.5

```
import mock
import unittest

import icecreamapi

from flavors.exceptions import CantListFlavors
from flavors.utils import list_flavors_sorted

class TestIceCreamSorting(unittest.TestCase):

    # Set up monkeypatch of icecreamapi.get_flavors()
    @mock.patch.object(icecreamapi, "get_flavors")
    def test_flavor_sort(self, get_flavors):
        # Instructs icecreamapi.get_flavors() to return an unordered list.
        get_flavors.return_value = ['chocolate', 'vanilla', 'strawberry', ]

        # list_flavors_sorted() calls the icecreamapi.get_flavors()
        #   function. Since we've monkeypatched the function,
 it will always
```

```
        #   return ['chocolate', 'strawberry', 'vanilla', ]. Which the.
        #   list_flavors_sorted() will sort alphabetically
        flavors = list_flavors_sorted()

        self.assertEqual(
            flavors,
            ['chocolate', 'strawberry', 'vanilla', ]

        )
```

Now let's demonstrate how to test the behavior of the `list_flavors_sorted()` function when the Ice Cream API is innaccessible.

Example 22.6

```
    @mock.patch.object(icecreamapi, "get_flavors")
    def test_flavor_sort_failure(self, get_flavors):
        # Instructs icecreamapi.get_flavors() to throw a FlavorError.
        get_flavors.side_effect = icecreamapi.FlavorError()

        # list_flavors_sorted() catches the icecreamapi.FlavorError()
        #   and passes on a CantListFlavors exception.
        with self.assertRaises(CantListFlavors):
            list_flavors_sorted()
```

As an added bonus for API authors, here's how we test how code handles two different **python-requests** connection problems:

Example 22.7

```
    @mock.patch.object(requests, "get")
    def test_request_failure(self, get)
        """Test if the target site is innaccessible."""
        get.side_effect = requests.exception.ConnectionError()

        with self.assertRaises(CantListFlavors):
            list_flavors_sorted()
```

```python
@mock.patch.object(requests, "get")
def test_request_failure(self, get)
    """Test if we can handle SSL problems elegantly."""
    get.side_effect = requests.exception.SSLError()

    with self.assertRaises(CantListFlavors):
        list_flavors_sorted()
```

22.3.9 Use Fancier Assertion Methods

Comparing two lists (or tuples) is a very common use case. However, if the lists are allowed to have different sort orders, then we have to sort the lists to match, then run `self.assertEqual(control_list, candidate_list)` right?

Not if we know to use **unittest**'s `ListItemsEqual()` assertion method! In fact, Python and Django's unittest documentation includes handy links to the very useful assertion types we get for free:

- https://docs.python.org/2/library/unittest.html#assert-methods
- https://docs.python.org/3/library/unittest.html#assert-methods
- https://docs.djangoproject.com/en/1.8/topics/testing/tools/#assertions

We've found the following assert methods extremely useful:

- `assertRaises`
- Python 2.7: `ListItemsEqual()`, Python 3+ `assertCountEqual()`
- `assertDictEqual()`
- `assertFormError()`
- `assertContains()` Check status 200, checks in `response.content`.
- `assertHTMLEqual()` Amongst many things, ignores whitespace differences.
- `assertJSONEqual()`

22.3.10 Document the Purpose of Each Test

Just as it is a good idea to document the purpose of a class, method, or function with docstrings, it is also a good idea to document the purpose the test analogs of these items. If undocumented code makes a project somewhat harder to maintain, undocumented test code can make a project impossible to test. To remedy this, a little bit of docstring can go a long way.

If you think this is boring, well, we've found that a good way to deal with an impossible-to-debug problem is to document the related tests. By the time the tests are documented, you have either figured out the problem or you have documented tests. Either case is a win!

22.4 What About Integration Tests?

Integration testing is when individual software modules are combined and tested as a group. This is best done after unit tests are complete. Examples of integration tests can include:

- Selenium tests to confirm that an application works in the browser.
- Actual testing against a third-party API instead of mocking responses. For example, Django Packages conducts periodic tests against GitHub, BitBucket, and PyPI API to ensure that its interaction with those systems is valid.
- Interacting with `requestb.in` or `http://httpbin.org/` to confirm the validity of outbound requests.
- Using `runscope.com` to validate that our API is working as expected.

Integration tests are a great way to confirm that 'all the pieces' are working. We can confirm that our users will see what they are supposed to see and our APIs are functioning correctly.

The downside of integration tests are:

- Setting up integration tests can take a lot of time.
- Compared to unit tests, integrations are extremely slow. That's because instead of testing the smallest components, integration tests are, by definition, testing the whole system.
- When errors are thrown by integration tests, uncovering the problem is harder than unit tests. For example, a problem affecting a single type of browser might be caused by a unicode transformation happening at the database level.
- Integration tests are fragile compared to unit tests. A small change in a component or setting can break them. We've yet to work on a significant project where at least one person seemed forever blocked from running them successfully.

Even with these problems, integration tests are useful and worth considering adding to our testing stack.

22.5 Continuous Integration

For projects of any size, we recommend setting up a continuous integration (CI) server to run the project's test suite whenever code is committed and pushed to the project repo. See chapter 32, *Continuous Integration* for more details.

22.6 Who Cares? We Don't Have Time for Tests!

"*Tests are the Programmer's stone, transmuting fear into boredom.*" –Kent Beck

Let's say you are confident of your coding skill and decide to skip testing to increase your speed of development. Or maybe you feel lazy. It's easy to argue that even with test generators and using tests instead of the shell, they can increase the time to get stuff done.

Oh, really?

What about when it's time to upgrade?

That's when the small amount of work you did up front to add tests saves you a lot of work.

For example, in the summer of 2010, Django 1.2 was the standard when we started Django Packages (`http://www.djangopackages.com`). Since then we've stayed current with new Django versions, which has been really useful. Because of our pretty good test coverage, moving up a version of Django (or the various dependencies) has been easy. Our path to upgrade:

- Upgrade the version in a local instance of Django Packages.
- Run the tests.
- Fix any errors that are thrown by the tests.
- Do some manual checking.

If Django Packages didn't have tests, any time we upgraded *anything* we would have to click through dozens and dozens of scenarios manually, which is error-prone. Having tests means we can make changes and dependency upgrades with the confidence that our users (i.e. the Django community) won't have to deal with a buggy experience.

This is the benefit of having tests.

22.7 The Game of Test Coverage

A great, fun game to play is trying get **test coverage** as high as possible. Every day that we increase our test coverage is a victory, and every day that the coverage goes down is a loss.

22.8 Setting Up the Test Coverage Game

Yes, we call test coverage a game. It's a good tool for developers to push themselves. It's also a nice metric that both developers and their clients/employers/investors can use to help evaluate the status of a project.

We advocate following these steps because most of the time we want to only test our own project's apps, not all of Django and the myriad of third-party libraries that are the building blocks of our project. Testing those 'building blocks' takes an enormous amount of time, which is a waste because most are already tested or require additional setup of resources.

22.8.1 Step 1: Start Writing Tests

We've done that already, right?

22.8.2 Step 2: Run Tests and Generate Coverage Report

Let's try it out! In the command-line, at the *<project_root>*, type:

Example 22.8

```
$ coverage run manage.py test --settings=twoscoops.settings.test
```

If we have nothing except for the default tests for two apps, we should get a response that looks like:

Example 22.9

```
Creating test database for alias "default"...
..
-----------------------------------------------
Ran 2 tests in 0.008s

OK

Destroying test database for alias "default"...
```

This doesn't look like much, but what it means is that we've constrained our application to only run the tests that you want. Now it's time to go and look at and analyze our embarrassingly low test coverage numbers.

22.8.3 Step 3: Generate the Report!

coverage.py provides a very useful method for generating HTML reports that don't just provide percentage numbers of what's been covered by tests, it also shows us the places where code is not tested. In the command-line, at the *<project_root>*:

Example 22.10

```
$ coverage html --omit="admin.py"
```

Ahem...don't forget to change *<project-root>* to match the development machine's structure! For example, depending on where one does things, the *<path-to-project-root>* could be:

- */Users/audreyr/code/twoscoops/twoscoops/*
- */Users/pydanny/projects/twoscoops/twoscoops/*
- *c:\ twoscoops*

After this runs, in the *<project_root>* directory there is a new directory called *htmlcov/*. In the *htmlcov/* directory, open the *index.html* file using any browser.

What is seen in the browser is the test results for our test run. Unless we already wrote some tests, the total on the front page will be in the single digits, if not at 0%. Click into the various modules listed and we should see lots of code that's red-colored. *Red is bad.*

Let's go ahead and admit that our project has a low coverage total. If your project has a low coverage total, you need to admit it as well. It's okay just so long as we also resolve to improve the coverage total.

In fact, there is nothing wrong in saying publicly that you are working to improve a project's test coverage. Then, other developers (including ourselves) will cheer you on!

22.9 Playing the Game of Test Coverage

The game has a single rule:

> *Mandate that no commit can lower test coverage.*

If we add a feature or bug fix and coverage is 65% when we start, we can't merge our code in until coverage is at least 65% again. At the end of each day, if test coverage goes up by any amount, it means we're winning.

Keep in mind that the gradual increase of test coverage can be a very good thing over huge jumps. Gradual increases can mean that we developers aren't putting in bogus tests to bump up coverage numbers; instead, we are improving the quality of the project.

22.10 Alternatives to unittest

All the examples in this chapter thus far have used the unittest library. While every known authority on testing agrees that unittest is a very powerful, useful tool, not all of them like it. The specific reason, and one we fully comprehend, is that it requires too much boilerplate.

Fortunately, there are alternatives that require a lot less boilerplate. These are:

- `https://pypi.python.org/pypi/pytest-django/`
- `https://pypi.python.org/pypi/django-nose`

These two libraries are wrappers around the **pytest** and **nose** libraries. In return for a little bit of extra setup, these libraries allow for not just the running of unittest-based tests, but also for running any function (and class/directory/module) prefixed with "**test_**". For example, you could write a simple test that looks like this:

EXAMPLE 22.11

```
# test_models.py
from pytest import raises

from cones.models import Cone

def test_good_choice():
    assert Cone.objects.filter(type='sugar').count() == 1

def test_bad_cone_choice():
    with raises(Cone.DoesNotExist):
        Cone.objects.get(type='spaghetti')
```

While this example is based on pytest, similar functionality can be used with nose and it's `nose.tools.raises` decorator.

A possible downside of the simplicity of these function-based tests is the lack of inheritance. If a project needs to have similar behavior over a lot of different tests, then writing tests this way may not make sense.

22.11 Summary

All of this might seem silly, but testing can be very serious business. In a lot of developer groups this subject, while gamified, is taken very seriously. Lack of stability in a project can mean the loss of clients, contracts, and even employment.

In the next chapter we cover a common obsession of Python developers: documentation.

23 Documentation: Be Obsessed

Given a choice between ice cream and writing great documentation, most Python developers would probably choose to write the documentation. That being said, writing documentation while eating ice cream is even better.

When you have great documentation tools like **reStructuredText** and **Sphinx**, you actually can't help but want to add docs to your projects.

> **PACKAGE TIP: Install Sphinx Systemwide**
>
> We've found that simply installing *Sphinx* fetches for us all the pieces you need to document our Django (or Python) project. We recommend **pip** installing Sphinx systemwide, as you'll want to have it handy for every Django project.

23.1 Use reStructuredText for Python Docs

You'll want to learn and follow the standard Python best practices for documentation. These days, reStructuredText (**RST**) is the most common *markup* language used for documenting Python projects.

What follows are links to the formal reStructuredText specification and a couple sample projects which benefit from using it:

- `http://2scoops.co/restructured-text-specification`
- `https://docs.djangoproject.com/en/1.8/`
- `http://docs.python.org`

While it's possible to study the formal documentation for reStructuredText and learn at least the basics, here is a quick primer of some very useful commands you should learn.

Example 23.1

```
Section Header
==============

**emphasis (bold/strong)**

*italics*

Simple link: http://django.2scoops.org
Fancier Link: `Two Scoops of Django`_

.. _Two Scoops of Django: https://django.2scoops.org

Subsection Header
-----------------

#) An enumerated list item

#) Second item

* First bullet

* Second bullet

  * Indented Bullet

  * Note carriage return and indents

Literal code block::

    def like():
        print("I like Ice Cream")

    for i in range(10):
        like()
```

```
Python colored code block (requires pygments):

code-block:: python

    # You need to "pip install pygments" to make this work.

    for i in range(10):
        like()

JavaScript colored code block:

code-block:: javascript

    console.log("Don't use alert()");
```

23.2 Use Sphinx to Generate Documentation From reStructuredText

Sphinx is a tool for generating nice-looking docs from your *.rst* files. Output formats include **HTML**, **LaTeX**, manual pages, and plain text.

Follow the instructions to generate Sphinx docs: http://sphinx-doc.org/.

TIP: Build Your Sphinx Documentation at Least Weekly

You never know when bad cross-references or invalid formatting can break the Sphinx build. Rather than discover that the documentation is unbuildable at an awkward moment, just make a habit of creating it on a regular basis.

23.3 What Docs Should Django Projects Contain?

Developer-facing documentation refers to notes and guides that developers need in order to set up and maintain a project. This includes notes on installation, deployment, architecture, how to run tests or submit pull requests, and more. We've found that it really helps to place this documentation in all our projects, private or public. Here we provide a table that describes what we consider the absolute minimum documentation:

Filename or Directory	Reason	Notes
README.rst	Every Python project you begin should have a README.rst file in the repository root.	Provide at least a short paragraph describing what the project does. Also, link to the installation instructions in the docs/ directory.
docs/	Your project documentation should go in one, consistent location. This is the Python community standard.	A simple directory.
docs/deployment.rst	This file lets you take a day off.	A point-by-point set of instructions on how to install/update the project into production, even if it's done via something powered by Ruby, Chef, Fabric, or a Makefile.
docs/installation.rst	This is really nice for new people coming into a project or when you get a new laptop and need to set up the project.	A point-by-point set of instructions on how to onboard yourself or another developer with the software setup for a project.
docs/architecture.rst	A guide for understanding what things evolved from as a project ages and grows in scope.	This is how you imagine a project to be in simple text and it can be as long or short as you want. Good for keeping focused at the beginning of an effort.

Table 23.1: Documentation Django Projects Should Contain

Figure 23.1: Even ice cream could benefit from documentation.

23.4 Additional Documentation Resources

- http://www.python.org/dev/peps/pep-0257 Official specification on docstrings.
- https://readthedocs.org/ Read the Docs is a free service that can host your Sphinx documentation.
- http://pythonhosted.org/ Python Hosted is another free service for documentation hosting.

23.5 The Markdown Alternative

Markdown is a plain text formatting syntax not too dissimilar to reStructuredText. While it doesn't have all the built-in features of reStructuredText, it does have the advantage of being easier to learn. While used infrequently in the Python and Django communities, it's very popular in tangential places including the JavaScript and technical book-writing community.

When using Markdown instead of reStructuredText for open source projects, keep the following in mind:

- **PyPI** will not format the `long_description` if it's written in anything except reStructuredText.
- Many Python and Django developers will search reStructuredText-powered documentation sources before Markdown-powered ones.

23.5.1 README.md to README.rst: Using Pandoc for Packages Uploaded to PyPI

Pandoc is a command-line tool that allows us to convert files from one markup format into another. We can write a README in one format, and for uploading to PyPI, display it in another. Here's how some people use pandoc in their ***setup.py*** module:

Example 23.2

```
# setup.py
import subprocess
import sys

if sys.argv[-1] == 'md2rst':
    subprocess.call('pandoc README.md -o README.rst', shell=True)
...
```

To convert a README.md to README.rst, just run `python setup.py md2rst`. Then we upload the package to PyPI as per the normal process.

23.5.2 Markdown Resources

- https://en.wikipedia.org/wiki/Markdown
- http://www.mkdocs.org/ is a static site generator geared towards project documentation written in markdown.
- http://documentup.com will host README documents written in Markdown format.
- http://progrium.viewdocs.io/ allows for Markdown documents to be organized and displayed in a Sphinx-like format. Also provides free hosting.

- http://johnmacfarlane.net/pandoc/ is a great tool for converting between Markdown to other formats, but it's not perfect. It's great for converting README.md to README.rst, which we describe in the previous subsection

23.6 Wikis and Other Documentation Methods

For whatever reason, if you can't place developer-facing documentation in the project itself, you should have other options. While wikis, online document stores, and word processing documents don't have the feature of being placed in version control, they are better than no documentation.

Please consider creating documents within these other methods with the same names as the ones we suggested in the table on the previous page.

23.7 Summary

In this chapter we went over the following:

- The use of reStructuredText to write documentation in plaintext format.
- The use Sphinx to render your documentation in HTML and EPUB formats. If you know how to install LaTeX you can even render it as PDF. For reference, installing LaTeX is easy to do on Linux and Windows and a bit harder on Mac OS X.
- Advice on the documentation requirements for any Django project.
- Using Markdown for documentation, and converting README.md to README.rst.

Next, we'll take a look at common bottlenecks in Django projects and ways to deal with them.

24 | Finding and Reducing Bottlenecks

This chapter covers a few basic strategies for identifying bottlenecks and speeding up your Django projects.

24.1 Should You Even Care?

Remember, premature optimization is bad. If your site is small- or medium-sized and the pages are loading fine, then it's okay to skip this chapter.

On the other hand, if your site's user base is growing steadily or you're about to land a strategic partnership with a popular brand, then read on.

24.2 Speed Up Query-Heavy Pages

This section describes how to reduce bottlenecks caused by having too many queries, as well as those caused by queries that aren't as snappy as they could be.

We also urge you to read up on database access optimization in the official Django docs: `http://2scoops.co/1.8-db-optimization`

24.2.1 Find Excessive Queries With Django Debug Toolbar

You can use **django-debug-toolbar** to help you determine where most of your queries are coming from. You'll find bottlenecks such as:

- Duplicate queries in a page.
- ORM calls that resolve to many more queries than you expected.
- Slow queries.

You probably have a rough idea of some of the URLs to start with. For example, which pages don't feel snappy when they load?

Install django-debug-toolbar locally if you don't have it yet. Look at your project in a web browser, and expand the SQL panel. It'll show you how many queries the current page contains.

> **PACKAGE TIP: Packages for Profiling and Performance Analysis**
>
> **django-debug-toolbar** is a critical development tool and an invaluable aid in page-by-page analysis. We also recommend adding **django-cache-panel** to your project, but only configured to run when ***settings/dev.py*** module is called. This will increase visibility into what your cache is doing.
>
> **django-extensions** comes with a tool called `RunProfileServer` that starts Django's runserver command with hotshot/profiling tools enabled.
>
> **silk** (`https://github.com/mtford90/silk`) Silk is a live profiling Django app that intercepts and stores HTTP requests and database queries before presenting them in a user interface for further inspection.

24.2.2 Reduce the Number of Queries

Once you know which pages contain an undesirable number of queries, figure out ways to reduce that number. Some of the things you can attempt:

- Try using `select_related()` in your ORM calls to combine queries. It follows `ForeignKey` relations and combines more data into a larger query. If using CBVs, **django-braces** makes doing this trivial with the `SelectRelatedMixin`. Beware of queries that get too large by explicitly passing the related field names you are interested in. Only the specified relations will be followed. Combine that with careful testing!

- For many-to-many and many-to-one relationships that can't be optimized with `select_related()`, explore using `prefetch_related()` instead.
- If the same query is being generated more than once per template, move the query into the Python view, add it to the context as a variable, and point the template ORM calls at this new context variable.
- Implement caching using a key/value store such as **Memcached**. Then write tests to assert the number of queries run in a view. See `http://2scoops.co/1.8-test-num-queries` for instructions.
- Use the `django.utils.functional.cached_property` decorator to cache in memory the result of method call for the life of an object instance. This is incredibly useful, so please see subsection 29.3.5, '`django.utils.functional.cached_property`' in chapter 29.

24.2.3 Speed Up Common Queries

The length of time it takes for individual queries can also be a bottleneck. Here are some tips, but consider them just starting points:

- Make sure your indexes are helping speed up your most common slow queries. Look at the raw SQL generated by those queries, and index on the fields that you filter/sort on most frequently. Look at the generated `WHERE` and `ORDER_BY` clauses.
- Understand what your indexes are actually doing in production. Development machines will never perfectly replicate what happens in production, so learn how to analyze and understand what's really happening with your database.
- Look at the query plans generated by common queries.
- Turn on your database's slow query logging feature and see if any slow queries occur frequently.
- Use django-debug-toolbar in development to identify potentially-slow queries defensively, before they hit production.

Once you have good indexes, and once you've done enough analysis to know which queries to rewrite, here are some starting tips on how to go about rewriting them:

1. Rewrite your logic to return smaller result sets when possible.
2. Re-model your data in a way that allows indexes to work more effectively.

❸ Drop down to raw SQL in places where it would be more efficient than the generated query.

TIP: Use EXPLAIN ANALYZE / EXPLAIN

If you're using PostgreSQL, you can use `EXPLAIN ANALYZE` to get an extremely detailed query plan and analysis of any raw SQL query. For more information, see:

- http://www.revsys.com/writings/postgresql-performance.html
- http://2scoops.co/craig-postgresql-perf2

The MySQL equivalent is the `EXPLAIN` command, which isn't as detailed but is still helpful. For more information, see:

- http://dev.mysql.com/doc/refman/5.6/en/explain.html

A nice feature of django-debug-toolbar is that the SQL pane has an `EXPLAIN` feature.

24.2.4 Switch ATOMIC_REQUESTS to False

The clear, vast majority of Django projects will run just fine with the setting of `ATOMIC_REQUESTS` to `True`. Generally, the penalty of running all database queries in a transaction isn't noticeable. However, if your bottleneck analysis points to transactions causing too much delay, it's time to change the project run as `ATOMIC_REQUESTS` to `True`. See subsection 7.7.2, 'Explicit Transaction Declaration,' for guidelines on this setting.

24.3 Get the Most Out of Your Database

You can go a bit deeper beyond optimizing database access. Optimize the database itself! Much of this is database-specific and already covered in other books, so we won't go into too much detail here.

24.3.1 Know What Doesn't Belong in the Database

Frank Wiles of Revolution Systems taught us that there are two things that should never go into any large site's relational database:

Logs. Don't add logs to the database. Logs may seem OK on the surface, especially in development. Yet adding this many writes to a production database will slow their performance. When the ability to easily perform complex queries against your logs is necessary, we recommend third-party services such as Splunk or Loggly, or use of document-based NoSQL databases.

Ephemeral data. Don't store ephemeral data in the database. What this means is data that requires constant rewrites is not ideal for use in relational databases. This includes examples such as django.contrib.sessions, django.contrib.messages, and metrics. Instead, move this data to things like Memcached, Redis, Riak, and other non-relational stores.

> **TIP: Frank Wiles on Binary Data in Databases**
>
> Actually, Frank says that there are three things to never store in a database, the third item being binary data. Storage of binary data in databases is addressed by `django.db.models.FileField`, which does the work of storing files on file servers like AWS CloudFront or S3 for you. Exceptions to this are detailed in subsection 6.2.5.

24.3.2 Getting the Most Out of PostgreSQL

If using **PostgreSQL**, be certain that it is set up correctly in production. As this is outside the scope of the book, we recommend the following articles:

- `http://wiki.postgresql.org/wiki/Detailed_installation_guides`
- `http://wiki.postgresql.org/wiki/Tuning_Your_PostgreSQL_Server`
- `http://www.revsys.com/writings/postgresql-performance.html`
- `http://2scoops.co/craig-postgresql-perf`
- `http://2scoops.co/craig-postgresql-perf2`

For further information, you may want to read the book "*PostgreSQL 9.0 High Performance*": `http://amzn.to/1fWctM2`

24.3.3 Getting the Most Out of MySQL

It's easy to get **MySQL** running, but optimizing production installations requires experience and understanding. As this is outside the scope of this book, we recommend the following book to help you:

- *"High Performance MySQL"* `http://amzn.to/188VPcL`

24.4 Cache Queries With Memcached or Redis

You can get a lot of mileage out of simply setting up Django's built-in caching system with Memcached or Redis. You will have to install one of these tools, install a package that provides Python bindings for them, and configure your project.

You can easily set up the per-site cache, or you can cache the output of individual views or template fragments. You can also use Django's low-level cache API to cache Python objects.

Reference material:

- `https://docs.djangoproject.com/en/1.8/topics/cache/`
- `https://github.com/sebleier/django-redis-cache/`

24.5 Identify Specific Places to Cache

Deciding where to cache is like being first in a long line of impatient customers at Ben and Jerry's on free scoop day. You are under pressure to make a quick decision without being able to see what any of the flavors actually look like.

Here are things to think about:

- Which views/templates contain the most queries?
- Which URLs are being requested the most?
- When should a cache for a page be invalidated?

Let's go over the tools that will help you with these scenarios.

24.6 Consider Third-Party Caching Packages

Third-party packages will give you additional features such as:

- Caching of QuerySets.
- Cache invalidation settings/mechanisms.
- Different caching backends.
- Alternative or experimental approaches to caching.

A couple of the popular Django packages for caching are:

- **django-cache-machine**
- **johnny-cache**

See `http://www.djangopackages.com/grids/g/caching/` for more options.

> **WARNING: Third-Party Caching Libraries Aren't Always the Answer**
>
> Having tried many of the third-party Django cache libraries, we have to ask our readers to test them very carefully and be prepared to drop them. They are cheap, quick wins, but can lead to some hair-raising debugging efforts at the worst possible times.
>
> Cache invalidation is hard, and in our experience, magical cache libraries are better for projects with more static content. By-hand caching is a lot more work, but leads to better performance in the long run and doesn't risk those terrifying moments.

24.7 Compression and Minification of HTML, CSS, and JavaScript

When a browser renders a web page, it usually has to load HTML, CSS, JavaScript, and image files. Each of these files consumes the user's bandwidth, slowing down page loads. One way to reduce bandwidth consumption is via compression and minification. Django even provides tools for you: `GZipMiddleware` and the **{% spaceless %}** template tag. Through the at-large Python community, we can even use **WSGI** middleware that performs the same task.

The problem with making Django and Python do the work is that compression and minification take up system resources, which can create bottlenecks of their own. A better approach is to use **Apache** and **Nginx** web servers configured to compress the outgoing content. If you are maintaining your own web servers, this is absolutely the way to go.

A very common middle approach that we endorse is to use a third-party Django library to compress and minify the CSS and JavaScript in advance. Our preference is django-pipeline which comes recommended by Django core developer Jannis Leidel.

Tools and libraries to reference:

- Apache and Nginx compression modules
- **django-pipeline**
- **django-compressor**
- **django-htmlmin**
- Django's built-in spaceless tag: `http://2scoops.co/1.8-spaceless-tag`
- `http://www.djangopackages.com/grids/g/asset-managers/`

24.8 Use Upstream Caching or a Content Delivery Network

Upstream caches such as **Varnish** are very useful. They run in front of your web server and speed up web page or content serving significantly. See `http://varnish-cache.org/`.

Content Delivery Networks (CDNs) like Fastly, Akamai, and Amazon Cloudfront serve static media such as images, video, CSS, and JavaScript files. They usually have servers all over the world, which serve out your static content from the nearest location. Using a CDN rather than serving static content from your application servers can speed up your projects.

24.9 Other Resources

Advanced techniques on scaling, performance, tuning, and optimization are beyond the scope of this book, but here are some starting points.

On general best practices for web performance:

- YSlow's *Web Performance Best Practices and Rules*:
  http://developer.yahoo.com/yslow/
- Google's Web *Performance Best Practices*:
  https://developers.google.com/speed/docs/best-practices/rules_intro

On scaling large Django sites:

- Written with a focus on scaling Django, the book "*High Performance Django*" espouses many good practices. Full of useful information and tricks, as well as questions in each section that force you to think about what you are doing.
  https://highperformancedjango.com
- David Cramer often writes and speaks about scaling Django at Disqus, Dropbox, and Sentry. Read his blog and keep an eye out for his talks, Quora posts, comments, etc.
  http://justcramer.com/
- Watch videos and slides from past DjangoCons and PyCons about different developers' experiences. Scaling practices vary from year to year and from company to company:
  http://lanyrd.com/search/?q=django+scaling

Figure 24.1: With your site running smoothly, you'll be feeling as cool as a cone.

TIP: For Sites With High Volume: High Performance Django

We want to reiterate that "High Performance Django" is worth getting if your site has enough traffic to cause issues. Peter Baumgartner and Yann Malet have written a good book, one that you should consider purchasing.

- https://highperformancedjango.com
- amazon.com/High-Performance-Django/dp/1508748128/

24.10 Summary

In this chapter we explored a number of bottleneck reduction strategies including:

- Whether you should even care about bottlenecks in the first place.
- Profiling your pages and queries.
- Optimizing queries.
- Using your database wisely.
- Caching queries.
- Identifying what needs to be cached.
- Compression of HTML, CSS, and JavaScript.
- Exploring other resources.

In the next chapter, we'll cover various practices involving **asynchronous task queues**, which may resolve our bottleneck problems.

25 Asynchronous Task Queues

An **asynchronous task queue** is one where tasks are executed at a different time from when they are created, and possibly not in the same order they were created. Here is an example of a human-powered asynchronous task queue:

1. In their spare time, Audrey and Daniel make ice cream cakes, taking orders from friends and family. They use an issue tracker to track their tasks for scooping, spreading, and decorating each cake.
2. Every so often, when they have spare time, they review the list of tasks and pick one to do. Audrey prefers scooping and decorating, always doing those tasks first. Daniel prefers scooping and spreading, finishing those before decorating. The result is asynchronous completion of cake-making tasks.
3. As a cake-making task is completed and delivered, they mark the issue as closed.

> ### TIP: Task Queue vs Asynchronous Task Queue
>
> In the Django world, both terms are used to describe **asynchronous task queue**. When someone writes *task queue* in the context of Django, they usually mean *asynchronous task queue*.

Before we get into best practices, let's go over some definitions:

Broker The storage for the tasks themselves. This can be implemented using any sort of persistence tool, although in Django the most common ones in use are **RabbitMQ** and **Redis**. In the human-powered example, the storage is an online issue tracker.

Producer The code that adds tasks to the queue to be executed later. This is application code, the stuff that makes up a Django project. In the human-powered example, this would be Audrey and Daniel, plus anyone they can get to pitch in to help.

Worker The code that takes tasks from the broker and performs them. Usually there is more than one worker. Most commonly each worker runs as a daemon under supervision. In the human-powered example, this is Audrey and Daniel.

25.1 Do We Need a Task Queue?

It depends. They add complexity but can really help user experience. Arguably it comes down to whether a particular piece of code causes a bottleneck and can be delayed for later when more free CPU cycles are available.

Here is a useful rule of thumb for determining if a task queue should be used:

Results take time to process: Task queue *should* probably be used.
Users can and should see results immediately: Task queue *should* not be used.

Let's go over some possible use cases:

Use Task Queue?	Issue
Yes	Sending bulk email
Yes	Modifying files (including images)
Yes	Fetching large amounts of data from third-party Ice Cream APIs
Yes	Inserting or updating a lot of records into a table
No	Updating a user profile
No	Adding a blog or CMS entry
Yes	Performing time-intensive calculations
Yes	Sending or receiving of webhooks

Table 25.1: Should a Project Have a Task Queue?

Please keep in mind there are site-traffic driven exceptions to all of these use cases:

- Sites with small-to-medium amounts of traffic may never need a task queue for any of these actions.
- Sites with larger amounts of traffic may discover that nearly every user action requires use of a task queue.

Determining whether or not a site or action needs a task is a bit of an art. There is no easy answer we can provide. However, knowing how to use them is a really powerful tool in any developer's toolkit.

25.2 Choosing Task Queue Software

Celery, Redis Queue, django-background-tasks, which to choose? Let's go over their pros and cons:

Software	Pros	Cons
`Celery`	Defacto Django standard, many different storage types, flexible, full-featured, great for high volume	Challenging setup, overkill for slower traffic sites
`Redis Queue`	Flexible, powered by Redis, lower memory footprint then Celery, great for high volume, can use django-rq or not	Not as many features as Celery, medium difficulty setup, Redis only option for storage
`django-background-tasks`	Very easy setup, easy to use, good for small volume or batch jobs, uses Django ORM for backend	Uses Django ORM for backend, absolutely terrible for medium-to-high volume

Table 25.2: Comparing Task Queue Software

Here is our general rule of thumb:

- For most high-to-low volume projects, we recommend Redis Queue.
- For high-volume projects with the need for complex task management, we recommend Celery.
- For small volume projects, especially for running of periodic batch jobs, we recommend django-background-tasks

Of course, your own experience and knowledge should be used to determine which task queue system you use for a project. For example, if you have a good amount of Celery experience and are comfortable with it, then by all means use it for small volume or toy projects.

25.3 Best Practices for Task Queues

While each of the different task queue packages has their own quirks, there are some constants we can apply to all of them. A nice feature about these practices is that they help with the portability of your task functions. This can be incredibly useful when that low traffic django-background-tasks powered site becomes high traffic and has to be converted to use Celery or Redis Queue.

25.3.1 Treat Tasks Like Views

Throughout this book we recommend that views contain as little code as possible, calling methods and functions from other places in the code base. We believe the same thing applies to tasks.

A common trap is for the code inside task functions to become long and ugly, because the assumption is that "the task queue hides it from the user." We've been guilty of this ourselves. To avoid this, you can put your task code into a function, put that function into a helper module, and then call that function from a task function.

All task queue packages do some kind of serialization/abstraction of our task functions and their arguments. This makes debugging them that much more difficult. By using our task functions to call more easily tested normal functions, we not only make writing and debugging our code easier, we also encourage more reuse.

25.3.2 Tasks Aren't Free

Remember that the memory and resources to process a task have to come from somewhere. Overly resource-heavy tasks might be hidden, but they can still cause site problems.

Even if resource-intensive code is executed from a task, it should still be written as cleanly as possible, minimizing any unnecessary resource usage. Optimization and profiling can help here.

25.3.3 Only Pass JSON-Serializable Values to Task Functions

Just like views, for task function arguments, only pass JSON-serializable values. That limits us to integers, floats, strings, lists, tuples, and dictionaries. Don't pass in complex objects. Here's why:

1. Passing in an object representing persistent data (ORM instances for example can cause a race condition. This is when the underlying persistent data changes before the task is run. Instead, pass in a primary key or some other identifier that can be used to call fresh data.
2. Passing in complex objects that have to be serialized into the task queue is time and memory consuming. This is counter-productive to the benefits we're trying to achieve by using a task queue.
3. We've found debugging JSON-serializable values easier than debugging more complex objects.
4. Depending on the task queue in use, only JSON-serializable primitives are accepted.

25.3.4 Learn How to Monitor Tasks and Workers

Gaining visibility into the status of tasks and workers is critical for debugging of task functions. Some useful tools:

- Celery: `https://pypi.python.org/pypi/flower`
- Redis Queue: `https://pypi.python.org/pypi/django-redisboard` for using Redis Queue directly.
- Redis Queue: `https://pypi.python.org/pypi/django-rq` for using django-rq.
- `django.contrib.admin` for django-background-tasks.

25.3.5 Logging!

Since task queues are working "behind the scenes," it can be hard to determine exactly what is going on. This is where logging (chapter 27) and tools like Sentry become really useful. In error-prone task code, it can be a good idea to log inside of each task function. This will make debugging production code easier.

25.3.6 Monitor the Backlog

As traffic increases, tasks can pile up if there aren't enough workers. When we see this happening, it's time to increase the number of workers. If our software only has one worker (django-background-tasks), then it is time to upgrade to Celery or Redis Queue.

25.3.7 Periodically Clear Out Dead Tasks

Sometimes a task is passed into a queue and then just sits there doing nothing for some reason. It could be caused by a bug, e.g. a resource being used by the task might no longer exist. However these things happen, they can build up over time, taking up space in our system.

Learn how your software cleans out dead tasks, and check to make sure it's running properly.

25.3.8 Ignore Results We Don't Need

When a task completes, the broker is designed to record whether it succeeded or failed. While useful for statistical purposes, this exit status is not the result of the job the task was performing. As recording this status takes up time and storage space, it's a feature we usually turn off.

25.3.9 Use the Queue's Error Handling

What happens when a task fails? It can be caused by a network error, a third-party API going down, or anything else that can be imagined. Look up how to do the following for your task queue software and learn how to set them:

- Max retries for a task
- Retry delays

Retry delays deserve a lot of consideration. When a task fails, we like to wait at least 10 seconds before trying again. Even better, if the task queue software allows it, increase the delay each time an attempt is made. We set things this way in order to give the conditions that caused a failure to resolve themselves.

25.3.10 Learn the Features of Your Task Queue Software

Celery and Redis Queue allow for definition of multiple queues, whereas django-background-tasks does not. Celery has fancy routing features that no other software package possesses.

If we don't take the time to explore, learn, and use these features, we're losing out on lots of secret sauce. Staying ignorant of these features can mean that instead of leaning on our package of choice, we end up writing code that duplicates what the package provides.

25.4 Resources for Task Queues

General:

- http://www.fullstackpython.com/task-queues.html
- http://www.2scoops.co/why-task-queues/ Slide presentation
- https://pypi.python.org/pypi/django-transaction-hooks
  Django database backends that permit registering post-transaction-commit hooks.

Celery:

- http://celeryproject.com Homepage of Celery
- https://denibertovic.com/posts/celery-best-practices/ Must-read article for anyone learning Celery
- https://pypi.python.org/pypi/flower A web-based tool for managing Celery clusters
- http://wiredcraft.com/blog/3-gotchas-for-celery/
- https://www.caktusgroup.com/blog/2014/06/23/scheduling-tasks-celery/

Redis-Queue:

- http://python-rq.org/ Homepage of Redis Queue
- http://racingtadpole.com/blog/redis-queue-with-django/

django-background-tasks:

- https://pypi.python.org/pypi/django-background-tasks

25.5 Summary

In this chapter we explored high-level practices for working with task queues. Because of the abstraction involved in using them, we advocate treating them like views, minimizing the amount of business logic within.

In the next chapter, we'll go over the basics of securing Django projects.

26 Security Best Practices

When it comes to security, Django has a pretty good record. This is due to security tools provided by Django, solid documentation on the subject of security, and a thoughtful team of core developers who are extremely responsive to security issues. However, it's up to individual Django developers such as ourselves to understand how to properly secure Django-powered applications.

This chapter contains a list of things helpful for securing your Django application. This list is by no means complete. Consider it a starting point.

26.1 Harden Your Servers

Search online for instructions and checklists for server hardening. Server hardening measures include but are not limited to things like changing your SSH port and disabling/removing unnecessary services.

26.2 Know Django's Security Features

Django 1.8's security features include:

- Cross-site scripting (XSS) protection.
- Cross-site request forgery (CSRF) protection.
- SQL injection protection.
- Clickjacking protection.
- Support for TLS/HTTPS/HSTS, including secure cookies.
- Secure password storage, using the PBKDF2 algorithm with a SHA256 hash by default.

- Automatic HTML escaping.
- An expat parser hardened against XML bomb attacks.
- Hardened JSON, YAML, and XML serialization/deserialization tools.

Most of Django's security features "just work" out of the box without additional configuration, but there are certain things that you'll need to configure. We've highlighted some of these details in this chapter, but please make sure that you read the official Django documentation on security as well: `https://docs.djangoproject.com/en/1.8/topics/security/`

26.3 Turn Off DEBUG Mode in Production

Your production site should not be running in **DEBUG** mode. Attackers can find out more than they need to know about your production setup from a helpful `DEBUG` mode stack trace page. For more information, see `http://www.2scoops.co/1.8-settings-debug/`.

Keep in mind that when you turn off DEBUG mode, you will need to set **ALLOWED_HOSTS** or risk raising a `SuspiciousOperation` error, which generates a 500 error that can be hard to debug. For more information on setting/debugging `ALLOWED_HOSTS` see:

- section 26.6, 'Use Django 1.8's Allowed Hosts Validation'
- subsection 33.2.4, 'That Troublesome `ALLOWED_HOSTS` Error'

26.4 Keep Your Secret Keys Secret

If your `SECRET_KEY` setting is not secret, this means you risk everything from remote code execution to password hacking. Your API keys and other secrets should be carefully guarded as well. These keys should not even be kept in version control.

We cover the mechanics of how to keep your `SECRET_KEY` out of version control in chapter 5, *Settings and Requirements Files*, section 5.3, 'Keep Secret Keys Out With Environment Variables,' and section 5.4, 'Loading Secrets from Files Instead of From Environment Variables.'

26.5 HTTPS Everywhere

It is always better to deploy a site behind HTTPS. Not having HTTPS means that malicious network users can sniff authentication credentials between your site and end users. In fact, all data sent between your site and end users is up for grabs.

There is also no guarantee that any of your users are seeing what you expect them to see: an attacker could manipulate anything in the request or the response. So HTTPS makes sense even if all your information is public, but you do care about the integrity of the information.

Your entire site should be behind HTTPS. Your site's static resources should also be served via HTTPS, otherwise visitors will get warnings about "insecure resources" which should rightly scare them away from your site. For reference, these warnings exist because they are a potential man-in-the-middle vector.

TIP: Jacob Kaplan-Moss on HTTPS vs HTTP

Django co-leader Jacob Kaplan-Moss says, "Your whole site should only be available via HTTPS, not HTTP at all. This prevents getting "firesheeped" (having a session cookie stolen when served over HTTP). The cost is usually minimal."

If visitors try to access your site via HTTP, they should be redirected to HTTPS. This can be done either through configuration of your web server or with Django middleware. Performance-wise, it's better to do this at the web server level, but if you don't have control over your web server settings for this, then redirecting via Django middleware is fine.

TIP: Use django.middleware.security.SecurityMiddleware

The tool of choice for projects on Django 1.8+ for enforcing HTTPS/SSL across an entire site through middleware is built right in. To activate this middleware just follow these steps:

1. Add `django.middleware.security.SecurityMiddleware` to the `settings.MIDDLEWARE_CLASSES` definition.
2. Set `settings.SECURE_SSL_HOST` to `True`.

WARNING: django.middleware.security.SecurityMiddleware Does Not Include static/media

As JavaScript, CSS, images, and other static assets are typically served directly by the web server (nginx, Apache), make certain that serving of such content is done via HTTPS. Providers of static assets such as Amazon S3 now do this by default.

You should purchase an SSL certificate from a reputable source rather than creating a self-signed certificate. To set it up, follow the instructions for your particular web server or platform-as-a-service.

26.5.1 Use Secure Cookies

Your site should inform the target browser to never send cookies unless via HTTPS. You'll need to set the following in your settings:

Example 26.1

```
SESSION_COOKIE_SECURE = True
CSRF_COOKIE_SECURE = True
```

Read https://docs.djangoproject.com/en/1.8/topics/security/#ssl-https for more details.

26.5.2 Use HTTP Strict Transport Security (HSTS)

HSTS can be configured at the web server level. Follow the instructions for your web server, platform-as-a-service, and Django itself (via `settings.SECURE_HSTS_SECONDS`).

WARNING: Choose Your HSTS Policy Duration Carefully

Remember that HSTS is a one-way switch. It's a declaration that for the next N seconds, your site will be HTTPS-only. Don't set a HSTS policy with a `max-age` longer than you are able to maintain. Browsers do not offer an easy way to unset it.

If you have set up your own web servers, Wikipedia has sample HSTS configuration snippets that you can use: https://en.wikipedia.org/wiki/HTTP_Strict_Transport_Security

When you enable HSTS, your site's web pages include a HTTP header that tells HSTS-compliant browsers to only connect to the site via secure connections:

- HSTS-compliant browsers will redirect HTTP links to HTTPS.
- If a secure connection isn't possible (e.g. the certificate is self-signed or expired), an error message will be shown and access will be disallowed.

To give you a better idea of how this works, here's an example of what a HTTP Strict Transport Security response header might look like:

EXAMPLE 26.2

```
-Strict-Transport-Security: max-age=31536000; includeSubDomains
```

Some HSTS configuration advice:

1. You should use HSTS' `includeSubDomains` mode if you can. This prevents attacks involving using non-secured subdomains to write cookies for the parent domain.
2. Set `max-age` to a small value like 3600 (1 hour) during initial deployment of a secured site to make sure you haven't screwed something up or forgotten to make some portion of the site available via HTTPS. We suggest this small value because once you set `max-age`, you can't unset it for users; their browsers control expiration, not you.
3. Once you've confirmed that your site is properly secured, set `max-age` to a large value like 31536000 (12 months) or 63072000 (24 months) if you can.

Note that HSTS should be enabled *in addition* to redirecting all pages to HTTPS as described earlier.

WARNING: Additional Warning for `includeSubDomains`

We recommend everyone to use HSTS with a long duration and to use `includeSubDomains`. However, especially in projects with lots of legacy componentss, the combination requires great care when configuring.

Example: Imagine we create a new Django website called *example.com*. Of course, the site is HTTPS with HSTS. We test the HSTS settings, which work fine, and then increase the duration to a year. Alas, after a month, someone realises *legacy.example.com* is still a production service and does not support HTTPS. We remove `includeSubdomains` from the header, but by now it's already too late: all clients inside the company have the old HSTS header remembered.

In short, before even considering `includeSubdomains`, one should be entirely aware of what might be hosted under the domain that HSTS is configured on.

26.5.3 HTTPS Configuration Tools

Mozilla provides a SSL configuration generator at the `2scoops.co/mozilla-ssl-config-generator`, which can provide a starting point for your own configuration. While not perfect, it expedites setting up HTTPS. As our security reviewers say, "In general, any HTTPS is better than plain HTTP."

Once you have a server set up (preferably a test server), use the Qualys SSL Labs server test at `https://www.ssllabs.com/ssltest/` to see how well you did. A fun security game is trying to score an **A+**. Especially as the official Two Scoops of Django reward for getting that good of a grade is a trip to the local favorite ice cream saloon.

26.6 Use Allowed Hosts Validation

In production you must set `ALLOWED_HOSTS` in your settings to a list of allowed host/domain names in order to avoid raising `SuspiciousOperation` exceptions. This is a security measure to prevent use of fake HTTP host headers to submit requests.

We recommend that you avoid setting wildcard values here. For more information, read the Django documentation on `ALLOWED_HOSTS` and the `get_host()` method:

- http://2scoops.co/1.8-allowed-hosts
- http://2scoops.co/1.8-get_host

26.7 Always Use CSRF Protection With HTTP Forms That Modify Data

Django comes with easy-to-use cross-site request forgery protection (CSRF) built in, and by default it is activated across the site via the use of middleware. We have some strong recommendations discussed in section 11.3, 'Always Use CSRF Protection With HTTP Forms That Modify Data'.

26.8 Prevent Against Cross-Site Scripting (XSS) Attacks

XSS attacks usually occur when users enter malignant JavaScript that is then rendered into a template directly. This isn't the only method, but it is the most common. Fortunately for us, Django by default escapes <, >, `'`, `"`, and `&`, which is all that is needed for proper HTML escaping.

The following are recommended by the Django security team:

26.8.1 Use Django Templates Over mark_safe

Django gives developers the ability to mark content strings as safe, meaning that Django's own safeguards are taken away. Even for small snippets of HTML, try to use the template rendering system, rather than `mark_safe`.

26.8.2 Don't Allow Users to Set Individual HTML Tag Attributes

If you allow users to set individual attributes of HTML tags, that gives them a venue for injecting malignant JavaScript.

26.8.3 Use JSON Encoding for Data Consumed by JavaScript

Rely on JSON encoding rather than finding ways to dump Python structures directly to templates. It's not just easier to integrate into client-side JavaScript, it's also safer.

26.8.4 Additional Reading

There are other avenues of attack that can occur, so educating yourself is important.

- http://2scoops.co/1.8-docs-on-html-escaping
- http://en.wikipedia.org/wiki/Cross-site_scripting

26.9 Defend Against Python Code Injection Attacks

We once were hired to help with a project that had some security issues. The requests coming into the site were being converted from `django.http.HttpRequest` objects directly into strings via creative use of the `str()` function, then saved to a database table. Periodically, these archived Django requests would be taken from the database and converted into Python dicts via the `eval()` function. This meant that arbitrary Python code could be run on the site at any time.

Needless to say, upon discovery the critical security flaw was quickly removed. This just goes to show that no matter how secure Python and Django might be, we always need to be aware that certain practices are incredibly dangerous.

26.9.1 Python Built-Ins That Execute Code

Beware of the `eval()`, `exec()`, and `execfile()` built-ins. If your project allows arbitrary strings or files to be passed into any of these functions, you are leaving your system open to attack.

For more information, read "Eval Really Is Dangerous" by Ned Batchelder:
http://nedbatchelder.com/blog/201206/eval_really_is_dangerous.html

26.9.2 Python Standard Library Modules That Can Execute Code

> *"Never unpickle data received from an untrusted or unauthenticated source."*
>
> – http://docs.python.org/2/library/pickle.html

You should not use the Python standard library's `pickle` module to deserialize anything which could have been modified by the user. As a general rule, avoid accepting pickled values from user for any reason. Specific warnings about `pickle` and security are listed below:

- https://lincolnloop.com/blog/playing-pickle-security/
- https://blog.nelhage.com/2011/03/exploiting-pickle/

26.9.3 Third-Party Libraries That Can Execute Code

When using PyYAML, only use `safe_load()`. While the use of **YAML** in the Python and Django communities is rare, it's not uncommon to receive this format from other services. Therefore, if you are accepting YAML documents, only load them with the `yaml.safe_load()` method.

For reference, the `yaml.load()` method will let you create Python objects, *which is really bad.* As Ned Batchelder says, `yaml.load()` should be renamed to `yaml.dangerous_load()`: http://nedbatchelder.com/blog/201302/war_is_peace.html

26.9.4 Be Careful With Cookie-Based Sessions

Typically most Django sites use either database- or cache-based sessions. These function by storing a hashed random value in a cookie which is used as a key to the real session value, which is stored in the database or cache. The advantage of this is that only the key to the session data is sent to the client, making it very challenging for malignant coders to penetrate Django's session mechanism.

However, Django sites can also be built using cookie-based sessions, which place the session data entirely on the client's machine. While this means slightly less storage needs for the server, it comes with security issues that justify caution. Specifically:

❶ It is possible for users to read the contents of cookie-based sessions.

❷ If an attacker gains access to a project's `SECRET_KEY` and your session serializer is JSON-based, they gain the ability to falsify session data and therefore, if authentication is used, impersonate any user.

❸ If an attacker gains access to a project's `SECRET_KEY` and your session serializer is pickle-based, they gain the ability to not only falsify session data and also execute arbitrary code. In other words, not only can they assume new rights and privileges, they can also upload working Python code. If you are using pickle-based sessions or are considering using them, please read the tip below.

❹ Another disadvantage of this configuration is that sessions can't be invalidated in a guaranteed way (except when they expire): you can try to override the cookie in the browser with a new value, but you can't enforce an attacker to use it: if they continue sending requests with the old cookie, the session backend won't know the difference.

TIP: Use JSON for Cookie-Based Sessions

The default cookie serializer for Django is JSON-based, meaning that even if an attacker discovers a project's `SECRET_KEY`, they can't execute arbitrary code. If you decide to write your own cookie serializer, stick to using JSON as the format.
Never, ever use the optional `pickle` serializer.

Resources on the subject:

- http://2scoops.co/1.8-http-session-serialization
- http://2scoops.co/1.8-settings-session-serializer

Another thing to consider is that cookie-based sessions are a potential client-side performance bottleneck. Transmitting the session data server-to-client is generally not an issue, but client-to-server transmissions are much, much slower. This is literally the difference between download and upload speeds all internet users encounter.

In general, we try to avoid cookie-based sessions.

Additional reading:

- http://2scoops.co/1.8-cookie-based-sessions
- http://2scoops.co/django-session-based-cookies-alert
- http://yuiblog.com/blog/2007/03/01/performance-research-part-3/

26.10 Validate All Incoming Data With Django Forms

Django forms should be used to validate all data being brought into your project, including from non-web sources. Doing so protects the integrity of our data and is part of securing your application. We cover this in section 11.1, "Validate All Incoming Data With Django Forms".

26.11 Disable the Autocomplete on Payment Fields

You should disable the HTML field autocomplete browser feature on fields that are gateways to payment. This includes credit card numbers, CVVs, PINs, credit card dates, etc. The reason is that a lot of people use public computers or their personal computers in public venues.

For reference, Django forms make this easy:

Example 26.3

```
from django import forms

class SpecialForm(forms.Form):
    my_secret = forms.CharField(
            widget=forms.TextInput(attrs={'autocomplete': 'off'}))
```

For any site that might be used in a public area (an airport for example), consider changing the form field itself to `PasswordInput`:

Example 26.4

```
from django import forms

class SecretInPublicForm(forms.Form):

    my_secret = forms.CharField(widget=forms.PasswordInput())
```

26.12 Handle User-Uploaded Files Carefully

The only way to completely safely serve user-provided content is from a completely separate domain. For better or worse, there are an infinite number of ways to bypass file type validators.

This is why security experts recommend the use of **content delivery networks** (CDNs): they serve as a place to store potentially dangerous files.

If you must allow upload and download of arbitrary file types, make sure that the server uses the "`Content-Disposition: attachment`" header so that browsers won't display the content inline.

26.12.1 When a CDN Is Not an Option

When this occurs, uploaded files must be saved to a directory that does not allow them to be executed. In addition, at the very least make sure the HTTP server is configured to serve images with image content type headers, and that uploads are restricted to a whitelisted subset of file extensions.

Take extra care with your web server's configuration here, because a malicious user can try to attack your site by uploading an executable file like a CGI or PHP script and then accessing the URL. This won't solve every problem, but it's better than the defaults.

Consult your web server's documentation for instructions on how to configure this, or consult the documentation for your platform-as-a-service for details about how static assets and user-uploaded files should be stored.

26.12.2 Django and User-Uploaded Files

Django has two model fields that allow for user uploads: `FileField` and `ImageField`. They come with some built-in validation, but the Django docs also strongly advise you to "pay close attention to where you're uploading them and what type of files they are, to avoid security holes."

If you are only accepting uploads of certain file types, do whatever you can do to ensure that the user is only uploading files of those types. For example, you can:

- Use the **python-magic** library to check the uploaded file's headers:
  https://github.com/ahupp/python-magic

- Validate the file with a Python library that specifically works with that file type. Unfortunately this isn't documented, but if you dig through Django's `ImageField` source code, you can see how Django uses PIL to validate that uploaded image files are in fact images.
- Use **defusedxml** instead of native Python XML libraries or lxml. See section 26.22.

WARNING: Custom Validators Aren't the Answer Here

Don't just write a custom validator and expect it to validate your uploaded files before dangerous things happen. Custom validators are run against field content after they've already been coerced to Python by the field's `to_python()` method.

If the contents of an uploaded file are malicious, any validation happening after `to_python()` is executed may be too late.

Further reading:

- https://docs.djangoproject.com/en/1.8/ref/models/fields/#filefield

26.13 Don't Use ModelForms.Meta.exclude

When using `ModelForms`, always use `Meta.fields`. Never use `Meta.exclude`. The use of `Meta.exclude` is considered a grave security risk, specifically a **Mass Assignment Vulnerability**. *We can't stress this strongly enough. Don't do it.*

One common reason we want to avoid the `Meta.exclude` attribute is that its behavior implicitly allows all model fields to be changed except for those that we specify. When using the excludes attribute, if the model changes after the form is written, we have to remember to change the form. If we forget to change the form to match the model changes, we risk catastrophe.

Let's use an example to show how this mistake could be made. We'll start with a simple ice cream store model:

Example 26.5

```
# stores/models.py
from django.conf import settings
```

```
from django.db import models

class Store(models.Model):
    title = models.CharField(max_length=255)
    slug = models.SlugField()
    owner = models.ForeignKey(settings.AUTH_USER_MODEL)
    # Assume 10 more fields that cover address and contact info.
```

Here is the *wrong way* to define the `ModelForm` fields for this model:

Bad Example 26.1

```
# DON'T DO THIS!
from django import forms

from .models import Store

class StoreForm(forms.ModelForm):

    class Meta:
        model = Store
        # DON'T DO THIS: Implicit definition of fields.
        #                Too easy to make mistakes!
        excludes = ("pk", "slug", "modified", "created", "owner")
```

In contrast, this is the *right way* to define the same `ModelForm`'s fields:

Example 26.6

```
from django import forms

from .models import Store

class StoreForm(forms.ModelForm):

    class Meta:
        model = Store
        # Explicitly specifying the fields we want
```

```
        fields = (
            "title", "address_1", "address_2", "email",
            "usstate", "postal_code", "city",
        )
```

The first code example, as it involves less typing, appears to be the better choice. It's not, as when you add a new model field you now you need to track the field in multiple locations (one model and one or more forms).

Let's demonstrate this in action. Perhaps after launch we decide we need to have a way of tracking store co-owners, who have all the same rights as the owner. They can access account information, change passwords, place orders, and specify banking information. The store model receives a new field as shown on the next page:

Example 26.7

```
# stores/models.py
from django.conf import settings
from django.db import models

class Store(models.Model):
    title = models.CharField(max_length=255)
    slug = models.SlugField()
    owner = models.ForeignKey(settings.AUTH_USER_MODEL)
    co_owners = models.ManyToManyField(settings.AUTH_USER_MODEL)
    # Assume 10 more fields that cover address and contact info.
```

The first form code example which we warned against using relies on us to remember to alter it to include the new `co_owners` field. If we forget, then anyone accessing that store's HTML form can add or remove co-owners. While we might remember a single form, what if we have more than one `ModelForm` for a model? In complex applications this is not uncommon.

On the other hard, in the second example, where we used `Meta.fields` we know exactly what fields each form is designed to handle. Changing the model doesn't alter what the form exposes, and we can sleep soundly knowing that our ice cream store data is more secure.

26.13.1 Mass Assignment Vulnerabilities

The problem we describe in this section is a **Mass Assignment Vulnerability**.

These occur when the patterns such as Active Record, designed to empower developers, create security risks for web applications. The solution is the approach we advocate in this section, which is explicit definition of fields that can be modified.

See https://en.wikipedia.org/wiki/Mass_assignment_vulnerability for more detail.

26.14 Don't Use `ModelForms.Meta.fields = "__all__"`

This includes every model field in your model form. It's a shortcut, and a dangerous one. It's very similar to what we describe in section 26.13, and even with custom validation code, exposes projects to form-based Mass Assignment Vulnerabilities. We advocate avoiding this technique as much as possible, as we feel that it's simply impossible to catch all variations of input.

26.15 Beware of SQL Injection Attacks

The Django ORM generates properly-escaped SQL which will protect your site from users attempting to execute malignant, arbitrary SQL code.

Django allows you to bypass its ORM and access the database more directly through raw SQL. When using this feature, be especially careful to escape your SQL code properly. This is of concern in these specific components of Django:

- The `.raw()` ORM method.
- The `.extra()` ORM method.
- Directly accessing the database cursor.

Reference:

- http://www.2scoops.co/1.8-sql-injection-protection/

26.16 Never Store Credit Card Data

Unless you have a strong understanding of the PCI-DSS security standards (`https://www.pcisecuritystandards.org/`) and adequate time/resources/funds to validate your PCI compliance, storing credit card data is too much of a liability and should be avoided.

Instead, we recommend using third-party services like Stripe, Braintree, Adyen, PayPal, and others that handle storing this information for you, and allow you to reference the data via special tokens. Most of these services have great tutorials, are very Python and Django friendly, and are well worth the time and effort to incorporate into your project.

> **TIP: Educate Yourself on PCI Compliance**
>
> Ken Cochrane has written an excellent blog post on PCI compliance. Please read `http://2scoops.co/guide-to-pci-compliant-web-apps`

> **TIP: Read the Source Code of Open Source E-Commerce Solutions**
>
> If you are planning to use any of the existing open source Django e-commerce solutions, examine how the solution handles payments. If credit card data is being stored in the database, even encrypted, then please consider using another solution.

26.17 Secure the Django Admin

Since the Django admin gives your site admins special powers that ordinary users don't have, it's good practice to make it extra secure.

26.17.1 Change the Default Admin URL

By default, the admin URL is *yoursite.com/admin/*. Change it to something that's long and difficult to guess.

> **TIP: Jacob Kaplan-Moss Talks About Changing the Admin URL**
>
> Django project co-leader Jacob Kaplan-Moss says (paraphrased) that it's an easy additional layer of security to come up with a different name (or even different domain) for the admin.
>
> It also prevents attackers from easily profiling your site. For example, attackers can tell which version of Django you're using, sometimes down to the point-release level, by examining the content of ***admin/*** on a project.

26.17.2 Use django-admin-honeypot

If you're particularly concerned about people trying to break into your Django site, **django-admin-honeypot** is a package that puts a fake Django admin login screen at ***admin/*** and logs information about anyone who attempts to log in.

See `https://github.com/dmpayton/django-admin-honeypot` for more information.

26.17.3 Only Allow Admin Access via HTTPS

This is already implied in the "Use SSL/HTTPS in Production" section, but we want to especially emphasize here that your admin needs to be SSL-secured. If your site allows straight HTTP access, you will need to run the admin on a properly-secured domain, adding to the complexity of your deployment. Not only will you need a second deployment procedure, but you'll need to include logic in your URLConf in order to remove the admin from HTTP access. In the experience of the authors, it's much easier to put the whole site on SSL/HTTPS.

Without SSL, if you log into your Django admin on an open WiFi network, it's trivial for someone to sniff your admin username/password.

26.17.4 Limit Admin Access Based on IP

Configure your web server to only allow access to the Django admin to certain IP addresses. Look up the instructions for your particular web server.

- Nginx instructions http://tech.marksblogg.com/django-admin-logins.html

An acceptable alternative is to put this logic into middleware. It's better to do it at the web server level because every middleware component adds an extra layer of logic wrapping your views, but in some cases this can be your only option. For example, your platform-as-a-service might not give you fine-grain control over web server configuration.

26.17.5 Use the allow_tags Attribute With Caution

The `allow_tags` attribute, which is set to `False` by default, can be a security issue. When `allow_tags` is set to `True`, in conjunction with `django.utils.html.format_html`, HTML tags are allowed to be displayed in the admin.

Our hard rule is `allow_tags` can only be used on system-generated data like primary keys, dates, and calculated values. Data such as character and text fields are completely out, as is any other user-entered data.

26.18 Secure the Admin Docs

Since the Django admin docs give your site admins a view into how the project is constructed, it's good practice to keep them extra-secure just like the Django admin. Borrowing from the previous section on the Django admin, we advocate the following:

- Changing the admin docs URL to something besides *yoursite.com/admin/doc/*.
- Only allowing admin docs access via HTTPS.
- Limiting admin docs access based on IP.

26.19 Monitor Your Sites

Check your web servers' access and error logs regularly. Install monitoring tools and check on them frequently. Keep an eye out for suspicious activity.

26.20 Keep Your Dependencies Up-to-Date

You should always update your projects to work with the latest stable release of Django and third-party dependencies. This is particularly important when a release includes security fixes. For that, we recommend `requires.io`, which automatically checks requirements files against the latest versions that PyPI provides.

> 'I've set up `requires.io` for distinct actions: it mails me once a week for each project with any outdated dependencies, and if it finds an insecure version it automatically creates a pull request in GitHub, so tests run automatically and I can deploy quickly.'
>
> – Erik Romijn, Django core and security reviewer for Two Scoops of Django 1.8

Useful links for updates to Django itself.

- The official Django weblog at `https://www.djangoproject.com/weblog/`
- The official django-announce mailing list at `http://2scoops.co/django-announce`

26.21 Prevent Clickjacking

Clickjacking is when a malicious site tricks users to click on a concealed element of another site that they have loaded in a hidden frame or iframe. An example is a site with a false social media 'login' button that is really a purchase button on another site.

Django has instructions and components to prevent this from happening:

- `https://docs.djangoproject.com/en/1.8/ref/clickjacking/`

26.22 Guard Against XML Bombing With defusedxml

Attacks against XML libraries are nothing new. For example, the amusingly titled but devastating 'Billion Laughs' attack (`http://en.wikipedia.org/wiki/Billion_laughs`) was discovered in 2003.

Unfortunately, Python, like many other programming languages, doesn't account for this or other venues of attack via XML. Furthermore, third-party Python libraries such as *lxml* are vulnerable to at least 4 well-known XML-based attacks. For a list of Python and Python library vulnerabilities see `http://2scoops.co/python-xml-vulnerabilities`.

Fortunately for us, Christian Heimes created **defusedxml**, a Python library designed to patch Python's core XML libraries and some of the third-party libraries (including lxml).

For more information, please read:

- `https://pypi.python.org/pypi/defusedxml`

26.23 Explore Two-Factor Authentication

Two-factor authentication requires users to authenticate by combining two separate means of identification.

For modern web applications, what that usually means is you enter your password as well as a value provided to you on your mobile device. A value that is either sent to your personal phone number or is reset every thirty seconds.

The advantage of 2FA is that it adds another component, one that changes frequently, to the authentication process, great for any site involving personal identity, finance, or medical requirements. The downside is that the user needs to have a charged mobile device with access to a network in order to log in to your site, making it not so ideal for users who may not have a charged mobile device or easy access to a network.

- `http://en.wikipedia.org/wiki/Two_factor_authentication`
- `https://pypi.python.org/pypi/django-two-factor-auth`

PACKAGE TIP: Look for TOTP in 2FA Products and Packages

TOTP is short for `2scoops.co/time-based-one-time-password-algorithm/`, which is an open standard used by Google Authenticator and many other services. TOTP does not require network access, which is useful for building certain kinds of Django projects. However, SMS implementations of course require cellular network access.

26.24 Embrace SecurityMiddleware

We've mentioned Django 1.8's new built in `django.middleware.security.SecurityMiddleware` several times already in this chapter. It replaces most of the functionality of the venerable **django-secure** package. We owe it to ourselves and our users to embrace and use this feature of Django.

26.25 Force the Use of Strong Passwords

A strong password is one that more than a list of characters. It is suitably complex, including punctuation, digits, and both character cases. Let's pledge to protect our users by enforcing the use of such passwords.

PACKAGE TIP: Tools for Strong Passwords

In order to expedite this practice, we encourage the use of **django-passwords**, a project created by core Django developer, pip/PyPI maintainer, and Two Scoops of Django 1.5 security reviewer, Donald Stufft.
Another gotcha with strong passwords is with automatically generated Django sites, such as those created by configuration management tools. Since the creation of superusers is bypassed, we always have to cook up our own work arounds. Fortunately, Roberto Rosario has provided us with **django-autoadmin**, which provides automatic admin users complete with passwords for Django projects.

- https://github.com/dstufft/django-passwords
- https://github.com/rosarior/django-autoadmin

26.26 Give Your Site a Security Checkup

Erik Romijn has created Pony Checkup, an automated security checkup tool for Django websites. There are several security practices that can easily be probed from the outside, and this is what his site checks for. It's not a security audit, but it's a great, free way to make certain that your production deployment doesn't have any gaping security holes.

If you have a Django site in production, we recommend that you go and try out:

- http://ponycheckup.com

26.27 Put Up a Vulnerability Reporting Page

It's a good idea to publish information on your site about how users can report security vulnerabilities to you.

GitHub's "Responsible Disclosure of Security Vulnerabilities" page is a good example of this and rewards reporters of issues by publishing their names:
`http://2scoops.co/responsible-disclosure-of-security-vulnerabilities`

26.28 Stop Using django.utils.html.remove_tag

Several months after the Django project decided to emphasize the potential danger of using this function, a similar issue prompted the deprecation of the `remove_tags()` function and related template tag. While you can use `remove_tags()` in Django 1.8, we recommend against its use. The Django core team agrees with us, which is why it will be removed in Django 2.0. Consider using `bleach`, a HTML-sanitizing tool instead.

- Django's `remove_tags` documentation.
- The `Remove Tags Advisory` on Django Project's blog.
- The `bleach` library on PyPI.

26.29 Have a Plan Ready for When Things Go Wrong

Handling security failures is incredibly stressful. There is a sense of urgency and panic that can overwhelm our better judgement, leading to snap decisions that can involve ill-advised 'bug fixes' and public statements that worsen the problem.

Therefore, it's critical that a point-by-point plan be written and made available to maintainers and even non-technical participants of a project. Here is a sample plan:

1. Shut everything down or put it in read-only mode.
2. Put up a static HTML page.
3. Back everything up.
4. Email security@djangoproject.com, even if it's your fault.
5. Start looking into the problem.

Let's go over these steps:

26.29.1 Shut Everything Down or Put It in Read-Only Mode

The first thing to do is remove the ability for the security problem to continue. That way, further damage is hopefully prevented.

On Heroku:

Example 26.8

```
$ heroku maintenance:on
Enabling maintenance mode for myapp... done
```

For projects you deploy yourself or with automated tools, you're going to have create this capability yourself. Fortunately, other people have faced this before so we come prepared with reference material:

- `http://2scoops.co/nginx-http503-page` for putting up maintenance 503 pages.
- **django-db-tools** is is great for flipping a project's database in and out of read-only mode.
- Other tools can be found at `http://2scoops.co/emergency-management`

26.29.2 Put Up a Static HTML Page

You should have a maintenance page formatted and ready to go when you launch your project. This way, when things go wrong and you've shut everything down, you can display that to the end user. If done well, the users might understand and give you the breathing room to work out the problem.

26.29.3 Back Everything Up

Get a copy of the code and then the data off the servers and keep it on a local hard drive or SSD. You might also consider a bonded, professional storage company.

Why? First, when you back things up at this stage, you are protecting your audit trail. This might provide you with the capability to determine where and when things went wrong.

Second, and this might be unpleasant to hear, but malignant staff can cause as many problems as any bug or penetration staff. What that means is that the best software-based security is useless against a developer who creates a backdoor or a non-technical staff level user who decides to cause trouble.

26.29.4 Email security@djangoproject.com, Even if It's Your Fault

Actually, don't worry about whose fault it is, just send a quick email summarizing the problem. Ask for help while you are at it.

There are a number of reasons why this is important:

- Writing up a quick summary will help you focus and gather your thoughts. You're going to be under an amazing amount of stress. The stress and urgency of the situation can make you attempt stupid things that can aggravate the problem.
- You never know, the Django security team might have good advice or even an answer for you.
- It might be a Django problem! If that is the case, the Django security team needs to know so they can mitigate the problem for everyone else before it becomes public.

TIP: Jacob Kaplan-Moss on Reporting to the Django Project

Django co-leader and Director of Security for Heroku Jacob Kaplan-Moss says, "I'd much rather have people send things that aren't actual problems in Django to security@djangoproject.com than accidentally disclose security issues publicly because they don't know better."

26.29.5 Start Looking Into the Problem

You've shut things down, backed everything up, are displaying a static HTML page, emailed security@djangoproject.com, and are looking at the problem. By following the above steps, you've given yourself (and possibly your team) time to breathe and figure out what really happened.

This will be a stressful time and people will be on the edge of panic. Start doing research, perhaps in this book, ask questions as per chapter 34, *Where and How to Ask Django Questions*, and find a resolution.

Before you implement a correction, it's often better to make sure you have a real, proper fix for the problem then do a rushed emergency patch that destroys everything. Yes, this is where tests and continuous integration shine.

Stay positive: now is the time for everyone to come together and fix the problem. Start taking notes, ask for help from the best people you know, remind yourself (or the team) that you have the will and the smarts to fix things, and make things right!

WARNING: The Nightmare of the Zero-Day Attack

Zero-day attacks are attacks on vulnerabilities that are known to the public or a closed list but still unpatched. For example:

- Attacks the day of a software update release, right before most people get around to installing the software update.
- Attacks right after a user writes up a blog post about a vulnerability they found, before package maintainers have the chance to write and release a patch.
- Attacks targeting vulnerabilities in discussion on a closed security mailing list.

With zero-day attacks, there is often no time to address and patch the vulnerability, making the compromise especially difficult to manage. If there was ever a reason to have a battle plan for handling security issues, this is it.

See `https://en.wikipedia.org/wiki/0day`

26.30 Obfuscate Primary Keys with UUIDs

Django 1.8 comes with very useful `models.UUIDField`. While a use case for using them as primary keys for large distributed systems exists, the rest of the time using them can be cumbersome. For example, we can easily remember that `User.objects.get(id=1)` but `User.objects.get(id='0b0fb68e-5b06-44af-845a-01b6df5e0967')` requires cut-and-paste. However, if we want to hide what our primary keys are from users, then `models.UUIDField` becomes really handy. Here is a sample model:

Example 26.9

```
import uuid as uuid_lib
from django.db import models
from django.utils.encoding import python_2_unicode_compatible

@python_2_unicode_compatible
class IceCreamPayment(models.Model):
    uuid = models.UUIDField(
        db_index=True,
        default=uuid_lib.uuid4,
        editable=False)

    def __str__(self):
        return str(self.pk)
```

And here is how we call that model:

Example 26.10

```
>>> from payments import IceCreamPayment
>>> payment = IceCreamPayment()
>>> IceCreamPayment.objects.get(id=payment.id)
<IceCreamPayment: 1>
>>> payment.uuid
UUID('0b0fb68e-5b06-44af-845a-01b6df5e0967')
>>> IceCreamPayment.objects.get(uuid=payment.uuid)
<IceCreamPayment: 1>
```

26.31 Reference Our Security Settings Appendix

Keeping track of everything that relates to security and Django is challenging. This chapter alone is nigh 30 pages long and at the beginning we make it very clear this is not an absolute reference.

In order to add clarity, we've created Appendix G: Security Settings Reference. This is where we put important and useful information on how to better configure the security settings of a Django project.

26.32 Keep Up-to-Date on General Security Practices

We end this chapter with some common-sense advice.

First, keep in mind that security practices are constantly evolving, both in the Django community and beyond. Subscribe to http://2scoops.co/django-announce and check Twitter, Hacker News, and various security blogs regularly.

Second, remember that security best practices extend well beyond those practices specific to Django. You should research the security issues of every part of your web application stack, and you should follow the corresponding sources to stay up to date.

TIP: Good Books and Articles on Security

Paul McMillan, Django core developer, security expert, and Two Scoops reviewer, recommends the following books:

- "*The Tangled Web: A Guide to Securing Modern Web Applications*": http://amzn.to/1hXAAyx
- "*The Web Application Hacker's Handbook*": http://amzn.to/1dZ7xEY

In addition, we recommend the following reference site:

- https://wiki.mozilla.org/WebAppSec/Secure_Coding_Guidelines

26.33 Summary

Please use this chapter as a starting point for Django security, not the ultimate reference guide. See the Django documentation's list for additional security topics: http://2scoops.co/1.8-additional-security-topics

Django comes with a good security record due to the diligence of its community and attention to detail. Security is one of those areas where it's a particularly good idea to ask for help. If you find yourself confused about anything, ask questions and turn to others in the Django community for help.

27 Logging: What's It For, Anyway?

Logging is like rocky road ice cream. Either you can't live without it, or you forget about it and wonder once in awhile why it exists.

Anyone who's ever worked on a large production project with intense demands understands the importance of using the different log levels appropriately, creating module-specific loggers, meticulously logging information about important events, and including extra detail about the application's state when those events are logged.

While logging might not seem glamorous, remember that it is one of the secrets to building extremely stable, robust web applications that scale and handle unusual loads gracefully. Logging can be used not only to debug application errors, but also to track interesting performance metrics.

Logging unusual activity and checking logs regularly is also important for ensuring the security of your server. In the previous chapter, we covered the importance of checking your server access and error logs regularly. Keep in mind that application logs can be used in similar ways, whether to track failed login attempts or unusual application-level activity.

27.1 Application Logs vs. Other Logs

This chapter focuses on application logs. Any log file containing data logged from your Python web application is considered an application log.

In addition to your application logs, you should be aware that there are other types of logs, and that using and checking all of your server logs is necessary. Your server logs, database logs, network logs, etc. all provide vital insight into your production system, so consider them all equally important.

27.2 Why Bother With Logging?

Logging is your go-to tool in situations where a stack trace and existing debugging tools aren't enough. Whenever you have different moving parts interacting with each other or the possibility of unpredictable situations, logging gives you insight into what's going on.

The different log levels available to you are `DEBUG`, `INFO`, `WARNING`, `ERROR`, and `CRITICAL`. Let's now explore when it's appropriate to use each logging level.

27.3 When to Use Each Log Level

In places other than your production environment, you might as well use all the log levels. Log levels are controlled in your project's settings modules, so we can fine tune this recommendation as needed to account for load testing and large scale user tests.

In your production environment, we recommend using every log level except for `DEBUG`.

Figure 27.1: Appropriate usage of CRITICAL/ERROR/WARNING/INFO logging in ice cream.

Since the same `CRITICAL`, `ERROR`, `WARNING`, and `INFO` logs are captured whether in production or development, introspection of buggy code requires less modification of code. This is important to remember, as debug code added by developers working to fix one problem can create new ones.

The rest of this section covers how each log level is used.

27.3.1 Log Catastrophes With CRITICAL

Use the `CRITICAL` log level only when something catastrophic occurs that requires urgent attention.

For example, if your code relies on an internal web service being available, and if that web service is part of your site's core functionality, then you might log at the `CRITICAL` level anytime that the web service is inaccessible.

This log level is never used in core Django code, but you should certainly use it in your code anywhere that an extremely serious problem can occur.

27.3.2 Log Production Errors With ERROR

Let's look at core Django for an example of when `ERROR` level logging is appropriate. In core Django, the `ERROR` log level is used very sparingly. There is one very important place where it is used: whenever code raises an exception that is not caught, the event gets logged by Django using the following code:

Example 27.1

```
# Taken directly from core Django code.
# Used here to illustrate an example only, so don't
# copy this into your project.
logger.error("Internal Server Error: %s", request.path,
    exc_info=exc_info,
    extra={
        "status_code": 500,
        "request": request
    }
)
```

How does Django put this to good use? Well, when `DEBUG=False` is in your settings, everyone listed in `ADMINS` immediately gets emailed the following:

- A description of the error
- A complete Python traceback from where the error occurred

- Information about the HTTP request that caused the error

If you've ever received one of those email notifications, you know how useful `ERROR` logs are when you need them most.

Similarly, we recommend that you use the `ERROR` log level whenever you need to log an error that is worthy of being emailed to you or your site admins. When your code catches the exception, log as much information as you can to be able to resolve the problem.

For example, an exception may be thrown when one of your views cannot access a needed third-party API. When the exception is caught, you can log a helpful message and the API's failure response, if any.

27.3.3 Log Lower-Priority Problems With WARNING

This level is good for logging events that are unusual and potentially bad, but not as bad as `ERROR`-level events.

For example, if you are using **django-admin-honeypot** to set up a fake *admin/* login form, you might want to log intruders' login attempts to this level.

Django uses the log level in several parts of `CsrfViewMiddleware`, to log events that result in a **403 Forbidden** error. For example, when an incoming POST request is missing its `csrf_token`, the event gets logged as follows:

Example 27.2

```
# Taken directly from core Django code.
# Used here to illustrate an example only, so don't
# copy this into your project.
logger.warning("Forbidden (%s): %s",
               REASON_NO_CSRF_COOKIE, request.path,
    extra={
        "status_code": 403,
        "request": request,
    }
)
```

27.3.4 Log Useful State Information With INFO

We recommend using this level to log any details that may be particularly important when analysis is needed. These include:

- Startup and shutdown of important components not logged elsewhere
- State changes that occur in response to important events
- Changes to permissions, e.g. when users are granted admin access

In addition to this, the `INFO` level is great for logging any general information that may help in performance analysis. It's a good level to use while hunting down problematic bottlenecks in your application and doing profiling.

27.3.5 Log Debug-Related Messages to DEBUG

In development, we recommend using `DEBUG` and occasionally `INFO` level logging wherever you'd consider throwing a `print` statement into your code for debugging purposes.

Getting used to logging this way isn't hard. Instead of this:

Bad Example 27.1

```
from django.views.generic import TemplateView

from .helpers import pint_counter

class PintView(TemplateView):

    def get_context_data(self, *args, **kwargs):
        context = super(PintView, self).get_context_data(**kwargs)
        pints_remaining = pint_counter()
        print("Only %d pints of ice cream left." % (pints_remaining))
        return context
```

We do this:

Example 27.3

```
import logging

from django.views.generic import TemplateView

from .helpers import pint_counter

logger = logging.getLogger(__name__)

class PintView(TemplateView):

    def get_context_data(self, *args, **kwargs):
        context = super(PintView, self).get_context_data(**kwargs)
        pints_remaining = pint_counter()
        logger.debug("Only %d pints of ice cream left." % pints_remaining)
        return context
```

Sprinkling `print` statements across your projects results in problems and technical debt:

- Depending on the web server, a forgotten print statement can bring your site down.
- *Print statements are not recorded.* If you don't see them, then you miss what they were trying to say.
- As the Django world migrates more and more to Python 3, old-style print statements like `print IceCream.objects.flavor()` will break your code.

Unlike `print` statements, logging allows different report levels and different response methods. This means that:

- We can write `DEBUG` level statements, leave them in our code, and never have to worry about them doing anything when we move code to production.
- The response method can provide the response as email, log files, console and `stdout`. It can even report as pushed HTTP requests to applications such as *Sentry*!

Note that there's no need to go overboard with debug-level logging. It's great to add `logging.debug()` statements while you're debugging, but there's no need to clutter your code with logging every single line.

Figure 27.2: Appropriate usage of DEBUG logging in ice cream.

27.4 Log Tracebacks When Catching Exceptions

Whenever you log an exception, it's usually helpful to log the stack trace of the exception. Python's logging module supports this:

1. `Logger.exception()` automatically includes the traceback and logs at `ERROR` level.
2. For other log levels, use the optional `exc_info` keyword argument.

Here's an example of adding a traceback to a `WARNING` level log message:

Example 27.4

```
import logging
import requests

logger = logging.getLogger(__name__)

def get_additional_data():
    try:
        r = requests.get("http://example.com/something-optional/")
    except requests.HTTPError as e:
```

```
        logger.exception(e)
        logger.debug("Could not get additional data", exc_info=True)
        return None
    return r
```

27.5 One Logger Per Module That Uses Logging

Whenever you use logging in another module, don't import and reuse a logger from elsewhere. Instead, define a new logger specific to the module like this:

Example 27.5

```
# You can place this snippet at the top
# of models.py, views.py, or any other
# file where you need to log.
import logging

logger = logging.getLogger(__name__)
```

What this gives you is the ability to turn on and off only the specific loggers that you currently need. If you're running into a strange issue in production that you can't replicate locally, you can temporarily turn on `DEBUG` logging for just the module related to the issue. Then, when you identify the problem, you can turn that logger back off in production.

27.6 Log Locally to Rotating Files

When you create a new Django project with `startproject`, your default settings file is configured to email `ERROR` and higher log messages to whomever you list in `ADMINS`. This occurs via a handler called `AdminEmailHandler` that comes with Django.

In addition to this, we recommend also writing logs of level `INFO` and higher to rotating log files on disk. On-disk log files are helpful in case the network goes down or emails can't be sent to your admins for some reason. Log rotation keeps your logs from growing to fill your available disk space.

A common way to set up log rotation is to use the UNIX **logrotate** utility with `logging.handlers.WatchedFileHandler`.

Note that if you are using a platform-as-a-service, you might not be able to set up rotating log files. In this case, you may need to use an external logging service such as Loggly: `http://loggly.com/`.

27.7 Other Logging Tips

- Control the logging in settings files per the Django documentation on logging: `https://docs.djangoproject.com/en/1.8/topics/logging/`
- While debugging, use the Python logger at `DEBUG` level.
- After running tests at `DEBUG` level, try running them at `INFO` and `WARNING` levels. The reduction in information you see may help you identify upcoming deprecations for third-party libraries.
- Don't wait until it's too late to add logging. You'll be grateful for your logs if and when your site fails.
- You can do useful things with the emails you receive when `ERROR` or higher level events occur. For example, you can configure a PagerDuty (`http://www.pagerduty.com/`) account to alert you and your team repeatedly until you've taken action.

PACKAGE TIP: Logutils Provides Useful Handlers

The **logutils** package by Vinay Sajip comes with a number of very interesting logging handlers. Features include:

- Colorizing of console streams under Windows, Linux and Mac OS X.
- The ability to log to queues. Useful in situations where you want to queue up log messages to a slow handler like `SMTPHandler`.
- Classes that allow you to write unit tests for log messages.
- An enhanced `HTTPHandler` that supports secure connections over HTTPS.

Some of the more basic features of logutils are so useful that they have been absorbed into the Python standard library!

27.8 Necessary Reading Material

- https://docs.djangoproject.com/en/1.8/topics/logging/
- http://docs.python.org/2/library/logging.html
- http://docs.python.org/2/library/logging.config.html
- http://docs.python.org/2/library/logging.handlers.html
- http://docs.python.org/2/howto/logging-cookbook.html

27.9 Useful Third-Party Tools

- Sentry (https://www.getsentry.com/) aggregates errors for you.
- App Enlight (https://appenlight.com/) tracks errors and performance issues in your app.
- loggly.com (http://loggly.com/) simplifies log management and provides excellent query tools.

27.10 Summary

Django projects can easily take advantage of the rich logging functionality that comes with Python. Combine logging with handlers and analysis tools, and suddenly you have real power. You can use logging to help you improve the stability and performance of your projects.

In the next chapter we'll discuss signals, which become much easier to follow, debug, and understand with the help of logging.

28 Signals: Use Cases and Avoidance Techniques

The Short Answer: Use signals as a last resort.

The Long Answer: Often when new Djangonauts first discover signals, they get signal-happy. They start sprinkling signals everywhere they can and feeling like real experts at Django.

After coding this way for a while, projects start to turn into confusing, knotted hairballs that can't be untangled. Signals are being dispatched everywhere and hopefully getting received somewhere, but at that point it's hard to tell what exactly is going on.

Many developers also confuse signals with asynchronous message queues such as what Celery (`http://www.celeryproject.org/`) provides. Make no mistake, *signals are synchronous and blocking*, and calling performance-heavy processes via signals provides absolutely no benefit from a performance or scaling perspective. In fact, moving such processes unnecessarily to signals is considered code obfuscation.

Signals can be useful, but they should be used as a last resort, only when there's no good way to avoid using them.

28.1 When to Use and Avoid Signals

Do not use signals when:

- The signal relates to one particular model and can be moved into one of that model's methods, possibly called by `save()`.

- The signal can be replaced with a custom model manager method.
- The signal relates to a particular view and can be moved into that view.

It might be okay to use signals when:

- Your signal receiver needs to make changes to more than one model.
- You want to dispatch the same signal from multiple apps and have them handled the same way by a common receiver.
- You want to invalidate a cache after a model save.
- You have an unusual scenario that needs a callback, and there's no other way to handle it besides using a signal. For example, you want to trigger something based on the `save()` or `init()` of a third-party app's model. You can't modify the third-party code and extending it might be impossible, so a signal provides a trigger for a callback.

> **TIP: Aymeric Augustin Thoughts on Signals**
>
> Django core developer Aymeric Augustin says: "I advise not to use signals as soon as a regular function call will do. Signals obfuscate control flow through inversion of control. They make it difficult to discover what code will actually run.
>
> Use a signal only if the piece of code sending it has positively no way to determine what its receivers will be."

28.2 Signal Avoidance Techniques

Let's go over some scenarios where you can simplify your code and remove some of the signals that you don't need.

28.2.1 Using Custom Model Manager Methods Instead of Signals

Let's imagine that our site handles user-submitted ice cream-themed events, and each ice cream event goes through an approval process. These events are set with a status of "Unreviewed" upon creation. The problem is that we want our site administrators to get an email for each event submission so they know to review and post things quickly.

We could have done this with a signal, but unless we put in extra logic in the post_save() code, even administrator created events would generate emails.

An easier way to handle this use case is to create a custom model manager method and use that in your views. This way, if an event is created by an administrator, they don't have to go through the review process.

Since a code example is worth a thousand words, here is how we would create such a method:

Example 28.1

```
# events/managers.py
from django.db import models

class EventManager(models.Manager):

    def create_event(self, title, start, end, creator):
        event = self.model(title=title,
                           start=start,
                           end=end,
                           creator=creator)
        event.save()
        event.notify_admins()
        return event
```

Now that we have our custom manager with its custom manager method in place, let's attach it to our model (which comes with a notify_admins() method:

Example 28.2

```
# events/models.py
from django.conf import settings
from django.core.mail import mail_admins
from django.db import models

from model_utils.models import TimeStampedModel

from .managers import EventManager

class Event(TimeStampedModel):
```

```
    STATUS_UNREVIEWED, STATUS_REVIEWED = (0, 1)
    STATUS_CHOICES = (
        (STATUS_UNREVIEWED, "Unreviewed"),
        (STATUS_REVIEWED, "Reviewed"),
    )

    title = models.CharField(max_length=100)
    start = models.DateTimeField()
    end = models.DateTimeField()
    status = models.IntegerField(choices=STATUS_CHOICES,
                                    default=STATUS_UNREVIEWED)
    creator = models.ForeignKey(settings.AUTH_USER_MODEL)

    objects = EventManager()

    def notify_admins(self):
        # create the subject and message
        subject = "{user} submitted a new event!".format(
                        user=self.creator.get_full_name())
        message = """TITLE: {title}
START: {start}
END: {end}""".format(title=self.title, start=self.start,
                        end=self.end)

        # Send to the admins!
        mail_admins(subject=subject,
            message=message,
            fail_silently=False)
```

Using this follows a similar pattern to using the `User` model. To generate an event, instead of calling `create()`, we call a `create_event()` method.

Example 28.3

```
>>> from django.contrib.auth import get_user_model
>>> from django.utils import timezone
```

```
>>> from events.models import Event
>>> user = get_user_model().get(username="audreyr")
>>> now = timezone.now()
>>> event = Event.objects.create_event(
...     title="International Ice Cream Tasting Competition",
...     start=now,
...     end=now,
...     user=user
...     )
```

28.2.2 Validate Your Model Elsewhere

If you're using a `pre_save` signal to trigger input cleanup for a specific model, try writing a custom validator for your field(s) instead.

If validating through a `ModelForm`, try overriding your model's `clean()` method instead.

28.2.3 Override Your Model's Save or Delete Method Instead

If you're using `pre_save` and `post_save` signals to trigger logic that only applies to one particular model, you might not need those signals. You can often simply move the signal logic into your model's `save()` method.

The same applies to overriding `delete()` instead of using `pre_delete` and `post_delete` signals.

28.2.4 Use a Helper Function Instead of Signals

We find this approach useful under two conditions:

1. *Refactoring*: Once we realize that certain bits of code no longer need to be obfuscated as signals and want to refactor, the question of 'Where do we put the code that was in a signal?' arises. If it doesn't belong in a model manager, custom validator, or overloaded model method, where does it belong?
2. *Architecture*: Sometimes developers use signals because we feel the model has become too heavyweight and we need a place for code. While Fat Models are a nice approach, we admit it's not much fun to have to parse through a 500 or 2000 line chunk of code.

This solution, suggested to us by Django core developer Aymeric Augustin, is to place the code in helper functions. If done right, this helps us write cleaner, more reusable code.

One interesting thing about this approach is to test the transition out of signals. Simply follow these steps:

1. Write a test for the existing signal call.
2. Write a test for the business logic of the existing signal call as if it were in a separate function.
3. Write a helper function that duplicates the business logic of the signal, matching the assertions of the test written in the second step.
4. Run the tests.
5. Call the helper function from the signal.
6. Run the tests again.
7. Remove the signal and call the helper function from the appropriate location.
8. Run the tests again.
9. Rinse and repeat until done.

This approach allows us to carefully remove the signal without breaking things. It also helps us identify when an existing signal is required for a specific process.

28.3 Summary

Signals are a powerful tool in any Django developer's toolbox. However, they are easy to misuse and it's good practice to delve into why and when to use them.

29 What About Those Random Utilities?

29.1 Create a Core App for Your Utilities

Sometimes we end up writing shared classes or little general-purpose utilities that are useful everywhere. These bits and pieces don't belong in any particular app. We don't just stick them into a sort-of-related random app, because we have a hard time finding them when we need them. We also don't like placing them as "random" modules in the root of the project.

Our way of handling our utilities is to place them into a Django app called ***core*** that contains modules which contains functions and objects for use across a project. (Other developers follow a similar pattern and call this sort of app ***common***, ***generic***, ***util***, or ***utils***.)

For example, perhaps our project has both a custom model manager and a custom view mixin used by several different apps. Our ***core*** app would therefore look like:

Example 29.1

```
core/
    __init__.py
    managers.py  # contains the custom model manager(s)
    models.py
    views.py  # Contains the custom view mixin(s)
```

> **TIP: Always make the core app a real Django app**
>
> We always make the core directory a Django app. At some point we inevitably end up doing at least one of the following:
>
> - Have non-abstract models in *core*.
> - Have admin auto-discovery working in *core*.
> - Have template tags and filters in *core*.

Now, if we want to import our custom model manager and/or view mixin , we import using the same pattern of imports we use for everything else:

Example 29.2

```
from core.managers import PublishedManager
from core.views import IceCreamMixin
```

29.2 Optimize Apps with Utility Modules

Synonymous with **helpers**, these are commonly called *utils.py* and sometimes *helpers.py*. They are places where we place functions and classes which make common patterns shorter and easier. Let's go into why this is helpful.

29.2.1 Storing Code Used in Many Places

There are times when we have functions or classes used in several places that doesn't quite fit in *models.py*, *forms.py*, or any other specifically named module. When this occurs, we put this logic in the *utils.py* module.

29.2.2 Trimming Models

This is best explained with an example.

We use the `Flavor` model frequently. We start attaching field after field, method after method, property after property, classmethod after classmethod. One day we notice that our *fat model* has reached brobdingnagian proprtions and is over a thousand lines of code. Debugging and maintenance have become hard. What do we do?

We start looking for methods (or properties or classmethods) whose logic can be easily encapsulated in functions stored in *flavors/utils.py*. The existing methods (or properties or classmethods) become simple wrappers calling functions from *flavors/utils.py*. The result is a more distributed code base that encourages code reuse as well as *easier testing*.

29.2.3 Easier Testing

A side effect of moving logic from more complex constructs into functions placed in isolated modules is that it becomes easier to test. By isolation we mean it is usually imported within the app, rather than doing in-app/in-project imports. This causes less business logic overhead, hence making it easier to write tests for what logic is present in the module.

TIP: Make Utility Code Constructs as Focused as Possible

Be it a function or a class, avoid allowing multiple behaviors or conditions. Each utility function should do one and only one thing well. Don't repeat yourself. Don't create utility functions that are duplicates of model behaviors.

29.3 Django's Own Swiss Army Knife

The Swiss army knife is a multi-purpose tool that is compact and useful. Django has a number of useful helper functions that don't have a better home than the `django.utils` package. It's tempting to dig into the code in `django.utils` and start using things, but don't. Most of those modules are designed for internal use and their behavior or inclusion can change between Django versions.

Instead, read https://docs.djangoproject.com/en/1.8/ref/utils/ to see which modules in there are stable.

TIP: Malcolm Tredinnick on Django's Utils Package.

Django core developer Malcolm Tredinnick liked to think of `django.utils` as being in the same theme as Batman's utility belt: indispensable tools that are used everywhere internally.

Figure 29.1: A utility belt for serious ice cream eaters.

There are some gems in there that have turned into best practices:

29.3.1 django.contrib.humanize

This is a set of localized template filters designed to give user presented data a more 'human' touch. For example it includes a filter called '`intcomma`' that converts integers to strings containing commas (or periods depending on locale) every three digits.

While `django.contrib.humanize`'s filters are useful for making template output more attractive, we can also import each filter individually as a function. This is quite handy when processing any sort of text, especially when used in conjunction with REST APIs.

29.3.2 django.utils.decorators.method_decorator(decorator)

Django has some really great function decorators. Many of us have written decorators for Django projects, especially when we're working with Function-Based Views. However, there comes a time when we discover that our favorite function decorator would also make sense as a method decorator. Fortunately, Django provides the `method_decorator`

29.3.3 django.utils.decorators.decorator_from_middleware(middleware)

Middleware is a wonderful tool, but is global in nature. This can generate extra queries or other complications. Fortunately, we can isolate the use of middleware on a per-view basis by using this view decorator.

Also see the related `decorator_from_middleware_with_args` decorator.

29.3.4 django.utils.encoding.force_text(value)

This forces Django to take anything and turn it into a plain `str` representation on Python 3 and `unicode` on Python 2. It avoids the display of a `django.utils.functional.__proxy__` object. For more details, see Appendix D.

29.3.5 django.utils.functional.cached_property

Reinout van Rees educated us about this incredibly useful method decorator introduced in Django 1.5. What it does is cache in memory the result of a method with a single `self` argument as a property. This has wonderful implications in regards to performance optimization of a project. We use it in every project, enjoying how it allows us to cache the results of expensive computations trivially.

For a description on how to use the `cached_property` decorator, the official Django documentation on the subject is excellent: http://2scoops.co/1.8-cached_property

In addition to the potential performance benefits, we've used this decorator to make sure that values fetched by methods remain static over the lifetime of their object. This has proven very useful when dealing with third-party APIs or dealing with database transactions.

WARNING: Careful Using cached_property Outside of Django

It is tempting to copy/paste the source code for `cached_property` for use outside of Django. However, when used outside a web framework, we discovered the code for this function has problems in multithreaded environments. Therefore, if coding outside of Django, you might want to take a look at the third-party `cached_property` library:

- https://github.com/pydanny/cached-property
- http://www.pydanny.com/cached-property.html

29.3.6 django.utils.html.format_html(format_str, args, **kwargs)

This is similar to Python's `str.format()` method, except designed for building up HTML fragments. All args and kwargs are escaped before being passed to `str.format()` which then combines the elements.

See http://2scoops.co/1.8-format_html for details on use.

29.3.7 django.utils.html.remove_tags(value, tags)

Deprecated for security reasons per section 26.27, *Stop Using django.utils.html.remove_tag.*

29.3.8 django.utils.html.strip_tags(value)

When we need to accept content from users and have to strip out anything that could be HTML, this function removes those tags for we while keeping all the existing text between tags.

WARNING: Security Advisory on strip_tags Safety

When using the `strip_tags` function, or the `striptags` template tage, make absolutely certain that the outputted content is not marked as safe. This especially applies if you have disabled automatic escaping in your templates. Reference:
https://djangoproject.com/weblog/2014/mar/22/strip-tags-advisory/

29.3.9 django.utils.six

Six is a Python 2 and 3 compatibility library by Benjamin Peterson. It's bundled directly into Django (hence its inclusion in Django's utils library), but we can also find it as an independent package for other projects.

- Six on PyPI: https://pypi.python.org/pypi/six
- Six documentation: http://pythonhosted.org/six/
- Six repo on BitBucket: https://bitbucket.org/gutworth/six
- Six in Django: https://github.com/django/django/blob/master/django/utils/six.py

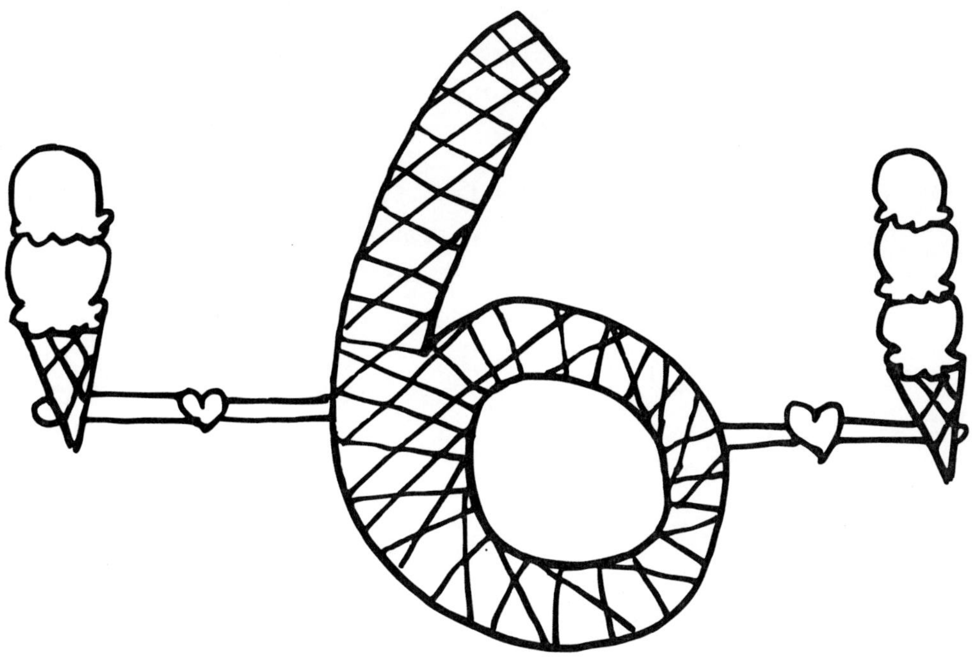

Figure 29.2: Six smooths over the differences between 2 and 3.

29.3.10 django.utils.text.slugify(value)

We recommend that whatever you do, don't write your own version of the `slugify()` function, as any inconsistency from what Django does with this function will cause subtle yet nasty problems in our data. Instead, we use the same function that Django uses and `slugify()` consistently.

It is possible to use `django.templates.defaultfilters.slugify()` in our Python code, as this calls the function described here. Nevertheless, we like to use the function directly from Django's utils directory, as it is a more appropriate import path.

However we decide to import this function, we try to keep it consistent across a project as there is a use case for when it has to be replaced, as described in the package tip on the next page.

PACKAGE TIP: slugify and languages Besides English

Tomasz Paczkowski points out that we should note that `slugify()` can cause problems with localization:

Example 29.3

```
>>> from django.utils.text import slugify
>>> slugify(u"straße") # German
u"strae"
```

Fortunately, **unicode-slugify**, is a Mozilla foundation-supported project that addresses the issue:

Example 29.4

```
>>> from slugify import slugify
>>> slugify(u"straße") # Again with German
u"straße"
```

There is also **awesome-slugify**, which shares similar functionality to **unicode-slugify**, but does not have Django as a dependency.

- https://github.com/mozilla/unicode-slugify
- https://github.com/dimka665/awesome-slugify

29.3.11 django.utils.timezone

It's good practice for us to have time zone support enabled. Chances are that our users live in more than one time zone.

When we use Django's time zone support, date and time information is stored in the database uniformly in UTC format and converted to local time zones as needed.

29.3.12 django.utils.translation

Much of the non-English speaking world appreciates use of this tool, as it provides Django's i18n support. See Appendix D for a more in-depth reference.

29.4 Exceptions

Django comes with a lot of exceptions. Most of them are used internally, but a few of them stand out because the way they interact with Django can be leveraged in fun and creative ways. These, and other built-in Django exceptions, are documented at https://docs.djangoproject.com/en/dev/ref/exceptions.

29.4.1 django.core.exceptions.ImproperlyConfigured

The purpose of this module is to inform anyone attempting to run Django that there is a configuration issue. It serves as the single Django code component considered acceptable to import into Django settings modules. We discuss it in both chapter 5 and Appendix E.

29.4.2 django.core.exceptions.ObjectDoesNotExist

This is the base `Exception` from which all `DoesNotExist` exceptions inherit from. We've found this is a really nice tool for working with utility functions that fetch generic model instances and do something with them. Here is a simple example:

Example 29.5

```
# core/utils.py
from django.core.exceptions import ObjectDoesNotExist

class BorkedObject(object):
    loaded = False

def generic_load_tool(model, pk):
    try:
        instance = model.objects.get(pk=pk)
```

```
    except ObjectDoesNotExist:
        return BorkedObject()
    instance.loaded = True
    return instance
```

Also using this exception, we can create our own variant of Django's `django.shortcuts.get_object_or_404` function, perhaps raising a HTTP 403 exception instead of a 404:

EXAMPLE 29.6

```
# core/utils.py
from django.core.exceptions import MultipleObjectsReturned
from django.core.exceptions import ObjectDoesNotExist
from django.core.exceptions import PermissionDenied

def get_object_or_403(model, **kwargs):
    try:
        return model.objects.get(**kwargs)
    except ObjectDoesNotExist:
        raise PermissionDenied
    except MultipleObjectsReturned:
        raise PermissionDenied
```

29.4.3 django.core.exceptions.PermissionDenied

This exception is used when users, authenticated or not, attempt to get responses from places they are not meant to be. Raising it in a view will trigger the view to return a `django.http.HttpResponseForbidden`.

This exception can prove useful to use in functions that are touching the sensitive data and components of a high-security project. It means that if something bad happens, instead of just returning a 500 exception, which may rightly alarm users, we simply provide a "Permission Denied" screen.

EXAMPLE 29.7

```
# stores/calc.py

def finance_data_adjudication(store, sales, issues):

    if store.something_not_right:
        msg = "Something is not right. Please contact the support team."
        raise PermissionDenied(msg)

    # Continue on to perform other logic.
```

In this case, if this function were called by a view and something was 'not right,' then the `PermissionDenied` exception would force the view to display the project's 403 error page. Speaking of 403 error pages, we can set this to any view we want. In the root URLConf of a project, just add:

EXAMPLE 29.8

```
# urls.py

# This demonstrates the use of a custom permission denied view. The default
# view is django.views.defaults.permission_denied
handler403 = 'core.views.permission_denied_view'
```

As always, with exception-handling views, because they handle all HTTP methods equally, we prefer to use function-based views.

29.5 Serializers and Deserializers

Whether it's for creating data files or generating one-off simple REST APIs, Django has some great tools for working with serialization and deserialization of data of JSON, Python, YAML and XML data. They include the capability to turn model instances into serialized data and then return it back to model instances.

Here is how we serialize data:

Example 29.9

```
# serializer_example.py
from django.core.serializers import get_serializer

from favorites.models import Favorite

# Get and instantiate the serializer class
# The 'json' can be replaced with 'python' or 'xml'.
# If you have pyyaml installed, you can replace it with
#   'pyyaml'
JSONSerializer = get_serializer("json")
serializer = JSONSerializer()

favs = Favorite.objects.filter()[:5]

# Serialize model data
serialized_data = serializer.serialize(favs)

# save the serialized data for use in the next example
with open("data.json", "w") as f:
    f.write(serialized_data)
```

Here is how we deserialize data:

Example 29.10

```
# deserializer_example.py
from django.core.serializers import get_serializer

from favorites.models import Favorite

favs = Favorite.objects.filter()[:5]

# Get and instantiate the serializer class
# The 'json' can be replaced with 'python' or 'xml'.
# If you have pyyaml installed, you can replace it with
#   'pyyaml'
JSONSerializer = get_serializer("json")
```

```
serializer = JSONSerializer()

# open the serialized data file
with open("data.txt") as f:
    serialized_data = f.read()

# deserialize model data into a generator object
#   we'll call 'python data'
python_data = serializer.deserialize(serialized_data)

# iterate through the python_data
for element in python_data:
    # Prints 'django.core.serializers.base.DeserializedObject'
    print(type(element))

    # Elements have an 'object' that are literally instantiated
    #   model instances (in this case, favorites.models.Favorite)
    print(
        element.object.pk,
        element.object.created
    )
```

Django already provides a command-line tool for using these serializers and deserializers: the `dumpdata` and `loaddata` management commands. While we can use them, they don't grant us the same amount of control that direct code access to the serializers provides.

This brings us to something that we always need to keep in mind when using Django's built-in serializers and deserializers: they can cause problems. From painful experience, we know that they don't handle complex data structures well.

Consider these guidelines that we follow in our projects:

- Serialize data at the simplest level.
- Any database schema change may invalidate the serialized data.
- Don't just import serialized data. Consider using Django's form libraries to validate incoming data before saving to the database.

Let's go over some of the features provided by Django when working with specific formats:

29.5.1 django.core.serializers.json.DjangoJSONEncoder

Out of the box, Python's built-in JSON module can't handle encoding of date/time or decimal types. Anyone who has done Django for a while has run into this problem. Fortunately for all of us, Django provides a very useful `JSONEncoder` class. See the code example below:

Example 29.11

```
# json_encoding_example.py
import json

from django.core.serializers.json import DjangoJSONEncoder
from django.utils import timezone

data = {"date": timezone.now()}

# If you don't add the DjangoJSONEncoder class then
# the json library will throw a TypeError.
json_data = json.dumps(data, cls=DjangoJSONEncoder)

print(json_data)
```

29.5.2 django.core.serializers.pyyaml

While powered by the third-party library, pyyaml, Django's YAML serializer tools handles the time conversion from Python-to-YAML that pyyaml doesn't.

For deserialization, it also uses the `yaml.safe_load()` function under the hood, which means that we don't have to worry about code injection. See subsection 26.9.3 *Third-Party Libraries That Can Execute Code* for more details.

29.5.3 django.core.serializers.xml_serializer

By default Django's XML serializer uses Python's built-in XML handlers. It also incorporates elements of Christian Heimes' **defusedxml** library, protecting usage of it from XML bomb attacks. For more information, please read section 26.22, 'Guard Against XML Bombing With defusedxml.'

29.6 Summary

We follow the practice of putting often reused files into utility packages. We enjoy being able to remember where we placed our often reused code. Projects that contain a mix of core, common, util, and utils directories are just that much harder to navigate.

Django's own 'utility belt' includes a plethora of useful tools, including useful functions, exceptions, and serializers. Leveraging them is on of the ways experienced Django developers accelerate development and avoid some of the tangles that can be caused by some of the very features of Django.

Now that we've covered tools to make things work, in the next chapter we'll begin to cover sharing a project with the world.

30 | Deployment: Platforms as a Service

If you're working on a small side project or are a founder of a small startup, you'll definitely save time by using a **Platform as a Service** (**PaaS**) instead of setting up your own servers. Even large projects can benefit from the advantages of using them.

First, a public service message:

> ### TIP: Never Get Locked Into a Platform as a Service
>
> There are amazing services which will host your code, databases, media assets, and also provide a lot of wonderful accessories services. These services, however, can go through changes that can destroy your project. These changes include crippling price increases, performance degradation, unacceptable terms of service changes, untenable service license agreements, sudden decreases in availability, or can simply go out of business.
>
> This means that it's in your best interest to do your best to avoid being forced into architectural decisions based on the needs of your hosting provider. Be ready to be able to move from one provider to another without major restructuring of your project.
>
> We try to make sure that our projects are not intrinsically tied to any hosting solution, meaning that we are not locked into a single vendor's pricing, policies, and functionality.

As a WSGI-compliant framework, Django is supported on many PaaS providers. The most commonly-used Django-friendly PaaS companies as of this writing are:

- Heroku (http://heroku.com) is a popular option in the Python community well known for its documentation and add-ons system. If you choose this option, please read http://www.theherokuhackersguide.com/ by Randall Degges.
- PythonAnywhere (https://www.pythonanywhere.com) is a Python-powered PaaS that is incredibly beginner-friendly.

Why do we like these services? We've evaluated them carefully for our needs. Your needs may be different, so read on about how to choose a PaaS.

30.1 Evaluating a PaaS

When a PaaS is chosen to host a project, that project forces architecture concessions in order for the application to work in their system. Therefore, even if we heed our warning at the top of this chapter, extracting ourselves from the PaaS takes effort and time.

Therefore, when a PaaS is chosen for a project, or while we are using a PaaS, we constantly consider the following:

30.1.1 Compliance

Before you begin evaluating any other aspect, it's critical to check to see if the PaaS meets local or federal mandates. Examples:

- Many medical-based projects in the United States require meeting HIPAA standards. If the PaaS doesn't meet HIPAA standards, and the project contains user medical data and a project is deployed there, *everyone involved is at risk for civil and criminal prosecution under Title II of HIPAA.* See https://en.wikipedia.org/wiki/HIPAA#Security_Rule
- Most e-commerce projects require at least SSL, and anything dealing with credit cards needs to adhere to PCI. While services like Stripe often make this moot, many projects require internal integration of credit card processing. Make sure the PaaS complies with the PCI specification. See http://2scoops.co/wikipedia-PCI-standard.

- For the European Union, if you are processing any identifiable data you'll need to follow EU Directive 95/46/EC on the protection of personal data into account. Amongst other things, this places restrictions on exporting such data outside the European Union, especially if your PaaS doesn't participate in the US-EU Safe Harbor. If in doubt, consult legal counsel.

30.1.2 Pricing

Most PaaS options provide a free tier for beginner and toy projects, and Heroku and PythonAnywhere are good examples of this trend. We've gotten a lot of mileage out of this, and it's been great. You can even add extra services for a reasonable monthly fee. However, if one loses track of projects and services, then this 'reasonable fee' can quickly add up to a hefty monthly service bill. Therefore, it's a good idea to keep up on service costs and your monthly provider bills.

At the other end of things, if high traffic is anticipated, it's a good idea to see how much a site will cost with all the settings dialed up. For example, Heroku maxed out on dynos and enterprise PostgreSQL will cost over $40,000 a month. While the chances of a project needing this much horsepower is slim, the fact that Heroku offers this means that it can and does happen.

While all of this is going on, keep in mind that PaaS companies are under no legal or moral obligation to keep their prices or pricing methods static. In fact, developers we know of have built architecture for projects to take advantage of how billing is done by a PaaS, only to face crippling bills when the said PaaS changes its terms. To make matters worse, because they had tied their internal infrastructure tightly to the billing structure of the PaaS, they lacked the option of quickly moving off.

30.1.3 Uptime

For PaaS this is a very tricky issue. They would really like to provide 99.999999% uptime (sometimes referred to as the 'nines'), but even with the best engineering, it's not entirely under their control:

- Most of them, including Heroku and PythonAnywhere, rent space from vendors such as AWS and Rackspace. If those services go down, then they go down.
- All of them are reliant on the physical infrastructure of the internet. Natural disasters or industrial accidents can bring everything to a halt.

Even if we ignore these factors, providing a PaaS infrastructure is a hard business. It's more than standing up servers or Linux containers, it's maintaining a billing system, customer-facing tools, customer contact systems, and a host of other systems. This volume of work, challenging in its own right, can conflict with the business of making sure our projects work and scale as we need them.

That said, because it is integral to their business to provide consistent service, they aim for as high a stability number as they can. In general most PaaS companies have pretty good uptime, slowly increasing over time as they make continual system improvements. Furthermore, the good companies provide status pages and publish formal reports about any outages or issues. Therefore, we don't bother with reading outage reports that are over a few months old, as they are not indicative of the current engineering status of a company.

However, if there are recent, multiple reports of outages, or a recent outage of an unacceptable duration, we consider other PaaS options.

WARNING: If You Need Very High Uptime

It's worth mentioning that for projects that are life-critical, i.e. people could die if they lack immediate access, then a PaaS is not the right solution. Instead, please use an infrastructure service that provides a formal Service License Agreement.

30.1.4 Staffing

Yes, it's important to know about the staffing level of a PaaS:

- If a PaaS lacks staff, then they can't provide 24x7 engineering support, especially across holidays. No matter how enthusiastic a small shop is, and the deals they offer, they can't fix problems when their engineer is sleeping.
- Do they have the staff to answer emails and problem tickets? If their engineering staff is managing all of these requests, when do they have time to maintain the system?

We recommend testing out their level of support and responsiveness by filing a support ticket early on. Use this opportunity to ask a thoughtful question about something that's unclear in their documentation, or get needed help from their staff.

30.1.5 Scaling

How easy is it to scale up? If an e-commerce site is mentioned on CNN or on national television, can the site be dialed up quickly?

On the flip side, how easy it is to scale back down? Sometimes a traffic spike is followed by slow periods and it should be easy to dial things back.

Finally, can we automate this process?

30.1.6 Documentation

In chapter 23, *Documentation: Be Obsessed* we make it pretty clear that we really care about documentation. While we readily admit to exploiting every channel we know to ask questions (see chapter 34, *Where and How to Ask Django Questions*), we want the services that we use to have good, maintained documentation. It's important to have this as readily-found reference material, and it demonstrates that the PaaS in question is serious about what they do.

TIP: Why We Don't Document How Each PaaS Works

Every PaaS changes their API and documentation over time, some more rapidly than others. Since the Django PaaS space is still evolving rapidly, specific PaaS commands and instructions are not listed here. We ask the reader to follow the documentation listed on the PaaS provider site.

30.1.7 Performance Degradation

Sometimes a project that has been running for a while under consistent load starts to slow down. When this occurs, it could be caused by one or more problems. We use the following workflow:

1. Check the project's commit history for changes could have caused a performance degradation. There may even be a major bug hiding.
2. Examine the project for undiscovered performance bottlenecks. See chapter 24, *Finding and Reducing Bottlenecks.*
3. Ask the PaaS support team to look into the problem. They might have a quick answer for you.
4. The physical hardware that the project is running on might have a problem. The 'cloud' is actually hardware and hardware breaks or gets old. Start up a new project instance, port the data, and update the DNS records to match if that resolves the issue.
5. Ask the PaaS support team for further assistance. It doesn't hurt to ask for help, especially as a paying customer.

If none of this works, consider running the project on another PaaS or your own servers. If it runs well in another environment, it might be time to move it off.

> **TIP: Free/Beginner Tiers Will Run Slowly**
>
> The free tier of any PaaS is not going to run fast or handle any significant load. That takes resources that cost the PaaS money. Even with the hefty angel or VC funding in the tech industry, it's just not going to happen. If the PaaS provides a free or inexpensive tier that handles very high loads, see the next section on 'Company Stability.'

30.1.8 Geography

Consider the location of primary usage compared to the location of the PaaS. For example, if the majority of users are in China, then a PaaS that only serves from US-based data centers isn't a good option. Latency issues can cause clients and users to become quickly unhappy with a project.

30.1.9 Company Stability

A PaaS is an enormous undertaking. When done well, it requires a lot of overhead. Engineers, servers, customer support, account, and marketing are all expensive business. Since the advent of PaaS solutions, we've seen a number of them fail because of lack of sales, over expenditure of funds, and sheer exhaustion by overworked staff. Fortunately, they've all provided a grace period during which projects were given time to move off, but it's not realistic to count on that.

Therefore, it behooves us to look at the pricing plans carefully. Once a PaaS is out of its beta or initial launch period, if there isn't a way to capture profitability, then using the PaaS is risky.

30.2 Best Practices for Deploying to PaaS

30.2.1 Aim for Identical Environments

The holy grail of deployment is identical environments between development and production. However, as soon as you decide to use a PaaS, this is no longer possible as the production system configuration is beyond your control. Nevertheless, the closer your can keep things identical between development and production the more maintainable your project will be.

Some PaaS platforms provide tools like Heroku's Foreman to provide a very loosely similar operating process. However, there is nothing like using Linux locally to replicate production. We cover this in section 2.5, *Identical Environments: The Holy Grail.*

30.2.2 Automate All the Things!

When it comes time to push an update to a production instance, it's never a good idea to do all the steps manually. It's simply too easy to make a mistake. Our solution is to use simple automation using one of the following tools:

- **Makefiles** are useful for simple projects. Their limited capability means we won't be tempted to make things too fancy. As soon as you need more power, it's time to use something else. Something like Invoke as described in the next bullet.
- **Invoke** is the direct descendant of the venerable **Fabric** library. It is similar to Fabric, but is designed for running tasks locally rather than on a remote server. Tasks are defined in Python code, which allows for a bit more complexity in task definitions (although it's easy to take things too far). It has full support for Python 3.4.

30.2.3 Maintain a Staging Instance

With automation often comes the ability to run staging instances of projects at a lower cost tier. This is a great place to test production deployments, not to mention a place to demo feature changes.

30.2.4 Prepare for Disaster With Backups and Rollbacks

Even with all the precautions we take, sometimes deployments just blow up. Therefore, before any change is pushed a live site, we make certain for a particular PaaS we know how to:

- Restore databases and user-uploaded files from backups.
- Roll back to a previous code push.

30.2.5 Keep External Backups

The great virtue of PaaS is that they abstract away many deployment and operational issues, allowing us to focus on writing our project. With that comes the risk that the PaaS might encounter their own problems. While some PaaS (including Heroku) provide the capability to generate backups, it's a good idea to periodically run backups to external services. This includes the databases and uploaded user files.

Suggestions for storing the data include Dropbox, Crashplan, Amazon S3, and Rackspace Cloud Files, but there are many more. Which service to choose should be based on architectural decisions such as the location of the PaaS (For example, Heroku-based projects would use Amazon services).

30.3 Summary

Platforms as a Service are a great way to expedite delivery of deployable projects. They allow for developers to quickly harness significant resources that are maintained by specialized operations teams. On the other hand, they do come with a price tag and various limitations. Therefore, deciding to use a PaaS should be based per the project and skill set at hand, not out of personal preference.

In addition, it's a good idea to honor the practices we provide in this chapter, or to listen carefully to peers to determine what they do to best utilize these services.

In the next chapter, we cover the nuts and bolts of deployment at a high level.

31 Deploying Django Projects

Deployment of Django projects is an in-depth topic that could fill an entire book on its own. Here, we touch upon deployment at a high level.

31.1 Single-Server for Small Projects

Single-server is the quickest way to get a small Django project up onto a server. It's also the cheapest Django deployment option.

The obvious drawback is that your server will go down if your website URL gets featured on Hacker News or any popular blog.

31.1.1 Should You Bother?

Typically we don't bother with the single-server setup even for small projects, because using `cookiecutter-django` with Heroku is less work and gives us peace-of-mind in the event of traffic spikes.

However, we highly recommend that you try setting up a single-server Django deployment in these situations:

- If you've never done it before. It's an extremely important learning experience. Doing it will give you a deeper understanding of how Python web applications work.
- If your Django project is more of a toy project or experiment. Websites with paying customers can't afford to risk downtime, but the risk of a temporary spike is bearable to non-paying side projects.

- If you're certain that one server is adequate for your site's traffic. For example, a Django site for your wedding guests will probably be fine on a single server.

31.1.2 Example: Quick Ubuntu + Gunicorn Setup

Here's an example of how we could deploy a single-server Django project easily with the following components:

- An old computer or cheap cloud server
- Ubuntu Server OS
- PostgreSQL
- Virtualenv
- Gunicorn

You can either use a computer that you have lying around your house, or you can use a cheap cloud server from a provider like DigitalOcean, Rackspace, or AWS.

Typicaly, we start out by installing the latest LTS version of Ubuntu Server onto a cloud server. Cloud server providers often have readymade disk images that are installable with a click, making this trivial. But doing this manually by downloading an installer like `http://www.ubuntu.com/server` works fine too.

We then install the Ubuntu packages needed. They can vary, but typically we end up installing at least these:

For pip/virtualenv `python-pip`, `python-virtualenv`
For PostgreSQL `postgresql`, `postgresql-contrib`, `libpq-dev`, `python-dev`

Notice how Gunicorn and Django aren't in that list. Whenever we can install a Python package rather than an Ubuntu package, we go with the Python package. It'll almost always be more recent.

Then we do all the server setup basics like updating packages and creating a user account for the project.

At this point, it's Django time. We clone the Django project repo into our user's home directory and create a virtualenv with the project's Python package dependencies, including Gunicorn. We create a PostgreSQL database for the Django project and run `python manage.py migrate`.

Then we run the Django project in Gunicorn. As of this writing, this requires a simple 1-line command. See:
`https://docs.djangoproject.com/en/1.8/howto/deployment/wsgi/gunicorn/`

At this point, we see the Django site running when we go to the server's IP address in a web browser. Then we can configure the server hostname and point a domain name at that IP address.

Of course, this is just a quick overview that leaves out many important details. Once you have a single-server setup working experimentally, you'll want to go back and read chapter 26, *Security Best Practices*, and then secure your server and site.

You'll also outgrow the single-server setup pretty quickly. At that point, you may get fancier with your setup, e.g. adding nginx, Redis, and/or memcached, or setting up Gunicorn behind an nginx proxy. Eventually, you'll want to either sign up for a PaaS or move to a multi-server setup.

TIP: Look Up the Specifics Online

Our aim here is to give you a general idea and example of how the most minimal Django deployment might work, rather than a detailed *how-to* guide.

Because commands and package names change quickly, and because this is not a tutorial book, we have not provided links to any particular setup instructions. But you should be able to find detailed instructions with a quick web search.

31.2 Multi-Server for Medium to Large Projects

Companies and growing startups who opt not to use a PaaS typically use a multi-server setup. Here is what a basic one might look like:

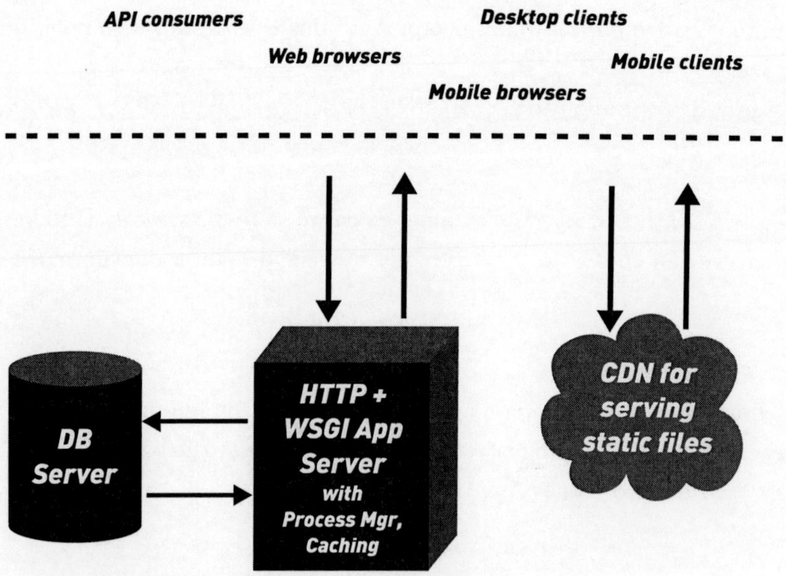

Figure 31.1: Example of a basic multi-server setup.

This is what you need at the most basic level:

- **Database server.** Typically PostgreSQL in our projects when we have the choice, though Eventbrite uses MySQL.
- **WSGI application server.** Typically uWSGI or Gunicorn with Nginx, or Apache with mod_wsgi.

Additionally, we may also want one or more of the following:

- **Static file server.** If we want to do it ourselves, Nginx or Apache are fast at serving static files. However, CDNs such as Amazon CloudFront are relatively inexpensive at the basic level.
- **Caching and/or asynchronous message queue server.** This server might run Redis, Memcached or Varnish.
- **Miscellaneous server.** If our site performs any CPU-intensive tasks, or if tasks involve waiting for an external service (e.g. the Twitter API) it can be convenient to offload them onto a server separate from your WSGI app server.

By having specialized servers that each focus on one thing, they can be switched out, optimized, or changed in quantity to serve a project's needs.

> **TIP: Using Redis for All Ephemeral Data**
>
> Redis has similar features to Memcached, but adds in the following:
>
> - Authentication, which Memcached doesn't have out of the box.
> - State is saved, so if a server is restarted the data doesn't go away.
> - Additional data types means it can be used as an asynchronous message queue, in conjunction with tools like **celery** and **rq**.

Finally, we also need to be able to manage processes on each server. We recommend in descending order of preference:

1. **Supervisord**
2. **init scripts**

Figure 31.2: Managing an ice cream replenishment process with Supervisord.

31.2.1 Advanced Multi-Server Setup

Here is an example of a much larger multi-server setup, complete with multiple servers of each type and load balancing:

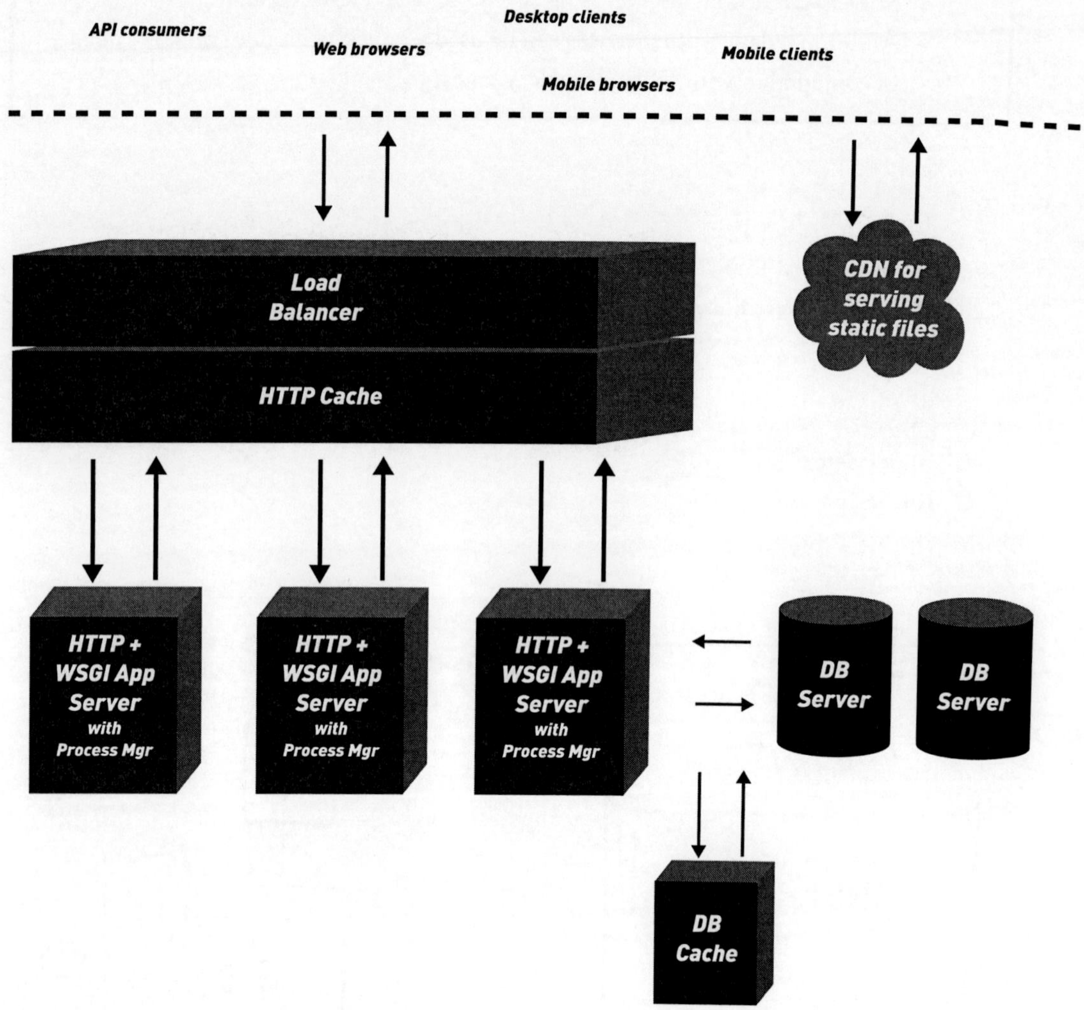

Figure 31.3: Example of an advanced multi-server setup.

Load balancers can be hardware- or software-based. Commonly-used examples include:

- **Software-based**: HAProxy, Varnish, Nginx

- **Hardware-based**: Foundry, Juniper, DNS load balancer
- **Cloud-based**: Amazon Elastic Load Balancer, Rackspace Cloud Load Balancer

TIP: Horizontal vs. Vertical Scaling

The above is an example of horizontal scaling, where more servers are added to handle load. Before scaling horizontally, it's good to scale vertically by upgrading your servers' hardware and maxing out the RAM on each server. Vertical scaling is relatively easy, since it's just a matter of throwing money at the problem.

TIP: Scaling Horizontally and Sessions

When scaling horizontally, make sure that users don't need sticky sessions. For example, if someone uploads a file to server 1, and then comes back thru the load balancer and lands on server 2, that shouldn't cause problems. Ways around this are storing uploaded media in a common shared drive or more commonly on cloud-based systems such as Amazon S3.

31.3 WSGI Application Servers

Always deploy your Django projects with **WSGI**.

Django 1.8's `startproject` command, sets up a *wsgi.py* file for us. This file contains the default configuration for deploying our Django project to any WSGI server. For what it's worth, the sample project templates we recommend in chapter 3, *How to Lay Out Django Projects* also includes a *wsgi.py* in its *config/* directory.

The most commonly-used WSGI deployment setups are:

1. **uWSGI** with **Nginx**.
2. **Gunicorn** behind a **Nginx** proxy.
3. **Apache** with **mod_wsgi**.

Here's a quick summary comparing the three setups.

Setup	Advantages	Disadvantages
uWSGI with Nginx	Lots of great features and options. Extremely configurable. Said to be better performing than the other setup options.	Documentation still growing. Not as time-tested as Apache. Not as beginner-friendly as the others.
Gunicorn (sometimes with Nginx)	Written in pure Python. Supposedly this option has slightly better memory usage, but your mileage may vary.	Documentation is brief for nginx (but growing). Not as time-tested as Apache.
Apache with mod_wsgi	Has been around for a long time and is tried and tested. Very stable. Works on Windows. Lots of great documentation, to the point of being kind of overwhelming.	Doesn't work with environment variables. Apache configuration can get overly complex. Lots of crazy conf files.

Table 31.1: Gunicorn vs Apache vs uWSGI

There's a lot of debate over which option is faster. Don't trust benchmarks blindly, as many of them are based on serving out tiny "Hello World" pages, which of course will have different performance from real web applications.

Ultimately, though, all three choices are in use in various high volume Django sites around the world. Configuration of any high volume production server can be very difficult, and if a site is busy enough it's worth investing time in learning one of these options very well.

The disadvantage of setting up our own web servers is the added overhead of extra sysadmin work. It's like making ice cream from scratch rather than just buying and eating it. Sometimes we just want to buy ice cream so we can focus on the enjoyment of eating it.

31.4 Performance and Tuning: uWSGI and Gunicorn

uWSGI and Gunicorn are very popular amongst Django developers looking to squeeze every last bit of performance out of their web servers. As of now, uWSGI is more configurable, but

Gunicorn is very configurable too, and arguably easier to configure.

Useful reading:

- http://uwsgi-docs.readthedocs.org
- https://docs.djangoproject.com/en/1.8/howto/deployment/wsgi/uwsgi/
- http://justcramer.com/2013/06/27/serving-python-web-applications/
  David Cramer's blog article arguing for using Nginx + UWSGI
- http://gunicorn.org/
- http://cerebralmanifest.com/uwsgi-vs-gunicorn/

31.5 Stability and Ease of Setup: Gunicorn and Apache

If you just want to get a Django site up and running fast, Gunicorn or Apache are your best bet. Apache used to be the easiest option, but Gunicorn has come a long way. These days, with Gunicorn and the default Django-provided *wsgi.py* file, the setup "just works" with zero or minimal debugging.

31.6 Common Apache Gotchas

WARNING: Do Not Use mod_python

The official Django documentation explicitly warns against using mod_python. Django's mod_python support was deprecated in Django 1.3. In Django 1.5, the mod_python request handler was removed from Django.

Unfortunately, there are still many online resources that talk about configuring Django with mod_python, causing many people confusion. Do not use mod_python. If using Apache, use mod_wsgi instead.

31.6.1 Apache and Environment Variables

Apache doesn't work with environment variables as described in chapter 5. You'll need to do something like load a local configuration file for secret values into your settings module written in .ini, .cfg, .json, or .xml formats. Please read section 5.4, 'When You Can't Use Environment Variables'.

31.6.2 Apache and Virtualenv

Thanks to the hard work of Graham Dumpleton, getting Apache to work with virtualenv is a task that's pretty straightforward:

- If using mod_wsgi 3.4 or newer and daemon mode, just add the following option to the `WSGIDaemonProcess` directive: `python-home=/some/path/to/root/of/virtualenv`
- If using embedded mode: `WSGIPythonHome /some/path/to/root/of/virtualenv`
- If using mod_wsgi 3.3 or older and daemon mode, instead use the following option to `WSGIDaemonProcess` where X.Y is the Python version: `python-path=/some/path/to/root/of/virtualenv/lib/pythonX.Y`

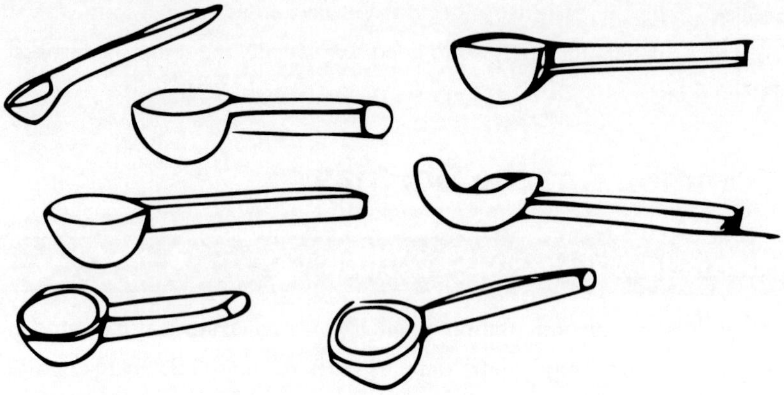

Figure 31.4: How ice cream is deployed to cones and bowls.

31.7 Automated, Repeatable Deployments

When we configure our servers, we really shouldn't be SSHing into our servers and typing in configuration commands from memory. It's too easy to forget what we've done. If servers configured this way go down and need to be recreated in an emergency, it's almost impossible to set them up identically to what we had before.

When you have a lot of moving parts, all those pieces need to be re-creatable in the event of a problem. Problems can and will occur. Relying on you or your system administrator's memory of how he or she set up everything a year ago is dangerous.

Instead, our server setup should be automated and documented in a way that makes it trivial to recreate everything from scratch. In the reader's case, you or your sysadmin should be able to set up everything without having to log into a single server manually.

Specifically, this means:

- We should be able to spin up and configure our entire server setup from scratch by running a command, then sitting back and watching as everything happens automatically.
- Even if it's just a single command, it should be documented precisely. Imagine that someone just got hired by our company. On their first day of work, without knowledge of our web application or servers, he or she should be able to open our ***deployment.rst*** document and set up our production servers.
- Each time we run the command, there should be no dependency on pre-existing server state.
- Any scripts should be idempotent, producing the same results no matter whether they are run for the first time or the hundredth time.

In order to achieve all of the above, companies who don't rely on a PaaS typically use one or more infrastructure automation and management tools.

Figure 31.5: Infrastructure automation can be very powerful.

WARNING: Caveat About the Rest of This Chapter

Our challenge in writing about automated deployments is twofold:

- Django is a web development framework, not a deployment system.
- The fact is that everything we wrote before has gotten stale. Web application deployment is a rapidly moving target.

Therefore, we're going to cover best practices at a very high level.

31.7.1 A Rapidly Changing World

As mentioned above, the world of automated deployments is evolving quickly. How quickly? Let's look at configuration management from the perspective of Two Scoops of Django:

Date	Milestone	Status of Config Management Tools
Through 2011	`Ancient History'	Chef/Puppet preferred, CFEngine predates the iPhone
2012	Work on Two Scoops commences	Chef/Puppet preferred, Salt/Ansible still very experimental
Jan 2013	Two Scoops of Django 1.5 Alpha	Chef and Puppet still strong, Salt/Ansible getting popular
Mar 2013	Two Scoops of Django 1.5 Final	Docker open sourced.
Jan 2014	Two Scoops of Django 1.6	Salt/Ansible are stable and popular, Chef/Puppet not so much, Docker still experimental, surges forward
Mar 2015	Two Scoops of Django 1.8 Early Release	Docker for identical environments, many use it for deployments, Salt/Ansible going strong, Chef/Puppet declining rapidly
June 2015	Two Scoops of Django 1.8 Final	Docker maturity? Will something new emerge?
2017	Projected Django 2.2 Release	Rise of tools yet imagined
2019	Projected Django 2.6 Release	Tools we use today may be relagated to the same boring place as CFEngine

Table 31.2: Timeline of DevOps Tools

If anything, this timeline makes it clear that it's a good idea for us not to tie our projects to a specific configuration management tool. Unfortunately, as a project grows over time, moving from one of these tools to another is a challenging process. Hence, we recommend choosing the tool of choice very carefully.

31.8 Which Automation Tool Should Be Used?

Because Python web application deployment is such a huge problem and pain point, the space has been flooded with tools attempting to solve it. We're hearing lots of big promises from every tool, but at this point no particular tool has gone mainstream as *The Easiest Way to Deploy, Self-Hosted*.

31.8.1 Too Much Corporate Fluff

In the past few years we've seen an vibrant ecosystem of companies dedicated to the issue of automating deployments. There is a lot of money to be made.

The result is that there are many good tools being built, but there is also a lot of corporate fluff to sift through. The creators of various tools each have their own corporate interests in mind, increasing with the amount of funding that they obtain from investors. Because a lot of money is involved, they each have their own marketing departments putting out a lot of convincing promises about what their tools have to offer.

This isn't a bad thing per se, but it can make it hard for us to determine what is the right tool for us.

31.8.2 Do Your Own Research

Great work is being done on great tools, but until these tools mature further, it's hard to figure out what's actually great and what's just a corporate promise. The only way to figure out what you like is to try everything, and to say "No, thanks!" when the "Kool-Aid" is being offered.

31.9 Current Infrastructure Automation Tools

Among Django users, Docker, Ansible, SaltStack, Puppet, and Chef are the most popular tools for automating deployments.

All of these automation tools tend to be complex to set up and use, with a steep learning curve. That's because they're designed to manage not just one server, but thousands or more.

Here is what these tools can perform at large scale:

Remote execution:

- Installing packages via apt-get or other system package management tools on remote servers
- Running commands on remote servers. For example, running the virtualenv command with the –no-site-packages option on staging/production servers.
- Starting services, and restarting them under certain conditions. For example, restarting an Nginx web server when the site's Nginx configuration file changes.
- When a command is executed remotely, logging and returning the response from the server.

Configuration management:

- Creating or updating conf files for services. For example, creating a pg_hba.conf file for a freshly installed PostgreSQL instance.
- Populating configuration values differently for different servers, based on variables like each server's particular IP address or OS-specific information.

Orchestration and targeting:

- Controlling which servers a job is sent to, and when it should be sent.
- Managing various components at a high level, creating pipelines to handle different workflows.
- Pushing jobs to servers from a master server, in push mode.
- Asking the master server what needs to occur, in pull mode.

Docker, Ansible, SaltStack, Puppet, and Chef are pretty similar and can perform all of the above. Let's explore what differentiates them:

Tool	Pros	Cons
Docker	Fast deployments due to only applying deltas. Containerization approach. YAML config. Large community. Open source.	Written in Go. Still immature enough to run into trouble spots.
SaltStack	Primarily push mode. Blazing fast transport via 0mq. YAML config. Lots of Salt states and examples online. Large community. Open source. Written in Python.	Complexity can be overwhelming. Still immature enough to run into trouble spots.
Ansible	Primarily push mode. Doesn't require daemons running on remote servers aside from OpenSSH. Easy to learn. YAML config. Open source. Written in Python.	Slower transport over SSH, but can use Fireball Mode which sets up a temporary 0mq daemon. Still immature enough to run into trouble spots.
Chef	Lots of recipes available. Large community. Open source.	Extremely steep learning curve. Written in Ruby, and recipes are written in Ruby. Extremely complex, often in a bad way.
Puppet	Large community. Open source.	Steep learning curve. Written in Ruby. Config is written in a custom DSL which can be difficult and painful to work with.

Table 31.3: Infrastructure Automation Tool Comparison

TIP: What About Fabric and Invoke?

Fabric and its Python 3-friendly successor Invoke are tools that allow you to execute remote commands. Smaller in scope than the above, it focuses on doing one thing well. It is frequently used in conjunction with all of the above tools.

A few years ago, the hot topic of every Python meetup seemed to be deployment configuration with Puppet, Chef, and Fabric. This combination is still in heavy use today by many companies.

The trend now seems to be Docker, SaltStack or Ansible. They all use YAML for configuraton. Since the latter two are written in Python, as a Python user it's easy to dig into their source code. The reality of development is that whenever you rely on a tool for long enough at large scale, you end up hitting bugs or interesting edge cases. When this happens, you'll be grateful that you can search the issue tracker, find others with the same problem, and look at or even modify source code if you need to.

Keep in mind that things are evolving quickly. If you spend a lot of your time on devops, you need to read blogs, follow other operations engineers on Twitter, attend infrastructure-related meetups, and keep the pulse of new developments.

Figure 31.6: Hopefully, one day someone will invent a one-button machine that deploys Django projects and makes ice cream.

31.10 Other Resources

The following are useful references for deploying projects.

- https://highperformancedjango.com
- http://www.fullstackpython.com/deployment.html

31.11 Summary

In this chapter we provided a very high level overview for deploying Django projects, including basic descriptions of single and multi-server setups. We also covered different the three most popular WSGI application servers. Finally, we compared infrastructure automation and configuration management tools.

32 | Continuous Integration

Continuous integration (CI) is one of those things where, to explain the concept, we quote one of its originators:

> Continuous integration is a software development practice where members of a team integrate their work frequently, usually each person integrates at least daily — leading to multiple integrations per day. Each integration is verified by an automated build (including test) to detect integration errors as quickly as possible. Many teams find that this approach leads to significantly reduced integration problems and allows a team to develop cohesive software more rapidly.
>
> — Martin Fowler, `http://2scoops.co/martin-fowler-continuous-integration`

Here's a typical development workflow when using continuous integration:

1. Developer writes code, runs local tests against it, then pushes the code to an instance of a code repository such as Git or Mercurial. This should happen at least once per day.
2. The code repository informs an automation tool that a new commit is ready for integration.
3. Automation integrates the code into the project, building out the project. Any failures during the build process and the commit are rejected.
4. Automation runs developer-authored tests against the new build. Any failures of the tests and the commit is rejected.
5. The developer is notified of success or the details of failure. Based on the report, the developer can mitigate the failures. If there are no failures, the developer celebrates and moves to the next task.

The advantages of this process are immediately clear. Thanks to continuous integration, we have the following:

- Earlier warnings of bugs and breakdowns.
- Deployment-breaking issues in the code are more frequently caught.
- Daily merges to the main trunk mean that no one person's code dramatically changes the code base.
- Immediate positive and negative feedback is readily available about the project.
- Automation tools that make this possible include a lot of metrics that make both developers and managers happy.

32.1 Principles of Continuous Integration

Now that we've gone over why continuous integration is great, let's go over some key components when using this work process. This is our interpretation of principles explored Martin Fowler's discussion of the topic at `http://2scoops.co/ci-practices`

32.1.1 Write Lots of Tests!

One of the nice things about continuous integration is that it ties so well with everything we discuss in chapter 22. Without comprehensive tests, continuous integration simply lacks that killer punch. Sure, some people would argue that without tests, continuous integration is useful for checking if a deployment would succeed and keeps everyone on the same branch, but we think they are thinking from the perspective of statically-typed languages, where a successful compilation already provides significant guarantees regarding the functionality of the software.

32.1.2 Keeping the Build Fast

This is a tricky one. Your tests should arguably be running against the same database engine as your production machine. However, under certain circumstances, tests can take a minute or ten. Once a test suite takes that long, Continuous Integration stops being advantageous, and starts becoming a burden.

It's at this point that developers (including the authors) begin considering using Sqlite3 in-memory for tests. We'll admit that we've done it ourselves. Unfortunately, because SQLite3's behaves significantly differently than **PostgreSQL** or **MySQL**, this can be a mistake. For example, field types are not constrained the same way.

Here are a few tips for speeding up testing on large projects:

- Avoid fixtures. This is yet another reason why we advise against their use.
- Avoid `TransactionTestCase` except when absolutely necessary.
- Avoid heavyweight `setUp()` methods.
- Write small, focused tests that run at lightning speed, plus a few larger integration-style tests.
- Learn how to optimize your database for testing. This is discussed in public forums like Stack Overflow: http://stackoverflow.com/a/9407940/93270

32.2 Tools for Continuously Integrating Your Project

Use the following tools:

32.2.1 Tox

http://tox.readthedocs.org/

This is a generic virtualenv management and testing command-line tool that allows us to test our projects against multiple Python and Django versions with a single command at the shell. You can also test against multiple database engines. It's how the authors and oodles of developers around the world check the compatibility of their code against different versions of Python.

If that isn't enough to convince you:

- Tox checks that packages install correctly with different Python versions *and interpreters*. Check on Python 2.7, 3.4, and PyPy all in one go!
- Tox runs tests in each of the environments, configuring your test tool of choice.

- Tox can act "as a frontend to continuous integration servers, reducing boilerplate and merging CI and shell-based testing."

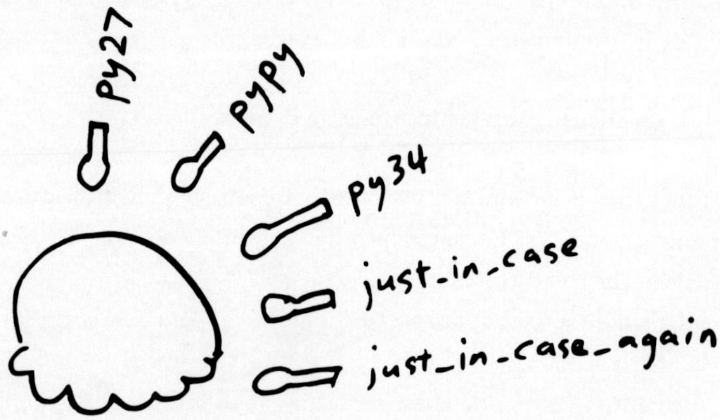

Figure 32.1: It's easy to get carried away. Pictured are two absolutely unnecessary Tox environments, just so we could get extra tastes.

32.2.2 Jenkins

http://jenkins-ci.org/

Jenkins is a extensible continuous integration engine used in private and open source efforts around the world. It is the standard for automating the components of Continuous Integration, with a huge community and ecosystem around the tool. If an alternative to Jenkins is considered, it should be done so after careful consideration.

32.3 Continuous Integration as a Service

Jenkins is an awesome tool, but sometimes you want to have someone else do the work in regards to setting it up and serving it. There are various services that provide automation tools powered by Jenkins or analogues. Some of these plug right into popular repo hosting sites like GitHub and BitBucket, and most provide free repos for open source projects. Some of our favorites include:

Service	Python Versions Supported	Link
Travis-CI	3.3, 3.2, 2.7, 2.6, PyPy	https://travis-ci.org
AppVeyor (Windows)	3.4, 3.3, 2.7	http://www.appveyor.com/
CircleCI	3.4, 3.3, 2.7, 2.6, PyPy, many more	https://circleci.com
Drone.io	2.7, 3.3	https://drone.io/
Codeship	3.4, 2.7	https://codeship.com

Table 32.1: Continuous Integration Services

32.3.1 Code Coverage as a Service

When we use continuous integration through one of the above CI services, what we don't get back is our code coverage. This causes problems with section 22.7, 'The Game of Test Coverage'. Fortunately for us, services like `codecov.io` can generate coverage reports and the game can continue.

32.4 Additional Resources

- http://en.wikipedia.org/wiki/Continuous_Integration
- http://jenkins-ci.org/
- http://www.caktusgroup.com/blog/2010/03/08/django-and-hudson-ci-day-1/
- http://ci.djangoproject.com/
- http://docs.python-guide.org/en/latest/scenarios/ci/

32.5 Summary

Continuous integration has become a standard for open source and private projects around the world. While there is the cost of doing work up front, the benefits of safer deployments and more robust projects easily outweigh the investment. Furthermore, there are enough resources and recipes that setting up continuous integration is faster than ever.

One final note: even if tests are not written for a project, the practice of continual project building makes continuous integration worth the setup.

33 | The Art of Debugging

Whether they are on a brand new shiny project or a legacy Django system that's a decade old, debugging just happens. This chapter provides useful tips we can do to make the debugging process better and easier.

33.1 Debugging in Development

These are common tricks and tools for debugging locally.

33.1.1 Use django-debug-toolbar

We've already mentioned this invaluable package repeatedly. It is arguably the easiest/fastest way to display various debug information about the current request/response cycle. If you want to know how fast your templates are rendering, what queries are being made, and what variables are being used, this is the tool.

If you don't have it set up and configured, stop everything else you are doing and add it to your project.

- `https://pypi.python.org/pypi/django-debug-toolbar`
- `http://django-debug-toolbar.readthedocs.org`

33.1.2 That Annoying CBV Error

If you are using `CBVs` this is an error you might see in the console or a view test:

Example 33.1

```
twoscoopspress$ python discounts/manage.py runserver 8001
Starting development server at http://127.0.0.1:8001/
Quit the server with CONTROL-C.

Internal Server Error: /
Traceback (most recent call last):
  File "/.envs/oc/lib/python2.7/site-packages/django/core/handlers/base.py",
        line 132, in get_response response = wrapped_callback(request,
        *callback_args, **callback_kwargs)
  File "/.envs/oc/lib/python2.7/site-packages/django/utils/decorators.py",
        line 145, in inner
    return func(*args, **kwargs)
TypeError: __init__() takes exactly 1 argument (2 given)
```

This is a bug that djangonauts of all skill levels introduce into their codebases.

The first thing we do when we see `TypeError: __init__() takes exactly 1 argument (2 given)` in the console is we check our ***urls.py*** modules. Chances are somewhere we are defining URLs where we forgot to add the `as_view()` method to our CBV routing.

Example of `TypeError` generating code:

Bad Example 33.1

```
# Forgetting the 'as_view()' method
url(r'^$',  HomePageView, name="home"),
```

Example of fixed code:

Example 33.2

```
url(r'^$',  HomePageView.as_view(), name="home"),
```

33.1.3 Master the Python Debugger

Also known as just **PDB**, this in essence provides an enhanced REPL for interacting with source code at breakpoints you specify. You can also step forward in the code to see how things change as the code is executed. In regards to Django, there tends to be three places PDB is used:

1. Inside of test cases.
2. During an HTTP request against development breakpoints allow you to examine at our own pace the process of evaluating the request.
3. To debug management commands.

WARNING: Before Deploying Check for PDB

Having PDB breakpoints in code that reaches production is disastrous as it will stop completion of user requests. Therefore, before deployment, search the code for 'pdb'. You can also rely on tools like **flake8** to automatically check for existence of pdb (and other problems).

While PDB is useful, it becomes dramatically more powerful when extended by third-party packages such as **ipdb**. What ipdb does is add the **ipython** interface to the PDB interface, turning a handy tool into a something worth celebrating with ice cream.

References:

- Python's pdb documentation: https://docs.python.org/2/library/pdb.html
- Using PDB with Django: https://mike.tig.as/blog/2010/09/14/pdb/

Packages:

- IPDB: https://pypi.python.org/pypi/ipdb
- Using IPDB with pytest https://pypi.python.org/pypi/pytest-ipdb

33.1.4 Remember the Essentials for Form File Uploads

Unless we consistently work on file uploads, there are two easily forgotten items that will cause file uploads to fail silently. This can be very frustrating, as code that fails silently is harder to debug. Anyway, should there be any problems with file uploads, check the following:

1. Does the `<form>` tag include an encoding type?

Example 33.3

```
<form action="{% url 'stores:file_upload' store.pk %}"
        method="post"
        enctype="multipart/form-data">
```

2. Do the views handle `request.FILES`? In Function-Based Views?

Example 33.4

```
# stores/views.py

from django.shortcuts import render, redirect, get_object_or_404
from django.views.generic import View

from stores.forms import UploadFileForm
from stores.models import Store

def upload_file(request, pk):
    """Simple FBV example"""
    store = get_object_or_404(Store, pk=pk)
    if request.method == 'POST':
        # Don't forget to add request.FILES!
        form = UploadFileForm(request.POST, request.FILES)
        if form.is_valid():
            store.handle_uploaded_file(request.FILES['file'])
            return redirect(store)
    else:
        form = UploadFileForm()
    return render(request, 'upload.html', {'form': form, 'store': store})
```

Or what about Class-Based Views?

Example 33.5

```
# stores/views.py
```

```python
from django.shortcuts import render, redirect, get_object_or_404
from django.views.generic import View

from stores.forms import UploadFileForm
from stores.models import Store

class UploadFile(View):
    """Simple CBV example"""
    def get_object(self):
        return get_object_or_404(Store, pk=self.kwargs['pk'])

    def post(self, request, *args, **kwargs):
        store = self.get_object()
        form = UploadFileForm(request.POST, request.FILES)
        if form.is_valid():
            store.handle_uploaded_file(request.FILES['file'])
            return redirect(store)
        return redirect('stores:file_upload', pk=pk)

    def get(self, request, *args, **kwargs):
        store = self.get_object()
        form = UploadFileForm()
        return render(
            request,
            'upload.html',
            {'form': form, 'store': store})
```

TIP: Form-Based Class Based Generic Views

If a view inherits from one of the following then we don't need to worry about `request.FILES` in your view code. Django handles most of the work involved.

- `django.views.generic.edit.FormMixin`
- `django.views.generic.edit.FormView`
- `django.views.generic.edit.CreateView`
- `django.views.generic.edit.UpdateView`

In these examples we don't provide the code for the `store.handle_uploaded_file()` method. We're just demonstrating where we might place such a method call.

33.1.5 Lean on the Text Editor or IDE

When using a **Text Editor** like Sublime Text, Textmates, Vim, Emacs, or many other choices, find Python and Django specific options or plugins and use them. Even if all they do is highlight code and identify PEP-8 violations, that will help immensely.

When using an **IDE** (Integrated Development Environment) like PyCharm, PyDev, WingIDE, Komodo, etc., then all of the IDE's capabilities with Python and Django should be embraced and used. That means use breakpoints and other advanced features. If we aren't using the IDE to the fullest, then why are we bothering with the effort of setting up the IDE?

Just make sure not to code to the IDE (or Text Editor). See subsection 1.7.2.

TIP: What is The Best IDE or Text Editor?

"*Whatever you prefer the most.*"

Each of us is an individual. Whatever flavor of ice cream or source code editor we prefer the most is our own unique expression. The only right answer is the one chosen for ourselves.

For what it is worth, as of 2015 Audrey prefers Textmate and Daniel prefers Sublime Text.

33.2 Debugging Production Systems

There are some bugs that turn up in production that seem impossible to duplicate in development. This happens when there are specific conditions that cannot be easily duplicated locally, including load conditions, third-party APIs, and the size of data. Debugging these problems can be really frustrating and time consuming. This section provides some tips on things that can be done to ease the pain.

33.2.1 Read the Logs the Easy Way

The problem with diving into production log files is they can be so large they obfuscate the cause of errors. Instead, use a log aggregator like Sentry to get a better view into what is going on in your application.

33.2.2 Mirroring Production

This concept is to mirror production in an environment that can be accessed by the maintainers for the sake of debugging. The growing popularity of modern deployment techniques (PaaS, devops, identical environments) in theory makes this easier to do. Generally, when duplicating a production environment, the following steps are taken:

1. Behind a firewall or some other protective measure, set up a remote server identical to the production environment.
2. Copy production data over, taking special care to remove **Personally Identifying Information**. By this, we mean anything that can be used to identify critical details of individual users, including email addresses.
3. Provide shell access to those who need it.

Once these steps have been taken, try to replicate the reported bug. If the production mirror is completely inaccessible to anyone outside the product (i.e. behind a firewall), you can even consider changing the `settings.DEBUG` to `True`.

> **WARNING: Take Special Care With Email Addresses**
>
> Ludvig Wadenstein notes that email addresses "might not seem like a big deal to keep around on your dev server, but all it takes is one small mishap and you have sent emails to all of your users."

33.2.3 UserBasedExceptionMiddleware

What if you could provide superusers with access to the `settings.DEBUG=True` 500 error page in production? That would make debugging much easier, right? The problem, of course, is that having `settings.DEBUG=True` in production is serious security problem. However, thanks to Simon Willison, co-creator of Django, there is a way to use this powerful debugging tool in production.

Example 33.6

```
# core/middleware.py
import sys

from django.views.debug import technical_500_response

class UserBasedExceptionMiddleware(object):
    def process_exception(self, request, exception):
        if request.user.is_superuser:
            return technical_500_response(request, *sys.exc_info())
```

33.2.4 That Troublesome `settings.ALLOWED_HOSTS` Error

> I see that my old nemesis, `settings.ALLOWED_HOSTS`, has returned.
>
> – Daniel Roy Greenfeld

The `ALLOWED_HOSTS` setting is a list of strings representing the host/domain names that a Django site can serve. This is a wonderful security measure that only turns on when `settings.DEBUG` is `False`. Unfortunately, as soon as `settings.DEBUG` is `False`, a project with an incorrectly set `ALLOWED_HOSTS` will generate constant 500 errors. Checking the logs will show that `SuspiciousOperation` errors are being raised, but those errors don't come with a meaningful message.

So what is happening?

1. `settings.DEBUG` is `False`
2. Django can't match the host/domains named in `ALLOWED_HOSTS` with what is being served. A common example is when `ALLOWED_HOSTS` is an empty list and we're trying to serve pages from example.com
3. Django thinks that something suspicious is going on, and raises a `SuspiciousOperation` error.

Therefore, whenever a project is deployed for the first time and always returns a 500 error, check `settings.ALLOWED_HOSTS`. As for knowing what to set, here is a starting example:

Example 33.7

```
# settings.py
ALLOWED_HOSTS = [
    '.djangopackages.com',
    'localhost',  # Ensures we can run DEBUG = False locally
    '127.0.0.1'  # Ensures we can run DEBUG = False locally
]
```

Reference:

- https://docs.djangoproject.com/en/1.8/ref/settings/#allowed-hosts

33.3 Feature Flags

An incredibly powerful technique, **Feature Flags** allow us to turn a project's feature on or off via a web-based interface.

TIP: Simon Willison' Advice on Feature Flags

Django project co-creator Simon Willison says:

> "Feature flags offer the best bang-for-your-buck of anything I've ever added to a codebase."

Let's say we're adding a new feature to our site, perhaps the ability to remotely control a robot that serves ice cream. Works great on our laptops, fine on a QA server. Then we push the change to production, thousands of users start to command the robot and it goes haywire. Utter disaster unfolds as chocolate ice cream is served to vanilla ice cream aficionados. We quickly shut everything down then spend days cleaning up the mess. However, the damage is done as ice cream eaters around the world decide not to use our ice cream serving robot.

While a silly example, this kind of thing happens. Identical environments can help, but aren't always the answer. For example, it's not uncommon for users to discover a broken element of a new feature or bug fix that was missed in tests. Anyone who has pushed code to a production server experiences this from time to time. Of course, you can ask people to play around on a QA or staging server, but that isn't the same as having them use the production site for real. What if we could allow a subset of real users (i.e. 'beta users') defined through an admin-style interface to interact with a new feature before turning it on for everyone?

This is what feature flags are all about!

If fact, production problems have been uncovered by having a smaller set of users more willing to try a new, possibly buggy feature. This can include staff, friends of staff, and friendly users willing to try out beta-level features before anyone else gets a chance.

33.3.1 Feature Flag Packages

The two most common feature flag packages for Django are **django-gargoyle** and **django-waffle**. They both support a similar feature set, though Gargoyle offers more options for building custom segments in exchange for more complexity. Either of them are very useful tools worth adding to projects.

- `https://github.com/disqus/gargoyle`
- `https://github.com/jsocol/django-waffle`

33.3.2 Unit Testing Code Affected by Feature Flags

One gotcha with feature flags is running tests against code that are turned off by them. How do we know that our new feature is tested when the flag to run them is turned off? The answer to this question is that our tests should cover both code paths, with feature flags on or off. To do this, we need to familiarize ourselves with how to turn a feature flag on or off within the Django testing framework:

- `http://www.2scoops.co/testing-with-gargoyle/`
- `http://www.2scoops.co/testing-with-waffle/`

33.4 Summary

Still can't figure out the problem? No worries, in the next chapter we provide some great tips for asking questions.

34 | Where and How to Ask Django Questions

All developers get stuck at one point or another on something that's impossible to figure out alone. When you get stuck, don't give up!

34.1 What to Do When You're Stuck

Follow these steps to increase your chances of success:

1. Troubleshoot on your own as much as possible. For example, if you're having issues with a package that you just installed, make sure the package has been installed into your virtualenv properly, and that your virtualenv is active.
2. Read through the documentation in detail, to make sure you didn't miss something.
3. See if someone else has had the same issue. Check Google, mailing lists, and StackOverflow.
4. Can't find anything? Now ask on StackOverflow. Construct a tiny example that illustrates the problem. Be as descriptive as possible about your environment, the package version that you installed, and the steps that you took.
5. Still don't get an answer after a couple of days? Try asking on the django-users mailing list or in IRC.

34.2 How to Ask Great Django Questions in IRC

IRC stands for **Internet Relay Chat**. There are channels like #python and #django on the Freenode IRC network, where you can meet other developers and get help.

A warning to those who are new to IRC: sometimes when you ask a question in a busy IRC channel, you get ignored. Sometimes you even get trolled by cranky developers. Don't get discouraged or take it personally!

The IRC #python and #django channels are run entirely by volunteers. You can and should help out and answer questions there too, whenever you have a few free minutes.

1. When you ask something in IRC, be sure that you've already done your homework. Use it as a last resort for when StackOverflow doesn't suffice.
2. Paste a relevant code snippet and traceback into `https://gist.github.com/` (or another pastebin).
3. Ask your question with as much detail and context as possible. *Paste the link to your code snippet/traceback.* Be friendly and honest.

> **TIP: Use a Pastebin!**
>
> Don't ever paste code longer than a few characters into IRC. Seriously, don't do it. You'll annoy people. Use a pastebin!

4. When others offer advice or help, thank them graciously and make them feel appreciated. A little gratitude goes a long way. A lot of gratitude could make someone's day. Think about how you would feel if you were volunteering to help for free.

34.3 Feed Your Brain

Fill up your ice cream bowl with these tasty tidbits of Django and Python information. They'll help you keep up to date with the latest and greatest.

1. `https://www.djangoproject.com/community/` Django Project's Feeds
2. Subscribe to Lincoln Loop's Django Round Up, an excellent mailing list for find new articles and packages for Django projects.
3. Subscribe to PyCoders Weekly and Python Weekly, two excellent methods for finding new articles and packages on the Python programming language.

34.4 Insider Tip: Be Active in the Community

The biggest secret to getting help when you need it is simple: be an active participant in the Python and Django communities.

The more you help others, the more you get to know people in the community. The more you put in, the more you get back.

34.4.1 9 Easy Ways to Participate

1. Attend Python and Django user group meetings. Join all the local groups that you can find on `http://wiki.python.org/moin/LocalUserGroups`. Search meetup.com for Python and join all the groups near you.
2. Attend Python and Django conferences in your region and country. Learn from the experts. Stay for the entire duration of the sprints and contribute to open source projects. You'll meet other developers and learn a lot.
3. Contribute to open source Django packages and to Django itself. Find issues and volunteer to help with them. File issues if you find bugs.
4. Join #python and #django on IRC Freenode and help out.
5. Find and join other smaller niche Python IRC channels. There's #pyladies, and there are also foreign-language Python IRC channels listed on `http://www.python.org/community/irc/`.
6. Answer Django questions on StackOverflow.
7. Meet other fellow Djangonauts on Twitter. Be friendly and get to know everyone.
8. Join the Django group on LinkedIn, comment on posts, and occasionally post things that are useful to others.
9. Volunteer for diversity efforts. Get involved with Django Girls and PyLadies and help make the Python community more welcoming to women. Remember that there are many angles to diversity: something as small as helping with a PyCon in an underrepresented country can make a major difference.

Figure 34.1: The ice cream eating help desk.

34.5 Summary

One of the strengths of Django is the human factor of the community behind the framework. Assume a friendly, open stance when you need guidance and odds are the community will rise to the task of helping you. They won't do your job for you, but in general they will reach out and attempt to answer questions or point you in the right direction.

35 Closing Thoughts

While we've covered a lot of ground here in this third edition of the book. Yet this is just the tip of the ice cream cone. For starters we plan to write more technical books and grow our open source projects.

As for Two Scoops of Django, our current plan is to wait until Django 2.2 is released. The reason is that Django 1.8 is a Long Term Support version of Django, meaning that the content in this book will remain relevant for a long time.

We'd genuinely love to hear from you, and so would the rest of the Django community. For specific book content-related feedback, we're using GitHub issues to track submissions and commentary from readers. Report any of the following at `https://github.com/twoscoops/two-scoops-of-django-1.8/issues`:

- Did you find any of the topics unclear or confusing?
- Any errors or omissions that we should know about?
- What additional topics would you like us to cover in a future edition of this book?

We hope that this has been a useful and worthwhile read for you. If you enjoyed reading this book, please tell others by writing a positive reviews. We need and appreciate your support.

Cheers to your success with your Django projects!

Daniel Roy Greenfeld and Audrey Roy Greenfeld

- `pydanny.com` / `audreyr.com` / `twoscoopspress.com`
- GitHub: `@pydanny`, `@audreyr`, and `@twoscoopspress`
- Twitter: `@pydanny`, `@audreyr`, and `@twoscoopspress`
- Facebook: `https://www.facebook.com/twoscoopspress`

Appendix A: Packages Mentioned In This Book

This is a list of the third-party Python, Django, and front-end packages that we've described or mentioned in this book. We've also snuck in a few really useful packages that we don't mention in the book but that we feel are extremely useful.

As for the packages that we're currently using in our own projects: the list has some overlap with this list but is always changing. Please don't use this as the definitive list of what you should and should not be using.

Core

Django `https://djangoproject.com`
: The web framework for perfectionists with deadlines.

django-debug-toolbar `http://django-debug-toolbar.readthedocs.org/`
: Display panels used for debugging Django HTML views.

django-model-utils `https://pypi.python.org/pypi/django-model-utils`
: Useful model utilities including a time stamped model.

ipdb `https://pypi.python.org/pypi/ipdb`
: IPython-enabled pdb

Pillow `https://pypi.python.org/pypi/Pillow`
: Friendly installer for the Python Imaging Library.

pip `http://www.pip-installer.org`
: Package installer for Python. Comes built-in with Python 3.4 or higher.

Sphinx `http://sphinx-doc.org/`
: Documentation tool for Python projects.

virtualenv http://virtualenv.org
Virtual environments for Python.

virtualenvwrapper http://www.doughellmann.com/projects/virtualenvwrapper/
Makes virtualenv better for Mac OS X and Linux!

virtualenvwrapper-win https://pypi.python.org/pypi/virtualenvwrapper-win
Makes virtualenv better for Windows! win

Asynchronous

celery http://www.celeryproject.org/
Distributed task queue.

flower https://pypi.python.org/pypi/flower
Tool for monitoring and management of Celery tasks.

rq https://pypi.python.org/pypi/rq
RQ is a simple, lightweight, library for creating background jobs, and processing them.

django-rq https://pypi.python.org/pypi/django-rq
A simple app that provides django integration for RQ (Redis Queue).

django-background-tasks https://pypi.python.org/pypi/django-background-tasks
Database backed asynchronous task queue.

Database

django-db-tools https://pypi.python.org/pypi/django-db-tools
Great for flipping a site in and out of read-only mode.

psycopg2 https://pypi.python.org/pypi/psycopg2
PostgreSQL database adapter.

Deployment

circus https://pypi.python.org/pypi/circus
Program that lets you run and watch multiple processes and sockets. Used at Mozilla, complicated, and not for small projects.

dj-database-url https://pypi.python.org/pypi/dj-database-url
This simple Django utility allows you to easily use Heroku for database access.

django-heroku-memcacheify https://pypi.python.org/pypi/django-heroku-memcacheify
Easy Memcached settings configuration for Heroku.

Fabric https://pypi.python.org/pypi/Fabric
Simple tool for remote execution and deployment.

Invoke https://pypi.python.org/pypi/invoke
Like Fabric, also works in Python 3.

Paver https://pypi.python.org/pypi/invoke
Easy build, distribution and deployment scripting.

Supervisor http://supervisord.org/
Supervisord is a client/server system that allows its users to monitor and control a number of processes on UNIX-like operating systems.

Forms

django-crispy-forms http://django-crispy-forms.readthedocs.org/
Rendering controls for Django forms. Uses Twitter Bootstrap widgets by default, but skinnable.

django-floppyforms http://django-floppyforms.readthedocs.org/
Form field, widget, and layout that can work with django-crispy-forms.

django-forms-bootstrap https://pypi.python.org/pypi/django-forms-bootstrap
A simple form filter for using Django forms with Twitter Bootstrap.

django-forms-builder A Django reusable app providing the ability for admin users to create their own forms within the admin interface. https://github.com/stephenmcd/django-forms-builder

Front-End

JSCS http://jscs.info/
JavaScript code style linter.

CSScomb http://csscomb.com/
Coding style formatter for CSS.

Logging

logutils https://pypi.python.org/pypi/logutils
Adds useful handlers for logging.

Sentry http://getsentry.com
Exceptional error aggregation, with an open source code base.

App Enlight https://appenlight.com/ Track errors and performance issues in your project.

Newrelic http://newrelic.com
Realtime logging and aggregation platform.

Project Templates

cookiecutter-django https://github.com/pydanny/cookiecutter-django
The sample project layout detailed in chapter 3 of this book.

Cookiecutter http://cookiecutter.readthedocs.org
Not explicitly for Django, a command-line utility for creating project and app templates. It's focused, heavily tested and well documented. By one of the authors of this book.

django-kevin https://github.com/imkevinxu/django-kevin
Django project template optimized for Heroku deployments. Forked from the earlier (1.5, 1.6) Two Scoops project template

django-herokuapp https://github.com/etianen/django-herokuapp
A set of utilities and a project template for running Django sites on Heroku.

REST APIs

django-rest-framework http://django-rest-framework.org/
The defacto REST package for Django. Exposes model and non-model resources as a RESTful API.

django-jsonview https://github.com/jsocol/django-jsonview
Provides a simple decorator that translates Python objects to JSON and makes sure decorated views will always return JSON.

django-tastypie http://django-tastypie.readthedocs.org
Expose model and non-model resources as a RESTful API.

Security

bleach https://pypi.python.org/pypi/bleachbleach
An easy whitelist-based HTML-sanitizing tool.

defusedxml https://pypi.python.org/pypi/defusedxml

Must-have Python library if you are accepting XML from any foreign source.

django-autoadmin https://pypi.python.org/pypi/django-autoadmin

Automatic admin users for Django projects with autogenerated passwords, takes the headache out of providing secure access with auto-created sites.

django-admin-honeypot https://pypi.python.org/pypi/django-admin-honeypot

A fake Django admin login screen to notify admins of attempted unauthorized access.

django-axes https://github.com/django-pci/django-axes

Keep track of failed login attempts in Django-powered sites.

django-ratelimit-backend https://pypi.python.org/pypi/django-ratelimit-backend

Login rate-limiting at the auth backend level.

django-passwords https://pypi.python.org/pypi/django-passwords

A Django reusable app that provides validators and a form field that checks the strength of a password.

django-secure https://pypi.python.org/pypi/django-secure

Helps you lock down your site's security using practices advocated by security specialists. Much of its functionality has been subsumed by Django's `SecurityMiddleware` class.

django-two-factor-auth https://pypi.python.org/pypi/django-two-factor-auth

Complete Two-Factor Authentication for Django.

django-user-sessions https://pypi.python.org/pypi/django-user-sessions

Django sessions with a foreign key to the user.

peep https://pypi.python.org/pypi/peep

Uses only verified TLS to upload to PyPI protecting your credentials from theft. Has other useful features worth looking at.

Twine https://pypi.python.org/pypi/twine

Uses only verified TLS to upload to PyPI protecting your credentials from theft. Has other useful features worth looking at.

Testing

coverage http://coverage.readthedocs.org/

Checks how much of your code is covered with tests.

django-test-plus https://github.com/revsys/django-test-plus

Useful additions to Django's default TestCase, which the Two Scoops authors learned from the creator of this package and continue to use to this day. We're happy to see this bundled up for ease of use.

factory boy `https://pypi.python.org/pypi/factory_boy`
A package that generates model test data.

model mommy `https://pypi.python.org/pypi/model_mommy`
Another package that generates model test data.

mock `https://pypi.python.org/pypi/mock`
Not explicitly for Django, this allows you to replace parts of your system with mock objects. This project made its way into the standard library as of Python 3.4.

pytest `http://pytest.org/`
A mature full-featured Python testing tool that is very useful for Python and Django projects.

pytest-django `http://pytest-django.readthedocs.org/`
pytest-django is a plugin for py.test that provides a set of useful tools for testing Django applications and projects.

tox `http://tox.readthedocs.org/`
A generic virtualenv management and test command line tool that allows testing of projects against multiple Python version with a single command at the shell.

User Registration

django-allauth `http://django-allauth.readthedocs.org/`
General-purpose registration and authentication. Includes Email, Twitter, Facebook, GitHub, Google, and lots more.

python-social-auth `http://django-social-auth.readthedocs.org/`
Easy social authentication and registration for Twitter, Facebook, GitHub, Google, and lots more.

Views

django-braces `http://django-braces.readthedocs.org`
Drop-in mixins that really empower Django's class-based views.

django-extra-views `http://django-extra-views.readthedocs.org/`
Provides a number of additional generic class-based views to complement those provide by Django itself.

django-vanilla-views `http://django-vanilla-views.org/`
Simplifies Django's generic class-based views by simplifying the inheritance chain.

Time

python-dateutil https://pypi.python.org/pypi/python-dateutil
Provides powerful extensions to Python's datetime module.

pytz https://pypi.python.org/pypi/pytz/
Brings the Olson tz database into Python. This library allows accurate and cross platform timezone calculations. It also solves the issue of ambiguous times at the end of daylight saving time. Library Reference

Miscellaneous

awesome-slugify https://pypi.python.org/pypi/awesome-slugify
A flexible slugify function.

dj-stripe https://pypi.python.org/pypi/dj-stripe
Django + Stripe made easy.

django-compressor http://django-compressor.readthedocs.org/
Compresses linked and inline JavaScript or CSS into a single cached file.

django-extensions http://django-extensions.readthedocs.org/
Provides `shell_plus` management command and a lot of other utilities.

django-haystack http://django-haystack.readthedocs.org/
Full-text search that works with SOLR, Elasticsearch, and more.

django-pipeline http://django-pipeline.readthedocs.org/
Compression of CSS and JS. Use with cssmin and jsmin packages.

django-htmlmin https://pypi.python.org/pypi/django-htmlmin
HTML minifier for django.

django-reversion https://pypi.python.org/pypi/django-reversion
An extension to the Django web framework that provides comprehensive version control facilities.

django-watson https://github.com/etianen/django-watson
Full-text multi-table search application for Django using SQL database features.

envdir http://envdir.readthedocs.org/ A Python port of daemontools' envdir.

flake8 https://pypi.python.org/pypi/flake8
Checks code quality by using PyFlakes, pep8, and other tools.

pathlib https://pypi.python.org/pypi/pathlib Object-oriented filesystem paths being merged into Python as of release 3.4.

pip-tools `https://github.com/nvie/pip-tools`
: A set of tools to keep your pinned Python dependencies fresh.

pyyaml `https://pypi.python.org/pypi/PyYAML`
: YAML parser and emitter for Python.

requests `http://docs.python-requests.org`
: Easy-to-use HTTP library that replaces Python's urllib2 library.

silk `https://github.com/mtford90/silk`
: Silk is a live profiling and inspection tool for the Django framework. Silk intercepts and stores HTTP requests and database queries before presenting them in a user interface for further inspection.

unicode-slugify `https://github.com/mozilla/unicode-slugify`
: A Mozilla-supported slugifier that supports unicode characters.

Unipath `https://pypi.python.org/pypi/Unipath`
: Object-oriented alternative to os/os.path/shutil.

Appendix B: Troubleshooting Installation

This appendix contains tips for troubleshooting common Django installation issues.

Identifying the Issue

Often, the issue is one of:

- That Django isn't on your system path, or
- That you're running the wrong version of Django

Run this at the command line:

EXAMPLE 35.1

```
python -c "import django; print django.get_version()"
```

If you're running Django 1.8, you should see the following output:

EXAMPLE 35.2

```
1.8
```

Don't see the same output? Well, at least you now know your problem. Read on to find a solution.

Our Recommended Solutions

There are all sorts of different ways to resolve Django installation issues (e.g. manually editing your PATH environment variable), but the following tips will help you fix your setup in a way that is consistent with what we describe in chapter on The Optimal Django Environment Setup.

Check Your Virtualenv Installation

Is **virtualenv** installed properly on your computer? At the command line, try creating a test virtual environment and activating it.

If you're on a Mac or Linux system, verify that this works:

Example 35.3

```
$ virtualenv testenv
$ source testenv/bin/activate
```

If you're on Windows, verify that this works:

Example 35.4

```
C:\code\> virtualenv testenv
C:\code\> testenv\Scripts\activate
```

Your virtualenv should have been activated, and your command line prompt should now have the name of the virtualenv prepended to it.

On Mac or Linux, this will look something like:

Example 35.5

```
(testenv) $
```

On Windows, this will look something like:

Example 35.6

```
(testenv) >
```

Did you run into any problems? If so, study the Virtualenv documentation (http://virtualenv.org) and fix your installation of Virtualenv.

If not, then continue on.

Check if Your Virtualenv Has Django 1.8 Installed

With your virtualenv activated, check your version of Django again:

Example 35.7

```
python -c "import django; print django.get_version()"
```

If you still don't see 1.8, then try using pip to install Django 1.8 into testenv:

Example 35.8

```
(testenv) $ pip install Django==1.8
```

Did it work? Check your version of Django again. If not, check that you have **pip** installed correctly as per the official documentation (http://pip-installer.org).

Check for Other Problems

Follow the instructions in the official Django docs for troubleshooting problems related to running django-admin.py:
https://docs.djangoproject.com/en/1.8/faq/troubleshooting/

Appendix C: Additional Resources

This appendix lists additional resources that are applicable to modern Django and Python. Therefore, we will only list content that is current and applicable to Django 1.8, Python 2.7.x, or Python 3.4.x.

Two Scoops Academy

`Two Scoops Academy` makes learning Python, Django, JavaScript, CSS, and HTML as fun as ice cream. These are a growing series of beginner-to-advanced online courses by the authors of this book, Daniel and Audrey Roy Greenfeld. Subjects covered include:

- Building projects from start to finish following best practices.
- How to install, configure, use, and improve open source packages.
- Super-fast test authoring and test coverage checking.
- Fancy image uploads (drag and drop).
- Asynchronous tasks with Celery.
- Integrating with third-party APIs.
- Flagging spam and moderation queues.
- Advanced ORM query tricks.
- Advanced use of Cookiecutter and cookiecutter-django.
- Deployment with Docker.
- Much, much more.

`twoscoopsacademy.com`

Intermediate/Advanced Django Material

Video:

Two Scoops Academy

twoscoopsacademy.com

Learn intermediate and advanced Django from the authors of Two Scoops of Django. Two Scoops Academy has a growing series of courses on Django, Python, JavaScript, and more. For more detail, see the previous page.

GoDjango

godjango.com

A series of short videos that each focus on something challenging to do with Django. You can access more material by "going pro".

Books:

High Performance Django

amazon.com/High-Performance-Django/dp/1508748128/

https://highperformancedjango.com (ebook)

Written with a focus on scaling Django, this book espouses many good practices. Full of useful information and tricks, as well as questions in each section that force you to think about what you are doing.

Lightweight Django

amazon.com/Lightweight-Django-Julia-Elman/dp/149194594X

A good book by Django veterans Julia Elman and Mark Lavin that focuses heavily on the front-end. Amongst other things, a handy reference for making Django work with Web sockets.

Django Design Patterns and Best Practices

amazon.com/Django-Design-Patterns-Best-Practices/dp/1783986646

Arun Ravindran's book is a useful and quite funny book on design patterns.

Two Scoops of Django: Best Practices for Django 1.6 (print)

http://amzn.to/1dpCoIt

The second printed edition of this book.

We maintain a list of current and outdated Django books at:

twoscoopspress.org/pages/current-django-books

Web:

Django Packages

`https://www.djangopackages.com`

A directory of reusable apps, sites, tools, and more for your Django projects maintained by the authors of Two Scoops of Django.

Classy Class-Based Views

`http://ccbv.co.uk/`

A website that has provides detailed descriptions, with full methods and attributes, for each of Django's class-based generic views.

Classy Django REST Framework

`http://www.cdrf.co/`

Detailed descriptions, with full methods and attributes, for each of Django REST Framework's class-based views and serializers.

pydanny's blog

`http://pydanny.com/tag/django.html`

A good amount of this blog is about modern Django. As the author of this blog is also one of this book's authors, the style of the blog loosely resembles the content of this book.

Getting Started with Django Rest Framework and AngularJS

`http://www.2scoops.co/kevin-stone-django-angular-tutorial/` Kevin Stone's amazing Django + Angular tutorial is an epic piece of work. It is over 25 pages long when printed out, and great for kickstarting yourself into understanding Django, Django Rest Framework, and Angular.js.

Django Model Behaviors

`http://blog.kevinastone.com/django-model-behaviors.html`

Kevin Stone explores how to structure models and associated code in large Django projects.

Lincoln Loop's Django Best Practices

`http://lincolnloop.com/django-best-practices/`

This free website resource is a really good reference of practices similar to those espoused in this book.

Awesome-Django

`http://awesome-django.com/`

A curated list of awesome Django apps, projects and resources.

Beginner Django Material

We actively maintain this list at http://twoscoopspress.com/pages/django-tutorials

Video:

Two Scoops Academy

twoscoopsacademy.com

Learn the fundamentals of Django from the authors of Two Scoops of Django. For more detail see the first page of this appendix.

Django Basics

teamtreehouse.com/library/django-basics

A beginner's introduction to Django, including installation, working with models, templates, views, and tests.

Books:

Test-Driven Web Development with Python

http://amzn.to/1Dky362 A great way to revisit the Django tutorial and learn agile/TDD processes at the same time.

Real Python

http://www.realpython.com/ Advanced Web Development with Django 1.8, is a practical, real-world guide to Django 1.8.

Web:

Django Girls Tutorial

http://tutorial.djangogirls.org/

Created and maintained by the international Django Girls organization, this is an excellent resource no matter your gender.

TaskBuster Django Tutorial

http://www.marinamele.com/taskbuster-django-tutorial

An epic end-to-end tutorial on building a Django project. Not a common tutorial it dives into the deep end and has you create a complex project.

Official Django 1.8 Documentation

https://docs.djangoproject.com/en/1.8/

The official Django documentation is incredibly useful. If you've used a previous version of Django, make sure that you are reading the correct edition of the documentation.

Beginner Python Material

Learn Python the Hard Way

http://amzn.to/1OOYqYv

If you don't know Python, this is one of the best places to start. The author takes you through Python the same way he learned guitar, through rote and repetition. Don't worry about the title, this is a good way to get started with Python.

Learn Python the Hard Way Online Edition

http://learnpythonthehardway.org/

By going right to the source, this free for HTML, paid for video resources, is one of the best places to start. The video resources are especially useful.

Automate the Boring Stuff with Python

amazon.com/gp/product/1593275994

This fascinating book teaches Python by instructing on how to make boring computer tasks easy through automation. Why update 150 columns of a spreadsheet when Python can do it for you?

Useful Python Material

Effective Python

http://amzn.to/1NsiqVr

Instructs on many useful practices and techniques when coding in Python.

Python Cookbook, 3rd Edition

http://amzn.to/I3Sv6q

An incredible book by Python luminaries David Beazley and Brian Jones, it's filled with delicious ice cream recipes... err... incredibly useful Python recipes for any developer using Python 3.3 or greater.

Treading on Python Volume 2

http://amzn.to/1kVWi2a

Covers more advanced Python structures.

Writing Idiomatic Python 3.3

http://amzn.to/1aS5df4

Great tips for optimizing your code and increasing the legibility of your work. There are a few places it differs from our practices (imports being the largest area of difference), but overall we concur.

Writing Idiomatic Python 2.7

`http://amzn.to/1fj9j7z`
Idiomatic Python, but for Python 2.7

JavaScript Resources

Books:

Secrets of a JavaScript Ninja (Print and Kindle)
`http://amzn.to/18QzT0r`
Definitive Guide to JavaScript (Print and Kindle)
`http://amzn.to/1cGVkDD`
JavaScript: The Good Parts (Print and Kindle)
`http://amzn.to/1auwJ6x`
JavaScript Patterns (Print and Kindle)
`http://amzn.to/1dii9Th`

Web Resources:

Mozilla Developer Network
`https://developer.mozilla.org/en-US/docs/Web/JavaScript`
Learning JavaScript Design Patterns
`http://addyosmani.com/resources/essentialjsdesignpatterns/book/`
Stack Overflow
`http://stackoverflow.com/questions/tagged/javascript`

> **WARNING: Stay Away From W3Schools**
>
> One problem about JavaScript (and CSS) research on the web is that W3Schools will turn up at the top of search engine results. This is unfortunate, because much of the data there is outdated enough to be incorrect. Be smart and avoid this resource.
>
> We scan the results page for the Mozilla Developer Network (MDN) link, usually around the third position, and click on that one.

Appendix D: Internationalization and Localization

Django and Python provides a lot of very useful tools for dealing with **internationalization**, **localization**, and of course, **Unicode**.

This appendix, added as of the second edition, contains a list of things helpful for preparing your Django application for non-English readers and non-USA users. This list is by no means complete, and we invite the reader to provide additional feedback.

Start Early

It is always easier to start with and grow an internationalized, localized project than to convert an existing project.

Define Python Source Code Encodings

In PEP 263 we are given a formal specification for defining how encoding of Python modules is to occur. Amongst other things, this affects how Python handles unicode literals. To define this encoding in internationalized projects, at the top each module add:

EXAMPLE 35.9

```
# -*- coding: utf-8 -*-
```

Or as shown in the next code example:

Example 35.10

```
#!/usr/bin/python
# -*- coding: utf-8 -*-
```

More information can be found at http://www.python.org/dev/peps/pep-0263/

Wrap Content Strings with Translation Functions

Every string presented to end users should be wrapped in a translation function. This is described in-depth in the official Django documentation on `django.utils.translation` at http://2scoops.co/1.8-translation. Since that is a lot of text to swallow, the table on the following page is a reference guide for knowing when and where to use what translation function for what tasks.

Function	Purpose	Link
`ugettext()`	For content executed at runtime, e.g. form validation errors.	http://2scoops.co/33
`ugettext_lazy()`	For content executed at compile time, e.g. `verbose_name` in models.	http://2scoops.co/32
`string_concat()`	Replaces the standard `str.join()` method for joining strings. Rarely used.	http://2scoops.co/37

Table 35.1: django.utils.translation Function Reference

Convention: Use the Underscore Alias to Save Typing

As you know, normally we aren't fans of abbreviations or shortcuts. However, in the case of internationalizing Python code, the existing convention is to use a _, or underscore, to save on letters.

Example 35.11

```
# -*- coding: utf-8 -*-
from django.utils.translation import ugettext as _
```

```python
print(_("We like gelato."))
```

Don't Interpolate Words in Sentences

> The golden rule is always have as much grammar as possible in the string, don't let the code piece the grammar together; and generally verbs are the most problematic.
>
> – Patrick McLoughlan

We used to construct translation strings all the time, going so far as to include it in the 1.5 edition of the book. This is when you use slightly-clever code to construct sentences out of various Python objects. For reference, this was part of Example 8.7:

Bad Example 35.1

```python
# DON'T DO THIS!

# Skipping the rest of imports for the sake of brevity
class FlavorActionMixin(object):

    @property
    def action(self):
        msg = "{0} is missing action.".format(self.__class__)
        raise NotImplementedError(msg)

    def form_valid(self, form):
        msg = "Flavor {0}!".format(self.action)
        messages.info(self.request, msg)
        return super(FlavorActionMixin, self).form_valid(form)

# Snipping the rest of this module for the sake of brevity
```

While seemingly handy in that it makes for a self-maintaining mixin, it is overly clever in we can't internationalize the result of calling `self.__class__`. In other words, you can't just add `django.utils.translation` the following and expect it to produce anything meaningful for translators to work from:

Bad Example 35.2

```
# DON'T DO THIS!
from django.utils.translations import ugettext as _

# Skipping the rest of this module for the sake of brevity

    def form_valid(self, form):

        # This generates a useless translation object.
        msg = _("Flavor {0}!".format(self.action))
        messages.info(self.request, msg)
        return super(FlavorActionMixin, self).form_valid(form)

# Skipping the rest of this module for the sake of brevity
```

Rather than writing code that constructs sentences out of various Python constructs, now we write more meaningful dialogues that can be readily translated. This means a little more work, but the result is a more easily translatable project. Hence why we now follow this pattern:

Example 35.12

```
# -*- coding: utf-8 -*-
# Skipping the rest of imports for the sake of brevity
from django.utils.translation import ugettext as _

class FlavorActionMixin(object):

    @property
    def success_msg(self):
        return NotImplemented

class FlavorCreateView(LoginRequiredMixin, FlavorActionMixin,
                        CreateView):
    model = Flavor

    # Slightly longer but more meaningful dialogue
```

```
    success_msg = _("Flavor created!")

# Skipping the rest of this module for the sake of brevity
```

For reference, you can combine individual strings representing meaningful sentences and dialogues into larger values. However, you shouldn't build sentences by concatenating pieces, because other languages may require a different order. For the same reason, you should always include punctuation in translated strings. See as follows:

EXAMPLE 35.13

```
# -*- coding: utf-8 -*-
from django.utils.translation import ugettext as _

class FlavorActionMixin(object):

    @property
    def success_msg(self):
        return NotImplemented

class FlavorCreateView(LoginRequiredMixin, FlavorActionMixin,
                        CreateView):
    model = Flavor

    # Example combining strings
    part_one = _("Flavor created! ")
    part_two = _("Let's go try it!")
    success_msg = part_one + part_two

# Skipping the rest of this module for the sake of brevity
```

Unicode Tricks

Here are some things we've learned when dealing with unicode-related issues.

Python 3 Can Make Unicode Easier

In our experience Python 3 makes unicode handling much, much easier. While in theory things can and are back-ported to Python 2.7, we've found that when using Python 3 we just don't have the same kinds of problems. If working on a new project, this is as good a reason as any to consider switching to Python 3.

Use django.utils.encoding.force_text() Instead of unicode()

When you are working with Python 2.7.x or Python 3.3+ and need to ensure that a useful string-type value is returned, don't use the `unicode()` or `str()` built-ins. What can happen is that under certain circumstances, instead of returning a unicode or str object, Django will return a nigh-meaningless `django.utils.functional.__proxy__` object, which is a lazy instance of the data requested.

Instead, do as our friend Douglas Miranda suggested to us, and use `django.utils.encoding.force_text`. In the case that you are dealing with a proxy object or lazy instance, it resolves them as strings.

> **TIP: Django is Lazy**
>
> One of the ways that Django does optimizations is via lazy loading, a design pattern which defers initialization of an object until it is needed. The place where this is most obviously used is Django's ORM, as described at http://2scoops.co/1.8-querysets-are-lazy. This use of lazy objects can cause problems with display of content, hence the need for `django.utils.encoding.force_text()`.

Browser Page Layout

Assuming you've got your content and Django templates internationalized and localized, you can discover that your layouts are broken.

A good Django-based example is Mozilla and their various sites for supporting tools like Firefox. On these sites they handle translations for over 80 languages. Unfortunately, a title that fits the page in English breaks the site in more verbose languages such as German.

Mozilla's answer is to determine the width of a title container, then use JavaScript adjust the font size of the title text downwards until the text fits into the container with wrapping.

A simpler way of handling this issue is to assume that other languages can take up twice as much space as English. English is a pretty concise language that, because of its short words, handles text wrapping very well.

Appendix E: Settings Alternatives

Here a couple of alternative patterns for managing settings that we feel can be recommended. They avoid the **local_settings anti-pattern** and allow for management of configuration that will work with either the **Environment Variables Pattern** or the **Secrets File Pattern**.

> **WARNING: Converting Existing Settings is Hard**
>
> If you have an existing project using multiple settings modules and you want to convert it to the single settings style, you might want to reconsider. Migrating settings approaches is always a tricky process, and requires deep and wide test coverage. Even with the best test coverage, there is a chance it's not going to be worth it.
>
> For these reasons, we suggest being conservative about switching to new settings approaches. Only do it when the current settings management approach has become a pain point, not when a new method becomes popular.

Twelve Factor-Style Settings

If we're relying on environment variables, why not use the simplest *settings.py* system possible? Bruno Renié, creator of django-floppyforms and FeedHQ (`https://feedhq.org`), advocates an alternate approach to Django settings files, in which all environments use the same single settings file.

The argument for this approach is that when using the multiple settings files approach, you end up with environment-specific code. For instance, when doing local development, you're not running the code with production settings. This increases the chance of running into production-specific bugs when you update some code without updating the production settings accordingly.

This style involves using sensible default settings and as few environment specific values as possible. When combined with tools like **Vagrant** and **Docker**, it means that mirroring production is trivial.

It results in a much simpler settings file, and for Twelve Factor App fans, it's right in line with that approach.

If you want to see an example of the approach in action, check out FeedHQ's settings module: `https://github.com/feedhq/feedhq/blob/master/feedhq/settings.py`

We've enjoyed this approach for new and smaller projects. When done right, it makes things elegantly simple.

However, it's not a perfect solution for all problems:

- It doesn't provide much benefit for simplification when development environments are drastically different than production.
- It doesn't work as well with projects being deployed to more than one operating system.
- Complex settings on large projects are not really simplified or shortened by this approach. It can be challenging to use on large or complex projects.

If you would like to know more about this approach, we recommend the following articles:

- `http://bruno.im/2013/may/18/django-stop-writing-settings-files/`
- `http://12factor.net/config`

Appendix F: Working with Python 3

Django's official documentation has a well-written page that covers much of what's involved with working with Python 3. Here are some specific sections you should pay careful attention to:

Django Official Docs on Python 3 http://2scoops.co/1.8-python3
Coding Guidelines http://2scoops.co/1.8-python3-coding-guidelines
Writing Compatible Code with Six http://2scoops.co/1.8-python3-six

Here are some other things you should know.

Most Critical Packages Work with Python 3

As of the time of this writing, Django Packages lists over 205 packages that support Python 3. This includes such critical libraries as:

- Django itself
- Pillow
- django-braces
- django-crispy-forms
- django-debug-toolbar
- django-floppyforms
- django-rest-framework
- python-requests

You can see a list of Django specific libraries at https://www.djangopackages.com/python3/.

Checking for Python 3 Compatibility

Here are the steps we follow in rough order when determining if a third-party library actually works with Python 3:

- Check on `https://www.djangopackages.com/python3/`.
- Look up the package on **PyPI** and see if any of its trove classifiers mention Python 3 status.
- See if a pull request for Python 3 support is outstanding.
- Run the test suite using Python 3.4.
- If a Django project, check the models for `__str__()` methods. If it has them, it's a pretty good indicator that it's Python 3.4 friendly.

Converting a Library to Work with Python 3.4

How we convert Python 2 code to Python 3:

- Get the test harness working with Python 3.
- Lean on `django.contrib.six` as much as possible. Add a *compat.py* module only if absolutely needed.
- Fix any problems you find in the code. Try to keep solutions as simple as possible.
- Submit the pull request.
- Politely poke the package owner to accept the pull request.
- Once the owner accepts the pull request, gently poke the package owner to push the update to PyPI.

TIP: Dealing with Slow Maintainers

Ranting to or complaining about slow-moving maintainers is absolutely counter-productive. People have lives and jobs that sometimes get in the way of open source. It's more productive to be patient, be polite, and if necessary do an absolutely minimal fork or find a working alternative.

Use Python 3.3.3 or Later

Django is a large, complicated system. While it's heavily tested for multiple versions of Python 3, we've found that it just works better with more recent versions of the language. For example, `migrate` fails in curious ways with Python 3.3.0.

Working With Python 2 and 3

We usually encounter this scenario when we are writing a third-party package for use in Django or even just vanilla Python. However, there are use cases where an entire Django project might be deployed to Python 2.7 as well as Python 3.3. Fortunately, most of the following suggestions apply no matter the scale of the project.

Tests and Continuous Integration

If there isn't a working test harness and functioning continuous integration, now is the time to set it up. Testing compatibility across major Python versions simply requires automation.

Keep Compatibility Minimally Invasive

The last thing that a project needs is complex branches to deal with different versions of Python. Therefore, use the following imports at the top of a Python module to keep code identical:

Example 35.14

```python
# The __future__ imports in this module means that all code
# in this example will work identically in Python 2.7 and
# Python 3 or higher.

# Multi-Line and Absolute/Relative imports will work identically across
# Python versions.
from __future__ import absolute_import

# Any division will return float objects. Example 3 / 2 = 1.5
```

```
from __future__ import division

# All strings defined in Python 2 and 3 can use Python 3's name = 'django'
# syntax for defining unicode-friendly strings.
from __future__ import unicode_literals
```

When we do need more complexity or any sort of logic, that's when it's time to create a *compat.py* module.

Use django.utils.encoding.python_2_unicode_compatible in Models

Rather than write both `__str__()` and `__unicode__()` methods, use `django.utils.encoding.python_2_unicode_compatible` so it only has to be written once. See section 19.3, 'Viewing String Representations of Objects.'

Resources

The following are useful resources for Python 3 topics:

Porting to Python 3
: http://python3porting.com/
: Lennart Regebro's free HTML or paid e-book bundle on the subject of moving from Python 2 to 3.

Porting Django apps to Python 3
: http://youtu.be/cJMGvAYYUyY
: This is Jacob Kaplan-Moss' PyCon US 2013 video on the subject.

Python Cookbook, 3rd Edition
: http://amzn.to/I3Sv6q
: David Beazley and Brian Jones' book of handy recipes for Python 3.

Writing Idiomatic Python 3.3
: http://amzn.to/1aS5df4
: Jeff Knupp's guide to writing Python 3 code the 'right' way.

Appendix G: Security Settings Reference

Appendix G: Security Settings Reference

In Django, knowing which setting should be set to what value in development vs production requires an unfortunate amount of domain knowledge. This appendix is a reference for better understanding how to configure a Django project for both development and production.

Setting	Development	Production
ALLOWED_HOSTS	any list	See subsection 33.2.4
Cross Site Request Forgery protection	See next page	See next page
DEBUG	True	False
DEBUG_PROPAGATE_EXCEPTIONS	False	False
Email SSL	See next page	See next page
MIDDLEWARE_CLASSES	Standard	Add `SecurityMiddleware`
SECRET_KEY	Use cryptographic key	See section 5.3
SECURE_PROXY_SSL_HEADER	None	See next page
SECURE_SSL_HOST	False	True
SESSION_COOKIE_SECURE	False	True
SESSION_SERIALIZER	See below	See next page

Table 35.2: Security Settings Reference

Cross Site Request Forgery Protection Settings

For most cases, the standard Django defaults for these settings are adequate. This list provides references to edge cases and the CSRF setting documentation that might provide mitigation:

- Internet Explorer and CSRF failure: 2scoops.co/1.8-csrf-cookie-age
- Cross-subdomain request exclusion, (e.g. posting from `vanilla.twoscoopspress.com` to `chocolate.twoscoopspress.com`): 2scoops.co/1.8-csrf-cookie-domain
- Changing the default CSRF failure view: 2scoops.co/1.8-csrf-failure-view

Email SSL

Django now supports secure connections to SMTP servers. If emails from a site contains security-related material, we strongly suggest using this feature. Documentation on the following settings begins at https://docs.djangoproject.com/en/1.8/ref/settings/#email-use-tls

- `EMAIL_USE_TLS`
- `EMAIL_USE_SSL`
- `EMAIL_SSL_CERTFILE`
- `EMAIL_SSL_KEYFILE`

SESSION_SERIALIZER

Per subsection 26.9.4:

`SESSION_SERIALIZER = django.contrib.sessions.serializers.JSONSerializer`.

SECURE_PROXY_SSL_HEADER

For some setups, most notably Heroku, this should be:

```
SECURE_PROXY_SSL_HEADER = ('HTTP_X_FORWARDED_PROTO', 'https')
```

Acknowledgments

This book was not written in a vacuum. We would like to express our thanks to everyone who had a part in putting it together.

The Python and Django Community

The Python and Django communities are an amazing family of friends and mentors. Thanks to the combined community we met each other, fell in love, and were inspired to write this book.

Technical Reviewers for 1.8

Bartek Ogryczak is a Python user and fanatic from 2004. From university days working with distributed systems, be it investment bankers' computing grid, social network's servers or AWS cloud. Born in Warsaw, Poland, after 5 years in Madrid, Spain and another 5 in Amsterdam, the Netherlands has settled with family in East Bay, California.

Barry Morrison is a self-proclaimed geek, lover of all technology. He is a multidiscipline systems adminstrator with more than 10 years of experience with Windows, Linux, and storage in the public and private sectors. He is also a Python and Django afficianado and Arduino tinkerer. He lives in California.

Kevin Stone is a full-stack technologist with experience ranging from launching early stage startups to designing billion-dollar systems. He's been using Django since 2008. Currently employed at Eventbrite to architect their highly scalable ticketing platform, he adores tools that allow him to move faster, focusing on solving customer problems rather than implementation details. He regularly blogs about Django best practices and is frequent speaker at meetups and conferences.

Paul Hallett is a human living in London, UK. He's a Software Engineer with a passion for developing Web Services and RESTful APIs. His favourite ice cream flavour is salted caramel.

Saurabh Kumar from New Delhi, is a Python evangelist and programs for web. When he is not working for his clients, he likes to contribute to open-source projects and organizes programming workshops for school and college students. Along side his passion for programming, he is also an avid traveler. He utilizes his photography skills to capture the greatest moments around his life. He loves to see technology from design perspective and vice versa.

Security Reviewer for 1.8

Erik Romijn started using Django in the days of 1.2. His largest contribution to Django was GenericIPAddressField, and he has worked on all sorts of patches since. While developing with Django, he always keeps a little list of even the slightest Django frustrations, to tackle them at a later time and prevent other developers from having to deal with the same issues. He also enjoys helping ordinary developers to build safer web apps, for which Django is already a great start, and developed Erik's `http://ponycheckup.com/` with that goal in mind. Erik lives in Amsterdam, The Netherlands.

Contributors to 1.8

The following individuals helped us improve this edition: Kenneth Love, Patrick McLoughlan, Sebastián J. Seba, Kevin Campbell, Doug Folland, Kevin London, Ramon Maria Gallart Escolà, Eli Bendersky, Dan O'Donovan, Ryan Currah, Shafique Jamal, Russ Ferriday, Charles L. Johnson, Josh Wiegand, William Vincent, Tom Atkins, Martey Dodoo, Krace Kumar Ramaraju, Felipe Arruda Pontes, Ed Patrick Tan, Sven Aßmann, Christopher Lambacher, Colin O'Brien, Sebastien de Menten, Evangelos Mantadakis, Silas Wegg, Michal Hoftich, Markus Holterman, Pat Curry, Gaston Keller, Mihail Russu, Jean-Baptiste Lab, Kaleb Elwert, Tim Bell, Zuhair Parvez, Ger Schinkel, Athena Yao, Norberto Bensa, Abhaya Agarwal, Steve Sarjeant, Karlo Tamayo, Cary Kempston, José Padilla, Konstantinos Faliagkas, Kelsey Gilmore-Innis, Adam Bogdał, Tyler Davis, Javier Liendo, Kevin Xu, Michael Barr, Caroline Simpson, John Might, Tom Christie, Nicolas Pannetier, Marc Tamlyn, Loïc Bistuer, Arnaud Limbourg, Alasdair Nicol, and Ludvig Wadenstein.

If your name is not on this list but should be, please send us an email so that we can make corrections!

Technical Reviewers for 1.6

The following were critical in supporting the 1.6 edition of this book.

Aymeric Augustin
Barry Morrison
Ken Cochrane
Paul McMillan - Security Reviewer

Technical Reviewers for 1.5

The following individuals gave us their invaluable help, aid and encouragement for the initial release of this book. We give special recognition here to Malcolm for his contributions to this book and the world.

Malcolm Tredinnick lived in Sydney, Australia and spent much of his time travelling internationally. He was a Python user for over 15 years and Django user since just after it was released to the public in mid-2005, becoming a Django core developer in 2006. A user of many programming languages, he felt that Django was one of the better web libraries/frameworks that he used professionally and was glad to see its incredibly broad adoption over the years. In 2012 when he found out that we were co-hosting the first PyCon Philippines, he immediately volunteered to fly out, give two talks, and co-run the sprints. Sadly, he passed away in March of 2013, just two months after this book was released. His leadership and generosity in the Python and Django community will always be remembered.

The following were also critical in supporting the 1.5 edition of this book.

Kenneth Love
Lynn Root
Barry Morrison
Jacob Kaplan-Moss
Jeff Triplett
Lennart Regebro

Randall Degges
Sean Bradley

Chapter Reviewers for 1.5

The following are people who gave us an amazing amount of help and support with specific chapters during the writing of the 1.5 edition. We would like to thank Preston Holmes for his contributions to the User model chapter, Tom Christie for his sage observations to the REST API chapter, and Donald Stufft for his support on the Security chapter.

Final Reviewers for 1.5

During the Final period the following individuals sent us corrections, cleanups, bug fixes, and suggestions. This includes: Chris Jones, Davide Rizzo, Tiberiu Ana, Dave Castillo, Jason Bittel, Erik Romijn, Darren Ma, Dolugen Buuraldaa, Anthony Burke, Hamish Downer, Wee Liat, Álex González, Wee Liat, Jim Kalafut, Harold Ekstrom, Felipe Coelho, Andrew Jordan, Karol Breguła, Charl Botha, Fabio Natali, Tayfun Sen, Garry Cairns, Dave Murphy, Chris Foresman, Josh Schreuder, Marcin Pietranik, Vraj Mohan, Yan Kalchevskiy, Jason Best, Richard Donkin, Peter Valdez, Jacinda Shelly, Jamie Norrish, Daryl Yu, Xianyi Lin, Tyler Perkins, Andrew Halloran, Tobias G. Waaler, Robbie Totten, Gabriel Duman, Nick Smith, Lachlan Musicman, Eric Woudenberg, Jim Munro, Larry Prince, Hamid Hoorzad, Matt Harrison, Aymeric Augustin, Khee Chin, Douglas Miranda, Saul Shanabrook.

Beta Reviewers for 1.5

During the Beta period an awesome number of people sent us corrections, cleanups, bug fixes, and suggestions. This includes: Francisco Barros, Florian Apolloner, David Beazley, Alex Gaynor, Jonathan Hartley, Stefane Fermigier, Deric Crago, Nicola Marangon, Bernardo Brik, Zed Shaw, Zoltán Árokszállási, Charles Denton, Marc Tamlyn, Martin Bächtold, Carlos Cardoso, William Adams, Kelly Nichols, Nick August, Tim Baxter, Joe Golton, Branko Vukelic, John Goodleaf, Graham Dumpleton, Richard Cochrane, Mike Dewhirst, Jonas Obrist, Anthony Burke, Timothy Goshinski, Felix Ingram, Steve Klass, Vinay Sajip, Olav Andreas Lindekleiv, Kal Sze, John Jensen, Jonathan Miller, Richard Corden, Dan Poirier, Patrick Jacobs, R. Michael Herberge, and Dan Loewenherz.

Alpha Reviewers for 1.5

During the Alpha period an amazing number of people sent us corrections and cleanups. This list includes: Brian Shumate, Myles Braithwaite, Robert Węglarek, Lee Hinde, Gabe Jackson, Jax, Baptiste Mispelon, Matt Johnson, Kevin Londo, Esteban Gaviota, Kelly Nicholes, Jamie Norrish, Amar Šahinović, Patti Chen, Jason Novinger, Dominik Aumayr, Hrayr Artunyan, Simon Charettes, Joe Golton, Nicola Marangon, Farhan Syed, Florian Apolloner, Rohit Aggarwa, Vinod Kurup, Mickey Cheong, Martin Bächtold, Phil Davis, Michael Reczek, Prahlad Nrsimha Das, Peter Heise, Russ Ferriday, Carlos Cardoso, David Sauve, Maik Hoepfel, Timothy Goshinski, Francisco Barros, João Oliveira, Zed Shaw, and Jannis Leidel.

Typesetting

We thank Laura Gelsomino for helping us with all of our LaTeX issues and for improving upon the book layout.

Laura Gelsomino is an economist keen about art and writing, and with a soft spot for computers, who found the meeting point between her interests the day she discovered LaTeX. Since that day, she habitually finds any excuse to vent her aesthetic sense on any text she can lay her hands on, beginning with her economic models.

We originally typeset the alpha version of the first editions with iWork Pages. Later editions of the book were written using LaTeX. All editions have been written on the Macbook Air.

List of Figures

List of Tables

Index